PASSIONATE AMATEURS

THEATER: THEORY/TEXT/PERFORMANCE
Series Editors: David Krasner and Rebecca Schneider
Founding Editor: Enoch Brater

Recent Titles:

Passionate Amateurs

THEATRE, COMMUNISM, AND LOVE

Nicholas Ridout

THE UNIVERSITY OF MICHIGAN PRESS

Ann Arbor

First paperback edition 2015
Copyright © by the University of Michigan 2013
All rights reserved

Published in the United States of America by
The University of Michigan Press
Manufactured in the United States of America
⊗ Printed on acid-free paper

2018   2017   2016   2015   5   4   3   2

A CIP catalog record for this book is available from the British Library.

Library of Congress Cataloging-in-Publication Data

Ridout, Nicholas Peter.
    Passionate amateurs : theatre, communism, and love / Nicholas Ridout.
       pages cm. — (Theater—theory/text/performance)
    Includes bibliographical references and index.
    ISBN 978-0-472-11907-3 (cloth : alk. paper) — ISBN 978-0-472-02959-4 (e-book)
       1. Theater and society.   2. Communism and culture.   I. Title.
    PN2051.R53   2013
    792—dc23
                                                              2013015596

ISBN 978-0-472-03633-2 (pbk. : alk. paper)

For Isabel and Peter, my parents

Acknowledgments

Throughout the writing of this book I was fortunate to work in the Department of Drama at Queen Mary University of London. Colleagues and students alike made the department a truly stimulating and supportive place to be, to work, and to think. I am grateful to them all. I owe particular thanks, for conversations that contributed in tangible ways to the development of this work, to Bridget Escolme, Jen Harvie, Michael McKinnie, Lois Weaver, and Martin Welton. A sabbatical in the academic year 2010–11 made its realization possible.

During that sabbatical I was exceptionally fortunate to spend a year in the Department of Theatre Arts and Performance Studies at Brown University. For their hospitality and intellectual partnership in this, my second professional home, I will always be especially grateful to Michelle Carriger, Jim Dennen, John Emigh, Lindsay Goss, Hunter Hargraves, Ioana Jucan, Patrick McKelvey, Coleman Nye, Paige Sarlin, Rebecca Schneider, Eleanor Skimin, Andrew Starner, Hans Vermy, Anna Watkins Fisher, and Patricia Ybarra.

I have also been fortunate to enjoy a range of opportunities to present parts of this work, in progress, at Quorum (the Drama Department research seminar at Queen Mary), the London Theatre Seminar, the Andrew Mellon School of Theatre and Performance at Harvard University, CalArts, and the University of Kent, as well as at conferences including Performance Studies international (PSi) in Copenhagen (2008), PSi in Utrecht (2010), and the American Society for Theatre Research in Nashville (2012), and I am grateful to the organizers of all these events for the opportunities for conversation that these occasions afforded.

At such events and on numerous other occasions I have enjoyed conversations and other theatrical experiences with many people, related either directly or indirectly to my work on this book. Among them I especially want to thank Una Bauer, Claudia Castellucci, Romeo Castellucci, Kate Elswit, Chris Goode, James Harding, Wendy Hubbard, Shannon Jackson, Miranda Joseph, Eirini Kartsaki, Jen Mitas, Sophie Nield, Louise

Owen, Jim Peck, Paul Rae, Alan Read, Janelle Reinelt, Theron Schmidt, Shelley Trower, and Simon Vincenzi.

At the University of Michigan Press, LeAnn Fields is an editor with whom conversation has been a source of inspiration and assurance throughout. I am grateful, also, to her assistant, Alexa Ducsay, for her support through the production process. The series editors, David Krasner and Rebecca Schneider (again), have been supportive and critical friends throughout. I am grateful, too, to anonymous readers for the press for their comments on the manuscript and to Sarah Thomasson for invaluable support in its preparation.

From the beginning, Rebecca Schneider (again, again) has been a constant friend and incomparable intellectual partner, in London, Providence, and places in between. Joe Kelleher enriches my experiences of theatre, thought, and social life, always. Giulia Palladini has been a comrade in this project, in thought, on song, and in a little shared resistance to productivity.

Contents

Prologue

The Yetis came as a surprise. That they possessed redemptive power was also unexpected. They appeared about half an hour through the performance of *B.#03*, the Berlin episode of Socìetas Raffaello Sanzio's *Tragedia Endogonidia,* presented at the Hebbel Theater in 2003.[1] They were white, hairy, and amiable. They enclosed part of the stage—which had recently been transformed from a murky and cinematic darkness into a field of white—behind a low white picket fence, with the playful enthusiasm of children setting up a camp for the night. They carried flags, some of them white and emblazoned with black letters in a gothic-style font, one of them the German national flag. Then they brought the dead girl back to life, and she danced, in red shoes, on the lid of her white coffin, while in a recorded loop a choir of children sang again and again a song by Benjamin Britten about the cycle of a cuckoo's life: "In April I open my bill, in May I sing day and night, in June I change my tune, in July far, far I fly, in August away I must."[2]

This girl's death had inaugurated the action of a drama. Or, more properly speaking, the drama began when her mother awoke to find her dead. For half an hour, before the arrival of the Yetis, we had followed this anonymous mother through scenes of intense grief. We had watched the woman's desperate and supposedly solitary gestures of self-consolation. But who were or are "we"? According to a scholarly convention, "we" may be used by an author to include the readers of a text, sometimes a little presumptuously, in the experience or knowledge being affirmed. It gathers consent around the text in order to allow it to proceed. According to a less well-defined convention, "we" may also be used in writing about performances for an audience, in order to scale up the experience of a single spectator into an experience that may be imagined as having been shared by others, by an audience. In a book about theatre, therefore, especially one in which questions of, say, communism, might be at stake, an author might wish to be rather careful about the use of this "we," careful, that is, to assume neither that a solitary experience might have been shared by others nor that the act of writing really can gather its disparate, solitary, and occasional readers into any kind of collective. Sometimes, then, this problematic first-person plural may call for back-up, recruiting other authors or spectators by means of citation to corroborate or substantiate claims about experience that might be too fragile to stand alone, to justify with force of numbers the use of the word "we," to suggest the presence that might constitute even the most minimal form of audience: two people, on their own, together:

> The Berlin episode of Romeo Castellucci's *Tragedia Endogonidia* is a play about grief. A mother awakes to lose her daughter and her grief erupts, in full view and straight on. It comes, though, with a glacial slowness, and filtered through a haze of semi-transparent screens. It is sorrow played out like a history lesson we are unable or unwilling to comprehend, processed into a series of ritual actions: stepping out of bed, walking and rocking herself, before it all has to begin; putting on shoes and a dress; taking a child's toy (a wooden horse) from out of the tangle of sheets; attempting to wake the child; failing; putting on the rubber gloves; dragging the dead child from out of the bed and off the stage; showing us the hammer, balancing the hammer at the front of the stage (the weapon moves of its own accord); scrubbing the blood from the bed and floor; settling on the end of the bed to masturbate, or try to masturbate, first with fingers, then with the child's horse: an impossible attempt at self-abandon. As if history could be turned off at the tap and she could be in any other moment than this one, now.[3]

These scenes culminated in an encounter with a disembodied female voice that commanded the mother to "show yourself . . . cross the bridge . . . come here . . . closer to me . . . lean out of the window . . . take off the mask . . . eat my ash . . . eat my metal . . . drink my water."[4] The stage trembled as if in an earthquake and was transformed from a space of gray and black into a world of pure white, into which the Yetis emerged. During the scenes of Yeti redemption the mother stood alone, her head shrouded, as a kind of witness who cannot see, and the performance as a whole took on the tone, or rather the tense, of a demonstration of what might just, at the very margins of plausibility, be possible, in a dazzlingly improbable spectacle of resurrection:

> Perhaps if we keep looping the cuckoo song, spring and summer will always be coming, and will never pass into autumn and win-

ter. Amid the absolute whiteness of this winter scene a parenthesis of sunshine will be forever erected, within which we shall live the eternity of the promise. In the deep freeze of the state of emergency, a new and benign rule will come. All that it required is that we should have our eyes open when the Yetis appear: it is that simple. This is not Marx's vision of history repeating itself as farce, but tragedy presenting history as comic alternative, for those who have eyes to see and ears to hear. Not, perhaps, these blind and big-eared spectators who occupy the stalls, however. Here, row upon row of stuffed rabbits have taken all the most expensive seats. They, it seems, have paid to have this promise acted out, but in their dumbly belligerent way of not being there they make me all the more aware that I must, despite what I am feeling, be here after all. If they are not going to live up to their responsibilities to a tragedy that has moved the witnesses out of the dramatis personae and into the dark of the house, then I must.[5]

If the Yetis somehow embody an idea of a "good community" of love and care and an end to death, the rabbits in the stalls, audience and image of an audience at once, might embody an idea of "bad community," which, for all that it seems "all ears," just won't do what it is there to do and listen. Sitting in the circle, looking down across the impassive rabbit collective, one member of the human gathering attempted to make sense out of some disordered feelings about loss and grief, about solitude and collectivity, about Berlin and communism. After the event this attempt resolved into a very particular question. Why had an experience of deep sadness brought about by watching an image of impossible resurrection resembled so closely another experience from about fifteen years earlier, when, sitting on the edge of a bed early one November morning in the English south-coast town of Hastings, about to set off to run a workshop for a community opera in a local school, I had cried tears, not of joy but of loss, at news footage of people taking down the Berlin Wall? In 1989, I was a professional theatre worker, engaged in a project whose existence rested on the idea that theatre might be an instance of "good" community, responding to television representations of events taking place in the "real" world. In 2003 I was a professional theatre spectator, engaged in a project of writing about a theatre work that recognized its audience as "a non-community"[6] and that took a form—tragedy—for which "an authentic foundation is impossible today."[7] Both before and since I had entertained a fragile affiliation with a tradition of political and philosophical thought that bore the name of communism: as a teenager I had experienced the peculiar political solitude of trying to sell copies of the Communist Party of Great Britain's newspaper on the High Street of my solidly bourgeois hometown. What I experienced at this performance of *B.#03* was the very faint possibility and the powerful hope that theatre might offer an image of the unconstrained community of fellow-feeling that might ground a utopian politics—communism—to which I remained affectively attached. The intensity of my emotional response to the manifestation of this hope had been shaped by feelings about the faintness of the possibility substantially conditioned by the pervasive conviction that communism had "collapsed" in 1989.

This book is in part an extended attempt to make sense of these connections and, further, to understand what it means for such feelings to be produced at a particular interface between work and leisure under capitalism. I look at the theatre as a place and a practice where it might be possible to think disruptively about work and leisure, about work and love, and about the apparently separate realms of necessity and freedom:

> Freedom, in this sphere, can consist only in this, that socialized man, the associated producers, govern the human metabolism with nature in a rational way, bringing it under their collective control instead of being dominated by it as a blind power; accomplishing it with the least expenditure of energy and in conditions most worthy and appropriate for their human nature. But this always remains a realm of necessity. The true realm of freedom, the development of human powers as an end in itself, begins beyond it, though it can only flourish with this realm of necessity as its basis.[8]

The passionate amateurs of this book's title are those who attempt, "in this sphere" of capitalism, to realize something that looks and feels like the true realm of freedom—not the "free time" of capitalist leisure—but knowing, very often, that in that very attempt, they risk subsuming their labors of love entirely to the demands of the sphere of necessity in which they must make their living. Some, but not all, of these passionate amateurs will be found at work making theatre or trying to make, of the theatre, a fleeting realm of freedom within the realm of necessity and to make it, perhaps paradoxically, endure.

ONE | Theatre and Communism after Athens

We are sitting in the theatre, and we are worrying about community. We are not alone; much work has already preceded us in thinking about the relationship between our attendance at the theatre and our participation in both the social and the political dimensions of community. In this chapter my aim is to move between the first of the three terms with which this book announces itself to be concerned—theatre—and the second— communism. Notwithstanding my own leap to a certain understanding of historical communism as part of the scope (or mythical content) of *B.#03*, the task of justifying communism, as such, as a central concern of this book will eventually come to depend upon a more familiar conjunction, that between theatre and community. For, as should be clear by now, this is not a book about a communist theatre. It seeks communism in a certain potentiality within theatrical practice rather than in any theatre that would name itself "communist" (even if the "Proletarian Children's Theater" of chap. 3 might lead one to think otherwise). Communism here is not the given name of a party, nor, least of all, of any national political state under which theatre might be produced and presented. The communism in question here remains to be found, in relation to the practice of theatre, or rather, as a potential relation within the practice of theatre.

What is the experience of relation in the practice of theatre that might offer communist potential? It will need to be distinguished both from a more general feeling that those who gather in a theatre might share a sense of community, and also from what Jill Dolan has called "the utopian performative," in which participation in a live performance event produces a public among whom a sense of human potential beyond the constraints of the present is fleetingly captured.[1] Dolan's is already a considerable refinement of the idea of theatre *as* community, which is often as free of specific content as claims that a theatrical event puts people in touch with their "feelings" or makes them "think." It is grounded in specific and contemporary experiences of performance, often those in which social identities and subjectivities marginalized or excluded in a society in which power, rights, and resources are unevenly distributed according to gender, race, and sexuality. In naming this potential "communist," however, I am trying to understand it in rather different historical and political terms: in terms of a longer history of theatre in which opposition to capitalism as such—rather than to its specific contemporary oppressions and exclusions—is at stake. This will involve considerations of historical development, of the nature of theatrical time, and of the relation of both to the experience of work. The communist potential, then, has to do with an experience of work, under specific historical circumstances (industrial capitalism) and in a specific industry (theatre), where the "present" of theatrical time—the time of performance—is the product of a specific division of labor (as between actors and spectators, for example, or amateurs and professionals). The communist potential is to be found in theatre's occasional capacity to trouble some quite fundamental assumptions about both work and time—about the work of time and the time of work—that have come to shape social and cultural life at least since the consolidation of industrial capitalism in Europe from around the end of the eighteenth century. This capacity, I will argue, arises largely from the participation of the theatres in question in what I have already called here "industry," rather than from any position outside capitalism and its institutions. Or rather, the communist potential—the trouble it makes with work and time—is experienced as a fraught relationship with industry, with its institutions, and with capitalism itself, rather than as flight or freedom from them. The passionate amateur—who is the person, either knowingly or not, in pursuit of this communist potential—may be traced, historically, then, to one of the first moments of cultural and political resistance to the establishment of our now dominant understanding of the relations between work and time; traced, that is, to the moment at which industrial capitalism first started to assert its power. The passionate amateur of this book is a theatrical variant of a historical figure whom Michael Löwy and Robert Sayre have called the romantic anti-capitalist.[2]

Romantic anti-capitalism names a resistance to industrial capitalism, articulated on behalf of values, practices, and experiences, often those of a premodern, preindustrial, rural life, that industrial capitalism seemed determined to destroy. Because of its valorization of premodern conceptions of community and social relations, it has frequently been characterized—along with romanticism more broadly—as a conservative or politically retrograde tendency in critical thought. Many Marxists, in particular, especially those for whom a progressive model of historical development is a crucial dimension of their political analysis, have regarded the romantic anti-capitalist with great suspicion. Indeed, the first elaboration of the term "romantic anti-capitalist" is usually attributed to the Hungarian Marxist, György Lukács, for whom it described the sensibility or worldview of writers such as Dostoevsky, whose work contains an only partly articulated vision of community as a "world beyond estrangement" and which therefore falls short of an adequate materialist critique of capitalism.[3] The term is intended as derogatory. In the 1931 article in which the term first appears, a text that Löwy and Sayre characterize as a "document of dogmatic frenzy," Lukács writes that Dostoyevsky, a writer who had been a major source of positive inspiration for him in the early 1920s, had transformed "the problems of Romantic opposition to capitalism into internal spiritual problems" and that he had thereby made himself "the artistic representative of 'a petit bourgeois Romantic anticapitalist intellectual opposition,'" a social phenomenon more likely to lead toward the reaction of the fascist right than it could to the revolutionary left.[4] Löwy and Sayre's project is to redeem figures of romantic anti-capitalism from the pervasive conviction that romantic notions of community tend inevitably in a dangerous rightward direction. This is done, first, by locating the origins of the "worldview" as a critique of a specific historical situation, and, second, by organizing the field in a kind of political taxonomy, in which romantic figures of the right (Georges Bernanos, Edmund Burke, Gottfried Benn, Carl Schmitt) are distinguished from liberal, leftist, and revolutionary figures. The aim of both strategies is to identify a "romantic" legacy deep within the intellectual tradition of Marxism itself, in which "romantic" aspects of Marx's own thought and writing (largely in the earlier work) are understood as having been carried forward by figures such as Rosa Luxemburg, Ernst Bloch, Walter Benjamin (the clearest representative of this tradition included in the present book), Herbert Marcuse, and even, albeit in a profoundly contradictory way, Lukács himself.[5]

Among the key characteristics of romantic anti-capitalism are that its expressions of rebellion and its articulations of critique are directed against the damage wrought by industrial capitalism upon human individuals and communities from a perspective shaped by a deeply felt attachment to a mythical or imaginary precapitalist past: "Romanticism issues from a revolt against a concrete historical present. . . . What is rejected, in other words, is not the present in the abstract but a specifically capitalist present conceived in terms of its most important defining qualities."[6] The most important of capitalism's "defining qualities" is its organization of all human life around wage labor, in which human activity and creative capacity are primarily valued for what they can contribute to the accumulation of capital, and in which life is measured out in units of productive time.

The precapitalist past—the world before wage labor became the dominant work-relation—takes a number of forms and throws up a diversity of mythical antecedents as images of revolt or an alternative society. For many German, and indeed English participants in this tradition (like William Morris), heroic fantasies of a highly aestheticized medieval period proved especially appealing. For Bloch, the sixteenth-century radical Protestant leader Thomas Münzer became an exemplary figure. Others, including Lukács, Engels, and, at times, Marx himself, looked either to democratic Athens or to the "Homeric" era's "primitive communism" for metaphorical and ideological resources—a preference that a number of theatre makers and scholars almost inevitably share. Michael Löwy, returning to the theme of romantic anti-capitalism in a recent study of Walter Benjamin's "Theses on the Concept of History," makes a crucial observation about the nature of this kind of use of the past. It does not involve a desire that history should go into reverse, but rather the idea that a genuinely revolutionary move might involve something that theatre does rather well—an interruption or substitution of the present with something of the past, something consciously and deliberately repeated:

> One might define the Romantic *Weltanschauung* as a cultural critique of modern (capitalist) civilization in the name of pre-modern (pre-capitalist) values—a critique or protest that bears upon aspects which are felt to be unbearable and degrading: the quantification and mechanization of life, the reification of social relations, the dissolution of the community and the disenchantment of the world. Its nostalgia for the past does not mean it is necessarily retrograde: the Romantic view of the world may assume both reactionary and revolutionary forms. For revolutionary Romanticism the aim is not a *return* to the past, but a *detour* through the past on the way to a utopian future.[7]

I want to suggest that theatre can perform this "detour" in two ways. First, it can offer an image or enactment or repetition of some aspect of the past—or, indeed, any time that is not the time of the "present" that the time of theatrical "presence" replaces—in order to negate something of our present reality. Second, within the social and economic structure of industrial capitalism, it offers this negation of the present by way of an experience that is not normally experienced as work, but as some kind of nonwork or "play." Of course it is no such thing: it is work for those who make it, just as the nonpresent past or future summoned into the present by the act of theatre-making is also no such thing, but rather the present itself, experienced otherwise. The detour taken through the theatre leads through a past that is not past and is accomplished through work that looks like it is not work. This is why the theatre is a particularly good place for the passionate amateur or romantic anti-capitalist who wants to find some way of undoing, even if only for a moment, the time of her work and the work of time upon herself.[8]

The theatre is also a good (because perverse) place to go looking for communist potential—not, crucially, because it offers any kind of space beyond or outside capitalism, but precisely because it usually nestles so deeply inside it. Much romantic anti-capitalism looks to the past because it offers an image of an outside upon which a future utopia might be modeled. In the same gesture it also assumes that there exists some essential, whole, and unalienated humanity, from which capitalism has torn us and to which we may one day return through a restoration of past experiences and practices of community. This is the "romance of community" against which Miranda Joseph offers a powerful critique.[9] For Joseph community is best understood, not as some alternative to capitalism in which human beings will realize themselves and their social relations most fully, but rather, as its supplement. It is a resource that lies within capitalism, and upon which capitalist projects and enterprises of many different kinds can draw in order to encourage the performance of subjectivities that will assist them in the production and realization of surplus value. It is not available, therefore, as an unproblematic source of alternative value and good feeling for left or liberal social and political projects. But nor is it merely an unattainable fantasy from which it would be better if everyone abstained. As Joseph writes, just once or twice, the true name of this "supplement" or "specter" is "communism": a potential for the making of a life beyond the division of labor right where the division of labor rules. It was partly by accident that the personal experience that seems most richly to inform Joseph's critique was that of working as a volunteer in a nonprofit theatre in San Francisco. But it was a happy accident, not least for the present project, for which one of theatre's most significant characteristics is that the division of labor is not just visible there, but, literally, on show, night after night, right where people go looking for something very different. It is in this apparent contradiction—and it is a contradiction that opens up only the very tightest of spaces—that the communist potential of theatre might be found. If you can make it here, you can make it anywhere.

Others have also sought to locate this potential in aesthetic practice. Jean-Luc Nancy, for example, writing against a communism grounded in work, in class identity and the projected triumph of a revolutionary historical subject called the working class, proposes a "literary communism." At first glance this might appear to be a kind of joke, echoing "champagne socialism" and suggesting, perhaps, that the "communism" in question is little more than a luxury pose, indulged mainly by members of a bourgeois élite who enjoy fine wine and good books. Indeed, the vulnerability of the idea to such ridicule is perhaps part of its meaning. Instead of a communism in which community might be the objective of a project, the work of work, as it were, in which the members or participants are fused together in an organic or organized union (a state that Nancy calls "immanence"), Nancy offers the fragile proposition of an articulation of exposures. Instead of seeking communion with others, one opens oneself to the experience of encounters with others as marking simultaneously the limit of one's self, and the place where one's self, such as it is, begins. That is to say, in a recognition that one's self, as such, is constituted, not by its integrity and individuality, but precisely by its appearance in relation to others, a relation that Nancy will call, in later texts, "compearance."[10] The "literary" dimension of a "communism" based upon this conception of the self in relation, then, is to be found in the idea that writing marks space between things:

> What is at stake is the articulation of community. "Articulation" means, in some way, "writing," which is to say, the inscription of a meaning whose transcendence or presence is indefinitely and constitutively deferred.[11]

This constitutive deferral is the "unworking" that Nancy opposes to the "work" that seeks to achieve community, and from which he derives the title of the publication in which he presented the idea of "literary communism": *Le communeauté désoeuvrée* (translated, not without some difficulty, into English as *The Inoperative Community*).[12] In the title essay Nancy outlines the extent to which a work-propelled teleology has dominated both political and philosophical conceptions of both communism and community. There is, he writes,

> no form of communist opposition—or let us say rather "communitarian" opposition, in order to emphasize that the word should not

be restricted in this context to strictly political references—that has not been or is not still profoundly subjugated to the goal of a *human* community, that is to the goal of achieving a community of beings producing in essence their own essence as their work, and furthermore producing precisely this essence *as community.* An absolute immanence of man to man—a humanism—and of community to community—a communism—obstinately subtends, whatever be their merits or strengths, all forms of oppositional communism, all leftist and ultraleftist models, and all models based on the workers' council.[13]

In my attempt to account for how a communist potential might manifest itself in the particularly "literary" space of the theatre, and, most specifically, in relation to my interest in identifying this with a resistance to work, these texts of Nancy's have been particularly useful inasmuch as they suggest simultaneously the value of work that is not work and of a community which is not (yet) one. The theatre that possesses this potential, I will suggest, will first of all be a theatre in which work is somehow in question; in which the complementary relationship between work and leisure is not taken for granted, neither by unreflective professionalism nor by the conditioned amateurism of the recreational hobby. Second, it will be a theatre in which there is always some kind of distance; in which participants are always separated from one another rather than merged with one another in an achieved community of the event. Third, it may also be a theatre in which this distance is not just a spatial separation in the present, but also a temporal articulation, in which the apparent presentness of the present is complicated by the appearance within it of people, things, and feelings from other times. A "theatrical" communism, then, following Nancy, might involve the potential "compearance" of figures from both the past and the future.

Even before Nancy articulates the idea of "literary communism," a historical point of departure for it may be detected in the approach he takes, along with his coauthor Philippe Lacoue-Labarthe, to Romanticism, and, in particular, to the life and work of the Jena Romantics. This was a group of writers who came together in the university town of Jena at the very end of the eighteenth century—August Wilhelm and Friedrich Schlegel, Caroline Schlegel-Schelling, Dorothea Mendelssohn-Veit, Friedrich Schleiermacher, Ludwig Tieck, Novalis and Friedrich Schelling. Between 1798 and 1800 their activities centered around the publication of a journal, the *Athenaeum* (their affiliation with Athens, avowed in this choice of title, includes them in the ranks of those who, as I will shortly discuss, imagine themselves in some way to be "after Athens"). Lacoue-Labarthe and Nancy describe this circle as "a sort of 'cell,' marginal (if not altogether clandestine), like the core of an organisation destined to develop into a 'network' and serve as the model for a new style of life" and also as a "form of community," a kind of "secret society," and "the first 'avant-garde' group in history."[14] Lacoue-Labarthe and Nancy see the emergence of this kind of association as a response to a "triple crisis" in Germany: a social crisis facing a certain element within the bourgeoisie, who have aspirations of cultural leadership but are no longer able to find stable employment or exercise such leadership in either the church or the university; a political crisis brought about by the promise and threat of the French Revolution; and a philosophical crisis opened up by the critical philosophy of Kant. The Jena "cell" saw their literary project not merely as a response to a literary crisis, but rather as the "privileged locus of expression" for a radical repudiation of bourgeois life as they found it.[15] To live together, in literature, is a way of living a critique of this life, the expression of their ambition for "an entirely new social function for the writer . . . and consequently for a different society."[16] Lacoue-Labarthe and Nancy find this ambition expressed with particular precision in Mendelssohn-Veit's statement that "since it is altogether contrary to bourgeois order and absolutely forbidden to introduce romantic poetry into life, then let life be brought into romantic poetry; no police force and no educational institution can prevent this."[17] In this call romanticism seems to be the realization, in the present, of a collective mode of life—secured against law, education, and, I would add, the centrality of work to bourgeois social order—as a kind of "communist" enclave. Just as it does for Löwy and Sayre, then, romanticism itself emerges, historically, as a critique of capitalism, and therefore as a crucial affective and intellectual resource for communism.

More recently John Roberts, introducing a special issue of *Third Text* titled "Art, Praxis and the Community to Come," writes of contemporary manifestations of a similar conception of communism as an "enclave" practice.[18] Roberts notes a leftward shift in art theory and practice, associated with "the increasing democratic dissolution of the professional boundaries of art production itself," and suggests that a "new communism" developed from the 1980s by philosophers such as Nancy, Alain Badiou, and Antonio Negri has contributed to the resurgence of messianic or utopian communist thought in the present.[19] There is a melancholic dimension to this resurgence, in that much of its thinking takes shape in response to precisely the sense of loss and defeat for communism that I have located in my feelings as a spectator at *B.#03,* and that Nancy articulates in *The Inoperative Community.* As Roberts writes of this phenomenon in general, and of its tendency to locate itself in artistic practice:

> In conditions of political retreat or "closure" the function of the communist imaginary is to keep open the ideal horizon of egalitarianism, equality and free exchange; and art, it is judged, is one of the primary spaces where this "holding operation" is best able to take place.[20]

There is something about Jena, too, that suggests it may participate in a similar melancholy, *avant la lettre,* as if the "cell" based on bringing life into romantic poetry had formed itself in the knowledge that the "police order" had already defeated it in the so-called real world.

But Roberts also points to a much more optimistic articulation of this "cultural communism," particularly in its role as a major intellectual resource for the curatorial practice and theoretical writing of Nicolas Bourriaud. Bourriaud's idea of "relational aesthetics"—in which artists produce social relations rather than material objects—has been widely discussed in contemporary art theory, and, because of its interest in people doing things with one another, has also begun to be taken up in writing about theatre and performance.[21] Bourriaud's work has been subjected to the kind of critique that any discourse that achieves fashionable status in the contemporary art market must expect, and much of it is successful in pointing to the absence of a concrete politics and the risk that the curatorial and critical valorization of the art practices in question might end up subsuming whatever socially ameliorative potential they might possess to the logics of a mode of capitalism for which, as we shall have occasion to observe from time to time throughout this book, social creativity of this kind is a prized commodity.[22] But Roberts suggests that the underlying affiliation of this discourse with "new" or "enclave" communism "cannot be dismissed simply as yet another outbreak of speculative artworld silliness and idealism."[23] Stewart Martin, however, in an earlier edition of *Third Text,* offers a persuasive critique of Bourriaud's *Relational Aesthetics,* in which he argues that Bourriaud's idea, far from being original, is in fact a revival of aspects of Romanticism, and one that, in its "reversibility," offers a "utopianism" that "echoes the commodified friendship of customer services."[24]

Elsewhere Martin also develops a critique of what he calls "artistic communism." In his own contribution to the issue of *Third Text* introduced by Roberts's essay, Martin offers a "retrospective" writing of "artistic communism," predicated upon "a conjunction or correspondence, in particular between the post-Kantian conception of absolute art and Marx's early conception of communism."[25] This construction also begins, as do Lacoue-Labarthe and Nancy, with Jena at the end of the eighteenth century, and, in particular, with Schelling—whose "proposal of art as the summit of practical reason," Martin writes, "exposes a general relation of art to activity and production that is common after Kant, and indicates a fundamental affinity with Marx and his conception of communism as a society of free producers."[26] Martin goes on to propose that this "artistic communism" has largely been "subverted" by "artistic capitalism"—the name he gives to "the creeping subsumption of life under capital" in the present historical moment at which, as Martin affirms, rewriting Sartre, "capitalism is now the unsurpassable horizon of our times."[27] Martin notes the contribution of Paolo Virno, for whom practices of "virtuosity" represent some potential for artlike activity currently subsumed by capital to become a site for a renewed politics—"the communism of capital." He cautions, however, against "a certain subjective idealism" in this "autonomist" gesture toward the "general intellect"—that communicative capacity held in common that thinkers such as Negri and Virno identify as crucial to their hopes for a properly political resistance to capitalism.[28]

I share Martin's interest in this idea of "artistic communism" and share to a large degree his critical perspective. While I am also skeptical of the optimistic uses to which "autonomist" thought has often been put, part of my project here is, nonetheless, to see whether there is anything to be found within the practice of theatre that might actualize some of its political potential. Martin is particularly skeptical of its now quite pervasive use in mainstream contemporary art practices and discourses. Its pervasiveness in such circles might even be taken as an indication of the extent to which its political potential has been co-opted for broadly liberal and pro-capitalist rather than radical anti-capitalist ends. In turning to theatre, instead, I don't wish to suggest that theatre is any more likely than contemporary art to offer refuge from such co-option. However, I am interested in exploring the possibility that, at least in some theatre practices of the twentieth century (and even of today), the subsumption of labor under capitalism might not be as complete as Martin's account would suggest; that there may be some continued resistance on the part of "artistic communism" to the subversion wrought against it by "artistic capitalism." My articulation of the idea of the "passionate amateur" is an attempt to describe at least one part of the spectrum of such theatre practices (those that fall outside or undermine theatre's status as a professional activity).

My gamble then is that there might yet be something in what "literary," "cultural," or "artistic communism" proposes, that it may be possible to actualize in collective or socially oriented artistic practices something that is elsewhere only an idea or a vision of the future (often based on a romantic nostalgia for a mythical past): production and pleasure beyond the division of labor. One of the propositions of this book, then, is that some of that potentiality, or, at the very least, evidence of a desire for it, is to be found in the activities of passionate amateurs of the theatre. These passionate amateurs are those who work together for the production of value for one another (for love, that is, rather than money) in ways that refuse—sometimes rather quietly and perhaps even ineffectually— the division of labor that obtains under capitalism as usual.

Many attempts to articulate what this potentiality might be, arising as they do, most often, in the name of that community with which many theatre-makers and scholars have associated the theatre, will frequently find themselves "after" Athens. That is to say that they will dwell upon theatre and thought that simultaneously follow an idea of theatre taken to have been born in Athens and seek better to understand what this "Athens" might be that is so readily produced as the ground for the association of theatre with community. I will follow in these footsteps, then, but in being "after" Athens, I aim not merely to be in pursuit of this distant idea; I also seek to be on its case. In particular, I seek to take account of the critique offered by Salvatore Settis of the dominant uses to which the concept of the "classical" is often put. In *The Future of the "Classical"* Settis shows how what Novalis calls the "summoning" of an "antiquity" that "has not come down to us by itself" has enabled successive generations of Europeans to treat as given and preideological any set of contemporary values capable of being legitimized by reference to their origins in Graeco-Roman antiquity.[29] Settis does not offer any extended consideration of theatre, focusing instead on approaches to the "classical" by way of the plastic arts (Vasari, Winckelmann, and Warburg are key figures in his narrative, the last for his disruption of the Eurocentric interpretations favored by his predecessors). However, he does note that the "classical" is deployed in political thought too, such as in the writing of Hannah Arendt, who shares what Settis calls "a widespread belief that the Greeks sowed the seed that would blossom much later into events and values that today we identify with," when she claims, for instance, "that neither the American nor the French Revolution could have occurred without the example provided by 'classical' antiquity."[30] Arendt's thought is of particular significance for this project for two principal reasons, beyond its engagement with "classical" Greek thought and practice: first, because it constitutes an attempt to rethink conventional Marxist conceptions of politics as grounded in work and production; second, because it turns to the theatre as a way to understand or explain the concept of action, which, as opposed to labor (the necessary task of subsistence or reproduction) and work (the labor of production, or poesis, a making that includes "art"), is for her both the form and the content of politics.[31]

In *The Human Condition* Arendt offers an account of the *polis* that, in its transitory constitution from the exchange of human speech and action, seems to suggest a theatrical event—a temporary coming together that is both part of and yet somehow to one side of the run of the social and political everyday, and that, perhaps crucially for the present project, depends upon its participants' freedom from the demands of labor. This might be taken to suggest, I think, that the *polis* might itself be constituted in the action that is the making of theatre: theatre being one of those places where people appear to one another and participate in action, and being also the one very specific place in which such action is reenacted, so that it may be collectively reflected upon:

> the specific revelatory quality of action and speech, the implicit manifestation of the agent and speaker, is so indissolubly tied to the living flux of acting and speaking that it can be represented and "reified" only through a kind of repetition, the imitation or mimesis, which according to Aristotle prevails in all arts but is actually appropriate only to the drama, whose very name (from the Greek verb dran, "to act") indicates that playacting actually is an imitation of acting.[32]

Clearly, if the *polis* is to be thought of as theatrical in this way, it must not be a theatre of consumption alone, but one of participation. If the *polis* is, as Arendt claims, "not the city-state in its physical location,"[33] but rather "the organization of the people as it arises out of acting and speaking together,"[34] and if she is right that "its true space lies between people living together for this purpose,"[35] then one might want to imagine not simply that the constitution of an audience in front of a theatrical event is a kind of political potentiality, but that the act of dedicating oneself to acting and speaking together, the act, that is, of forming some kind of collective theatrical organization, is, in and of itself, a political act. I shall hope to show how this might be the case, for both producers and consumers, actors and spectators, in the chapters that follow.

To be more precise, such an act might be political when and as long as it is not work, as long as it is *praxis* (a processual action) rather than *poesis* (the making of something).[36] In the four chapters that comprise the core of this book—chapters 2–5—theatre within the specific social and economic circumstances of (mainly) European capitalism in the twentieth and early twenty-first centuries will be examined so as to highlight moments in which a movement or uncertainty between praxis and poesis makes itself known. These are moments where a politics might break out, not so much because of an absence of work or labor (which might have to be the case in an Arendtian perspective), but rather because the terms upon which the theatre is made, in these four chosen examples, unsettle our capacity to distinguish between work and nonwork, poesis and praxis, the professional and the amateur. The relation of such "moments" of theatre to community, when community is thought of in relation to communism, will always therefore have something to do with a critique of the division of labor within capitalism. In going "after" Athens, in the footsteps of Arendt, I am also following Paolo Virno, who, in an inversion of Arendt's thought, observes that the distinctive characteristic of work in "post-Fordist" capitalism is precisely its folding into itself of those capacities for communication that were for Arendt, purely political, rather than concurring with Arendt's account of modern life in which work has reduced almost to nothing the space of politics:

> So then, I maintain that things have gone in the opposite direction from what Arendt seems to believe: it is not that politics has conformed to labor; it is rather that labor has acquired the traditional features of political action. My reasoning is opposite and symmetrical with respect to that of Arendt. I maintain that it is in the world of contemporary labor that we find the "being in the presence of others," the relationship with the presence of others, the beginning of new processes, and the constitutive familiarity with contingency, the unforeseen and the possible. I maintain that post-Fordist labor, the productive labor of surplus, subordinate labor, brings into play the talents and the qualifications which, according to a secular tradition, had more to do with political action.[37]

I will also be "after" Athens with Jacques Rancière, like Arendt, a student of praxis, whose thought aims consistently at detaching identity from work (suggesting, perhaps, that "the human condition" is to be found elsewhere) and who sees this redistribution of the sensible (in which one is no longer perceived and "identified" by one's place in the organization of labor) as an act of politics.[38] For Rancière, this undoing of the terms by which identity is conferred upon a subject by the work that they do is the undoing of a political philosophy inaugurated in Athens by theatre's ever-faithful antagonist, Plato. Theatre, for Rancière, offers at least an image, and sometimes even the reality, of social relations between people who cannot be defined by the work they do. If they are actors, they are doing a job in which, as Plato complains of artists in general, they know nothing about what it is they are supposed to be doing, because they are pretending to know how to be someone they are not. But precisely because they are pretending to know how to be someone they are not, they are also demonstrating that they do know how to do something. They know how to pretend to be someone else. The point is, precisely, that the situation is confused, and that the confusion is about how people might be defined in terms of what they do. And even if they are spectators rather than actors, they are participating in a field of the social that is unusually hospitable to temporary identity reassignments, in which they may reach both above and beneath their stations.[39]

However, Rancière wishes to understand the relationship between theatre and community as a "presupposition" rather than as something that theatre might actually produce. This means that, on the one hand, he affirms the significance and historical persistence of the idea that theatre is an especially communitarian practice:

> Since German Romanticism thinking about theatre has been associated with this idea of the living community. Theatre emerged as a form of aesthetic constitution—sensible constitution—of the community. By that I mean the community as a way of occupying a place and a time, as the body in action as opposed to a mere apparatus of laws; a set of perceptions, gestures, and attitudes that pre-cede and pre-form laws and political institutions. More than any other art, theatre has been associated with the Romantic idea of an aesthetic revolution, changing not the mechanics of the state and laws, but the sensible forms of human experience. Hence reform of the theatre meant the restoration of its character as assembly or ceremony of the community.[40]

But on the other hand, he insists that "it is high time we examine this idea that the theatre is, in and of itself, a community site."[41] Rancière notes that the fact of living bodies addressing other living bodies in the same physical space seems to lead to an assumption that theatre has "a communitarian essence" (not altogether removed, I would suggest, from the "ontology of performance" similarly derived from assumptions about the primacy of liveness). Accepting this assumption means, he asserts, that the question of exactly what is going on between spectators and performers, and, indeed, between spectators themselves, is avoided.

Rancière's preliminary answer to this question is to propose that the "presupposition" of a community is the only thing that makes the gathering in the theatre different from people all watching the same television show at the same time in different locations. This community, however, is linked neither by their interaction (as some advocates of a more participatory theatre frequently hope) nor by membership in any kind of "collective body" of the kind that might once, in Castellucci's terms, have offered "foundations . . . for the invention of tragedy," but simply by a shared sense of one another's equal intellectual capacity: "It is the capacity of anonymous people, the capacity that makes everyone equal to everyone else." Anonymous (and perhaps not even identifying with their work), equal, "separate from one another":[42] such is the condition of spectators, according to Rancière. It is hard to find, in *The Emancipated Spectator*, much that would account for the particular pleasures of this condition, and it is for this reason that my concluding chapter, entitled "Solitude in Relation," seeks in the affective experience of spectatorship a more extended understanding of what might be at stake here, in what sounds like it might be an emancipation from, rather than in or through, community. For the time being, however, I want to develop Rancière's suggestion that theatre is about community to the extent that it contains a "presupposition" of community, by looking at two ways this presupposition is frequently articulated in discussions of theatre today: theatre and community—that's "classical"!—and theatre and community—that's "good"! Both of these articulations may be understood as myths. The aim here is not just to show that these are myths, but also to explore what these two myths might still have to offer, for any attempt to develop a new line in "critical romantic anti-capitalism."

1. THEATRE, COMMUNITY, AND THE "CLASSICAL"

The first myth is, precisely, that which makes Athens the model "after" which an understanding of the association between theatre and community is to be crafted. The act of making Athens a model may sometimes be a matter of choice, and, at others, a process of manufacture. Only rarely is it a case of wholly unexamined assumptions and myths of origin; most myth-makers know what it is they are making, after all, even if, as Settis notes, the "less explicitly" the legitimization of ideological material by way of the "classical" is done, the "more effective it is."[43] Theatre and performance scholarship—at least in English—has for some considerable time now taken its lead in matters of the tragic theatre of the Athenian city-state from the conjuncture of two propositions: that the theatre in Athens was an institution in which the relations of citizens to one another were represented and interrogated, and that social and political life in Athens was constituted by participatory practices—of which the theatre was just one—such that it might usefully be understood as a "performance culture." This lead may well have been given most decisively by the work of Jean-Pierre Vernant and Pierre Vidal Naquet; taken up, influentially, in the field of classical studies by Simon Goldhill; and carried on in work on Greek theatre and theatre more generally in numerous locations up to and including David Wiles's recent *Theatre and Citizenship,* the opening chapter of which, in a symptomatic move, is devoted to "Athens."[44] I clearly exhibit similar symptoms, in beginning, however apologetically, in the same place (even if, as so often, it appears first in the guise of Berlin). The predominance of this general view of the social and political function of theatre in Athens is not problematic in itself. However it should be understood, at least in some cases, as evidence either of a preference or predisposition toward a communitarian understanding of theatre (with which I am far from unsympathetic) or of a desire to ground an analysis of contemporary political experiences in Greek categories. Classicists and historians of antiquity are usually more circumspect than either political theorists (like Arendt) or theatre and performance scholars when it comes to suggesting continuities between the present and any specific past.

One succinct articulation of the association between theatre and community in Athens is Oddone Longo's:

> It may not be amiss to insist from the beginning on the collective or communitarian character of the Athenian theater public in the classical period: a public which is quite unparalleled in the history of drama in that it coincided—in principle and to a great extent in fact—with the civic community, that is the community of *citizens.*[45]

What Longo insists upon is that the "theater public" is the "community." This insistence is qualified, crucially, by the observation that this coincidence is "unparalleled." Even if—and this remains an open question—the "Athenian theater public" may rightly be considered to coincide with "the community of citizens," and whether or not this would allow an analysis of the theatre as an institution or practice of the kind of community a contemporary theorist or activist might wish to promote (with all its notorious exclusions), the key point here is that this coincidence has never been repeated. The situation in Athens cannot, then, be evoked to describe any subsequent real relationship between theatre and community. It may yet, however, point to a future horizon at which such a coincidence might reappear. And it is made to do so, in Longo's text, in a familiar maneuver by summoning the image of a prior "community" from which the tragic theatre is supposed to have developed.[46] In insisting "from the beginning" upon the "communitarian," Longo seems to allude to the idea that, even if the theatre, as it is actually practiced, is not fully or uncomplicatedly "communitarian," it still carries with it some trace of an earlier, perhaps unknowable "community."

For Longo, theatre in classical Athens involved the precipitation of two communities—actors and spectators—out of a single community that had, in "the earliest performances," been "the collective which acted the 'drama.'" So, although his account does not posit tragic drama as the origin of anything contemporary, Longo does locate it in relation to a precedent "origin," in which community seems to stand for a way of life without social division. Longo seeks to avoid what he cautions might become "a too simplistic interpretation of tragedy as a directly communitarian ritual, or to a reading of Attic drama as somehow expressive of a completely collective situation." In order to do so he notes that the theatre's development from a predominantly choral form toward one dominated by the discursive interplay of the actors representing individual characters "might be seen as the progressive integration of the drama into the more pluralistic system of the polis, where division of labor, social stratification, and class struggle reduce precisely the area of unanimity in the community." Theatrical drama, then, is not the expression of a nonexistent "solid collectivity free from contradictions and class conflict," but rather, theatre is constituted as an institution for encouraging social cohesion in the midst of everyday conflict, so that "the dramatic enactment brings into being a 'theatrical community,' which in a certain sense is the passing hypostasis of the actual *polis*, but without its inevitable conflicts and cleavages."[47] In this respect, this "communitarian theatre" does indeed look forward, in its production of an ideal *polis* toward which its public (or at least some of them), and subsequent readers, spectators, activists, and scholars, might be imagined to aspire. And it looks forward by gesturing backward to an imaginary community out of which the real divided society of the *polis* supposedly emerged. What is elided here is that the participants in "the earliest performances," however much they may appear to embody more fully "the community" than do the "actors" and "spectators" divided from one another in the theatrical auditorium, cannot themselves be understood fully to "coincide" with any kind of "solid collectivity." This is for two reasons, one historical, the other rhetorical: historical, in that, despite romantic constructions in which Greek prehistory contains a phase of "primitive communism," preceding societies were themselves characterized by clear social hierarchies and other divisions;[48] rhetorical, in that, as Longo himself has already noted, the "coincidence" of public and community he observes in Athenian theatre is "unparalleled." If the participants in "the earliest performances" did indeed constitute a community of some kind, it will have been one that was identical only with itself: that is to say it was almost certainly formed on the basis of—and may even have helped constitute—some kind of class division. The image of a fully collective and participatory theatrical and political community therefore lies both before and after the moment of classical tragedy—in a mythic past and an imagined future. The peculiar coincidence of public and community that Longo identifies in the "Athenian theater public" turns out not to be located in that "unparalleled" moment, after all, but rather in two nonexistent moments: in "the beginning" of "the earliest performances" and in the intimation of a possible future that the "passing hypostasis" induces in that fleeting collectivity he calls 'a "theatrical community."[49] But neither of these can "parallel" the "Athenian" moment itself, even as that very moment turns out no longer and not yet to be itself. This is both a romantic and a theatrical conceptualization of time, as I hope future chapters will show: romantic in its appeal to an idealized past as a resource for constructing a better future in response to a painful and alienating present; theatrical in its confusion of multiple temporalities in the moment of performance.[50]

Without entering too deeply and prematurely into the kinks of this kind of time—whose time will come in later chapters—it is perhaps simply worth observing here that implicit in Longo's understanding of the political value of tragedy is the idea that it offers its participants resources for making community, rather than an image of what community should be. In this respect it corresponds with an understanding of mimesis as the action of making rather than copying, in which mimesis doubles the process of creation rather than producing copies of what has already been created. A similar perspective may be identified in Goldhill's account too, where the City Dionysia is understood as being "in the full sense of the expression a civic occasion" because it places the principles of the polis "at risk" by putting them into dramatic relation with values with which they are in tension.[51] It is the enactment of this tension that might be said to offer community-making resources. David Wiles reaches a very similar conclusion, in which he offers an analysis of "fifth century tragedy as a performance practice that built community, with shared pleasure in discussion comprising but one aspect of communal polis life."[52]

More ambitious in its attempt to claim continuity between practices of theatre about two thousand years apart from one another is a volume entitled *Dionysus since 69*, which takes its title from the Performance Group's celebrated production of *Dionysus in 69*, directed by Richard Schechner, which is now widely regarded as a definitive example of the uses to which "classical" material was adapted by experimental theatre practitioners of the 1960s.[53] In her introduction to the collection, Edith Hall explains that the book responds to what its editors see as a resurgent interest in the production and adaptation of Greek tragedy since the 1960s, an interest that, they suggest, can now, "retrospectively" be understood as "a virtually inevitable consequence of this potent cultural coincidence of the hippie challenge to the traditional notion of theatre, the Performative Turn, and the exploration of non-western theatre conventions."[54] Hall is suggesting here, I think, that the myth-making as regards the origins of performance studies—in the conjuncture of anthropology with experimental theatre practice in the context of the counterculture of the 1960s—is intimately bound up with a desire to return to and remake the myths of origins for which the "classical" had already proved such a rich resource. However, attention to the role of "fabrication" in this process is somewhat occluded by the enthusiasm with which something that sounds very much like export-led globalization is introduced:

> Recently Dionysus, the theatre-god of the ancient Greeks, has transcended nearly all boundaries created by time, space, and cultural tradition, for staging Greek tragedy is now emphatically an international, even worldwide phenomenon. This seminal art-form, born two and a half thousand years ago in democratic Athens, rediscovered in the Renaissance as prestigious pan-European cultural property, has evolved in recent decades into a global medium.[55]

One of the difficulties here is the proposition that an "art-form" was "born" in Athens. Whatever was "born" there, it only became an art form much later, as a crucial element in a process in which, as Dipesh Chakbrabarty writes, "an entity called 'the European intellectual tradition' stretching back to the ancient Greeks is a fabrication of relatively recent European history."[56] A second difficulty arises because it is precisely the fact that theatre in Athens was just one element in a broader "performance culture" that lends itself to the kind of revival and reappropriation by Schechner and others in the name of "community." That is to say that it is the specific historical relationship between theatre and other social practices in the Athenian *polis* that constitutes the "unparalleled" character of the theatre in question. To abstract just the remaining plays from that situation and to suggest, on the basis of their proliferation in recent years, that these apparent parallels point to a continuity is a very different project even to Schechner's. Within the pages of *Dionysus since 69* additional perspectives point as much to interruption as they do to continuity: Lorna Hardwick writes of African and Caribbean adaptations of plays through which, she argues, Greek drama "has itself been decolonised," while Erika Fischer-Lichte, writing about productions by Klaus Michael Grüber and Peter Stein at the Schaubühne in Berlin in the 1970s, proposes that these works demonstrate the extent to which, whether it is desirable or not, the continuity affirmed by Hall is simply not possible:

> Our distance from the past of Greek tragedy and Greek culture, cannot, in principle, be bridged—at least not by theatre and its performances of ancient Greek plays. Thus the purpose of staging Greek—and other classical—texts is to remind us of this distance and to enable us to find ways of coping with it individually and perhaps to insert fragments of such texts into the context of our contemporary reflections, life and culture. It cannot accomplish a return to the origins—whatever they may have been. They are gone and lost forever.[57]

Thus in the very historical moment at which the idea of the "classical legacy" is under acute artistic and intellectual pressure—a postcolonial moment, above all—it is also returned into play as a potentially universalizing resource by artists and intellectuals who align themselves with postcolonial political pluralisms. While Schechner's adaptation of what Hall calls "non-western theatre conventions" has given rise to accusations that he is also complicit with aspects of globalization, Schechner's activity might, if it is to be seen in this light, be understood as import rather than export led. Whatever trade flows are carried by such traffic between cultural and historical location, and however "fabricated" or contested the idea of the "classical ideal" might be, the temptation to evoke it, either "explicitly" or not, remains powerful. Such evocation may best be understood as performative: it functions, as Novalis writes, as a summons. The idea that theatre might be community, or, more precisely, that it can make community, is a powerful mythic resource, but it doesn't transcend boundaries of space and time of its own accord; it must be appropriated in order to do its work. The most powerful of its appropriations, at least for present purposes, are those that seek to assert a particular and privileged relationship between theatre and community, and that make of that relationship a potential agent for revolutionary social and political change, what I call in the section that follows "the good." Darko Suvin, for example, writing in 1972 about "political drama," offers Aeschylus's *Oresteia* in evidence to claim that

> it would not be exaggerating to state that theatre and drama, as *communal* arts, are ontologically political, if politics means the health or sickness of the community which determines all human relations in it.[58]

"It would not be exaggerating"; "It may not be amiss": these disavowals in the midst of the most forceful assertion capture rather well the ambivalent character of the "classical" as a resource for a politics of community in the theatre. Something is "amiss," but it has been "summoned" anyway, again, in an act that has to insist that it is not "exaggerating" when it affirms, in language very similar to Arendt's, the political ontology of theatre: "the political art par excellence."[59]

2. THEATRE, COMMUNITY, AND THE "GOOD"

The idea that theatre might be a resource for making community, and that this is "good," is the second of the two myths about theatre and community. Its adherents include practitioners and advocates of the diverse field variously named as applied, socially engaged, political, activist, and, of course, community theatre, as well as many theorists and practitioners of performance and liberatory and countercultural action. As Eugene van Erven writes, concluding a collection of essays on practices of "community theatre" in a range of different national and cultural situations:

All of the community theatre projects discussed in this book, I suspect, would subscribe to the central aim of providing the members
of socially, culturally, ethnically, economically, sexually, culturally, or otherwise peripheral "communities" with the artistic
means to collectively and democratically express their concerns
and passions in their own, albeit aesthetically mediated, voices.[60]

Such projects are based on practices and political perspectives whose sub-
stantive origins van Erven locates firmly in the latter part of the twentieth
century. There are more or less the same set of circumstances as those to
which Hall attributes the resurgence of interest in Greek drama, even if
van Erven gestures briefly to the possibility that a differently oriented
scholarship might still wish to insist on "classical" origins too:

Although the usual anthropological arguments could be dusted off
to place the origins of community theatre, as indeed of all theatrical
expression, back in pre-colonial and Graeco-Roman times, its more
immediate antecedents lie buried in the various forms of countercultural, radical, anti- and post-colonial, educational and libera-
tional theatres of the 1960s and 1970s.[61]

However, one of the most influential practitioners in this field—
Augusto Boal—grounds his theoretical account of the "theatre of the oppressed" in a fierce polemic against what he sees as the "coercive" anti-
communitarianism of tragic theatre as described in Aristotle's *Poetics*.[62] In
the second English edition of *Theatre of the Oppressed* (published in 2000)
Boal introduces his account of the "coercive system of tragedy" with a
consciously imaginary or mythologizing account of the imposition of theatre's "hypocrisy" upon the "creative anarchy" of the workers' Dionysiac
song and dance. Boal's "myth" is in three parts. In the first, he describes
how the spontaneous postwork celebrations of Greek farm laborers had
to be brought under the control of the landowning aristocracy, and how
the dramatic poet and the choreographer were deployed as the agents of
this curtailment of an otherwise dangerous and anarchic freedom and
produced the choric order of the Dithyramb. In the second, more extended narrative, he tells of how the improvisations of Thespis spoke
truth in the face of the normative expressions of the dithyrambic chorus,
thus producing the protagonist, who, from behind his mask, could speak
the truth and disavow it at the same time. The third story tells of how
Aristotle, calmly deflecting Plato's rage against the hypocrisy of the ac-

tor's being two things at once, devised a system of theatre in which whatever subversive truth the actor might speak could be repurposed as the error from which the obedient spectator-citizen could learn to free himself. Boal's view of theatre's relation to community seems very similar to the romantic idealization of prepolitical harmony to be found in accounts of "primitive communism," in which, for good or ill, we must always return to the Athenian moment, even if primarily to understand it as a moment in which the establishment of the state concludes a process in which an earlier "communal" order has disintegrated through the gradual establishment of private property and the division of labor.

"Primitive communism," or, as it may be more accurately named, "communalism," refers primarily to the idea that human societies initially held property in common. Marx includes this proposition in the section of *Grundrisse* entitled "Forms which Precede Capitalist Production."[63] The tripartite developmental schema outlined here, in which an "Asiatic" mode of production is succeeded by a transitional "ancient" (Graeco-Roman) mode on the way to a feudal mode, is now challenged by subsequent research and archaeological discoveries. However, aspects of the theory of primitive communalism continue to exert an influence on the shape of subsequent thought, including Boal's. Three in particular are worth mentioning here.

The first is that primitive communalism is hierarchical rather than egalitarian. This is presumably why Ellen Meiksins Wood prefers this term rather than "communism," which suggests too strongly that any communism that might come will be a return to an Edenic state. As Wood notes of the early societies sketched by Marx, all featured "communal property embodied in a higher authority, typically a despotic state."[64] Boal's myth of the development of theatre in Greek societies before the emergence of the Athenian city-state does not, it is worth recalling, begin in an egalitarian moment, but rather a moment in which workers seek respite from the labor imposed upon them in an inegalitarian or perhaps even despotic state, ruled by a landowning aristocracy.

The second is that the category of "worker" is not strictly applicable in such societies. As Marx argues in *Grundrisse:*

> individuals relate not as workers but as proprietors—and members of a community, who at the same time work. The aim of this work is not the *creation of value*—although they may do surplus labour in order to obtain *alien*, i.e. surplus products in exchange—rather, its aim is sustenance of the individual proprietor and of his

family, as well as of the total community. The positing of the individual as a *worker*, in this nakedness, is itself a product of history.[65]

The idea that to be a "worker" is not a fixed identity but the alterable result of historical circumstances is central to this project, as it is for Rancière's work. As we shall see, it is the assumed or "naturalized" identity between a person and her work that gives rise to the figure of "the worker," while it is the capacity of the theatre to disrupt this assumption, which forms the basis for much of Rancière's interest in theatrical activities. It is my ambition for the figure of the "passionate amateur" that it should perform at least some modest disruption of identitarian categories. Boal's "workers," then, are workers only for as long as they work. When they are doing something else they are dancers or drinkers, or they are not defined at all in relation to what they do, and it is their freedom to remain undefined that is under threat as their celebratory performance is organized into theatre.

The third is that all these early forms of landed property possess as a "presupposition" that there already exists a spontaneous or "natural" community, which, Marx writes, "appears not as a *result* of, but as a *presupposition for the communal appropriation* (temporary) *and utilization of the land.*"[66] This "presupposition" seems to return in Rancière's account of the theatre public's self-understanding as community. If, as Sartre wrote of the twentieth century, "communism is the unsurpassable horizon of our time," might one dare say here that community has a tendency to appear, at least in the theatre, as an unsurpassable presupposition? If not that, then perhaps at least this: the experience of being with others in the theatre seems to offer participants in a capitalist society an intimation of their own presuppositions about a mode of collective existence in which the division of labor has not yet turned some of us into workers and others into proprietors, designated some of us professionals and others amateurs, or, to return to Boal's terms, made of some us actors and of others spectators.

What Boal's myth seems to suggest is that theatre is one of the places where this presupposition persists *as intimation,* or by way of an experience of *intimacy* in public, or, as I shall call it in the final chapter of the book, solitude in relation. Boal implies that theatre, in spite of its division of labor, retains affective traces of a communal practice in which labor is set aside and hierarchy temporarily resisted, and that the task of his own theatre is to reactivate those traces in the name of a contemporary political challenge to oppression grounded in a desire for community. As Eugene van Erven writes, seeking to draw some conclusions from the diverse practices represented in his collection of essays on community theatre:

> While it can never restore pre-modern communal harmony, which probably never existed in the first place, community theatre can be an effective medium to negotiate internal differences and represent these in artistic forms, in the creation of which local cohesion is enhanced and respect for "otherness" increased.[67]

Although there is no way back to the mythical past, even for Boal, the origins of theatre itself are nonetheless posited as drawing on energies that come from outside the realm of work and whose expression takes place in the interruption or suspension of work. This "outside" of work is of course constituted by the necessity of work, and by the regulation of time and association in the "teamwork" of the farm or construction worker.[68] It is an outside that is already an inside, and whose occupants are desperate to get out; to express themselves, become emancipated, together in the collective action of song, dance, and drinking. If there is a community presupposed in this performance, it is one that work interrupts, and that is, itself, an interruption of work. This is why the amateur—someone who interrupts his or her work in order to make theatre, rather than making theatre his or her work—may be a crucial figure for understanding the appearances of romantic anti-capitalism in theatre. Even if romantic anti-capitalism might long to locate its "good community" beyond capitalism itself, and to seek relief from alienation in an exit from its logics, it is almost always obliged to make do with what it can make within them. Something of this predicament is captured in the word *amateur*. On the one hand, the amateur acts out of love, in what Marx calls "the realm of freedom," making an unconditional commitment that affirms its own autonomy. On the other hand, the amateur also acts in relation to "the realm of necessity," her activity constantly defined in opposition either to the work of the "professional" who makes her living from theatre, or to the work she herself does to make her own living. This is because, to follow the logic of Marx's thought, the realm of freedom is always ultimately contingent upon the realm of necessity.[69]

Amateur theatre in its most familiar sense (as a leisure activity for those who earn their livings by other means) is not, however, the topic of this book. Amateur theatre is of course a huge field of activity of which there is probably much of interest to be written.[70] But for the purposes of the present work, it accedes too readily to the distinction between work and leisure that I wish to unravel here. The same may also be said of what in the United Kingdom is often called community theatre (a term that, in the United States, is more usually applied to what in the United Kingdom is normally called amateur theatre). Taken as a whole, community theatre in the United Kingdom—which often takes the form of performance events produced by specialist professionals in collaboration with nonprofessional participants—also tends to leave the work/nonwork distinction largely untroubled. Nonetheless, many of the affects, contradictions, resistances, and pleasures that I will try to account for in the discussion that follows may also be found in community theatre (in its UK sense), and I will end this introductory chapter by briefly indicating two of them that seem particularly significant. The first is that there seems to be something in the quality of the nonprofessional and often untrained theatrical performer that allows them to be experienced as the bearers of the values of community presupposed in the event. The second is the peculiar, and related effect, most notable in the kind of historically based community plays first developed in the United Kingdom by Ann Jellicoe and the Colway Theatre Trust and widely adopted elsewhere, in which the untrained performer, experienced as bearer of values associated with community, does so in the role of a figure from what is imagined to have been that community's past (by appearing as character from a well-known local history, for example). Both of these effects are usually reported as indices of a kind of pre- or anti-capitalist authenticity wherein the social and political value of such projects inheres. Jon Oram, who succeeded Ann Jellicoe as director of the Colway Theatre Trust (now called Claque), writes in a brief article on what he calls "the social actor":

> There are conditions about the amateur actors from the community that make the audience's transition from mere spectator to involved performer almost seamless. Whilst we might be in awe of professional celebrity, there's a feeling of equality and intimacy when the cast and the audience come from the same community. Amateurs especially non-actors are closer to natural social behaviour as opposed to heightened performance. I build on these conditions by ensuring that the subject of the play is about the history of everyone in the room, and that they all share the same space. To put it succinctly there is a sense of community ownership about the play.[71]

Ann Jellicoe, in the preface to her *Community Plays: How to Put Them On*, cites extensively from observations made by Baz Kershaw about the Colyford community play (*Colyford Matters,* by Dennis Warner, produced in 1983):

> The stylistic focus is possible because the unity of the event derives from a simple shift of focus, away from theatre, towards community. Hence, the typical situations presented provoke a historical awareness that rests on a curious identification between the live actors and the dead people they play. They come from the same community and so it seems, in performance, as if they are the same people. The result is a powerful sense of the mysterious—set within an active celebration of shared meanings. So the explicitly presented development of community in the past is implicitly animated in the present. The artistic unity consequently derives from the fact that the fundamental event is not the play itself, but the opportunity the play provides for the continuing evolution of Colyford as a community. In other words, community plays are a community-forming process. Thus theatre is created through community.[72]

Both of these observations would ordinarily tend to support a strongly romantic conception of community, grounded in "nature," "authenticity," "identification," and "unity." These are precisely the terms against which critics of community as such, including Miranda Joseph and Jean-Luc Nancy, direct their analysis. All the same, as Joseph notes, seeking to distance herself somewhat from Nancy's sense of the impossibility of community, some critical perspectives fail to account for the passion that attends such experiences.[73] What Oram and Kershaw capture are sources for such passion—the appearance of the "natural social" and the reappearance of "community in the past"—and perhaps even foundations for the kind of "utopian performative" sought by Jill Dolan. Where I hope to develop a further understanding of such experiences is in a consideration of how these feelings might make meaning in more obviously compromised situations, or, rather, in theatrical circumstances where the "presupposition of community" is not as powerfully present. Is it possible to experience such (intimate, public, political) feelings even where they are not explicitly summoned up in the name of a supposedly natural or authentic "community"? I am most interested, therefore, in what happens when such passions are set in motion in ways that seem unnatural or inauthentic (theatrical, even) or where the appearance of figures from another time is experienced as a disruption rather than an affirmation of historical continuity. This is because, in seeking to develop a *critical* romantic anti-capitalism, I cannot depend upon straightforward distinctions between the natural, the authentic, and a continuous historical experience, on the one hand, and the artificial, the constructed, and the discontinuous on the other. I will look for such experiences in just a few selected locations in the chapters that follow. The search begins in Moscow at the start of the twentieth century, where Chekhov's *Uncle Vanya* stages feelings about work at the dawn of theatre's industrialization, and then moves on to Berlin in 1928, where Walter Benjamin and Asja Lacis imagine a proletarian children's theatre that might perform a kind of deindustrialization of the soul. This discontinuous history of passionate amateurs resumes in Paris in 1967, with Jean-Luc Godard's film, *La chinoise,* in which a group of students play at being revolutionaries the summer before the real "events" of 1968. It ends in the present, more or less, wondering, first, about the nature of theatrical labor in an economy that has found ever more ingenious ways of commodifying such things as "community," by way of an account of the Nature Theatre of Oklahoma's *No Dice,* and then, in a final sequence, speculating on the extent to which a professional spectator such as myself might have any business writing about passionate amateurs.

TWO

Of Work and Time

It's all over. The Professor and his wife, Yelena, have gone to Kharkov, unable to stand life in the country a moment longer. The Professor fears, perhaps, that Vanya will take another pop at him with the gun. Yelena needs to escape from the potential entanglements arising from her feelings for the Doctor and Vanya's feelings for her. Feelings we might care to call love. The Doctor, Astrov, has taken a final drink of vodka and returned home, having promised Yelena, for Sonya's sake, that he will never return. At the end of Chekhov's *Uncle Vanya,* Sonya and Vanya return to work, filling out entries in account books they have neglected for the duration of the Professor's visit to the estate. Neither Sonya nor Vanya has anything more to say about their unrequited loves (for Astrov and for Yelena). It's all over:

> SONYA: We shall live, Uncle Vanya. We shall live out many, many
> days and long evenings; we shall patiently bear the trials that
> fate sends us; we shall labour for others both now and in our
> old age, knowing no rest, and when our time comes, we shall
> meekly die, and there beyond the grave we shall say that we
> suffered, that we wept, that we were sorrowful, and God will
> have pity on us, and you and I, dear Uncle, shall see a life that
> is bright and beautiful and full of grace, we shall rejoice and
> look back on our present woes with tenderness, with a smile—
> and we shall rest. [. . .] We shall rest!

> TELEGIN *quietly plays his guitar*

> We shall rest! [. . .] We shall rest . . . [*Hugs him.*] We shall rest!

> [*The night-watchman knocks.* TELEGIN *plays quietly;* MARIYA VASILYEVNA
> *makes notes in the margins of a pamphlet;* MARINA *knits a stocking.*]

We shall rest!

[*The curtain slowly falls.*][1]

It is all over, but it is also a beginning, even if it is the beginning of something that has been continuing before. It is a kind of circularity. It is a resumption of an activity that had been interrupted, one might say disrupted, by the events of the play itself, a return to the status quo ante. But it is also a complex opening outward. For Vanya and Sonya the work to which they return is a putting aside, or a putting behind them (perhaps forever) of the upheavals and disappointments of love (Vanya's for Yelena, Sonya's for Astrov). In a familiar gesture, they hope to be able to forget, to bury their pain in renewed activity, and to rededicate themselves to a worthy if modest joint project after having lost themselves in what turned out to be fruitless (unproductive) projects of the heart.

The play ends, then, with two of its principal actors announcing their departure from the space of unproductive labor (play), through the commitment given by the characters they have produced on stage, to the work they are to undertake. With the departure of the idle and unproductive couple of the Professor and his wife, Vanya and Sonya resolve to abstain from theatrical behaviors brought on by the presence of this couple (doomed love affairs, bungled shootings) and to renounce the indolence that had overcome the household during their visit. In this sense, work is the grim but safe antithesis to the risks and excitements of love. It is duty, rather than passion. It might also be understood, coming as it does at the end of the play, as a gesture toward the mundane world that the play of theatrical production temporarily suspends. Let us get back to the day-world of work after this brief sojourn in the night of play.

The gesture of the actors, then, doubles the movement of their characters and, at the same time, the action the audience is about to take in making its way back to the working day: a renunciation of nonwork, an end to the suspension of production. Yet this doubling is also a contradiction, since it is in fact, for the actors, the very moment at which their productive labor comes to an end, at least for tonight. They appear to set themselves back to work at precisely the moment at which they are about to stop working. The last lines of the play complicate this situation further, as Sonya conjures a vision of daily work continuing to the grave, beyond which, she repeats, "We shall rest [. . .] We shall rest." As the actors clock off, might they be inviting the spectators, moving now from the end of the play toward the beginning of the working day, to take up the burden of their labor or to take a rest, and if so, what kind of labor and what sort of rest might this be? In what kind of labor might both actors and spectators jointly participate? And what kind of rest might follow?

To prepare the ground for an attempt to answer these questions I will sketch out some ideas about work in general in industrial capitalism, about some particular aspects of work in the context of an industrializing Russia in the 1890s, and finally, about the nature of work in the theatre, both in industrial capitalism generally and in the specific context of an industrializing theatre in Moscow at the time of the first production of *Uncle Vanya* in 1899. By this rather circuitous route I hope to be able to show that in the industrial capitalism of the late nineteenth and twentieth centuries the figure of the passionate amateur took on a new and significant form, in the person of the professional for whom life, work, and politics came to be inextricably entwined with one another. In the particular case of the theatre industry, I aim to suggest how such passionate amateurs might participate in and contribute to affective experiences of productive consumption that revive a kind of romantic anti-capitalism. These ✳ passionate amateurs are to be found both onstage and off: as fictional figures produced by the labor of the actor; as actors (and other theatrical professionals) working at the production of play; and, crucially, as spectators for whom the consumption of the theatrical production is itself a form of production, of subjectivities rather than commodities.

WORK IN INDUSTRIAL CAPITALISM

In chapter 10 of *Capital,* simply called "The Working Day," Marx presents both a *longue durée* history of political struggle over the very concept of the "working day" and a more contemporary account of a political struggle over its length.[2] In both cases the histories in question, as so often in *Capital,* are drawn from the English experience, since England represented at the time the clearest and most advanced example of a capitalist society, enjoying levels of industrialization with which Russia, famously, would only compete much later (hence the supposed historical irony of a socialist revolution taking place in Russia rather than in England, where students and followers of Marx might reasonably have most expected it). Let us consider this as just one anachronism among several, following those already alluded to in the differential movements toward and away from the "working day" in the case of a performance of *Uncle Vanya* and in anticipation of others to come later in this chapter.

Marx's history of the working day begins in 1349 with a "Statute of Labourers," introduced during the reign of Edward III, which "found its immediate pretext (not its cause, for legislation of this kind outlives its pretext by centuries)" in the "great plague that decimated the population," thus, supposedly, requiring a more coordinated and disciplined effort on the part of the survivors to supply the needs of a feudal economy. It is worth noting here, in anticipation of there being a relationship between the length of the working day and the length of the working life, that this first attempt to standardize a working day seems to arise from (even if it is not caused by) the premature death of actual workers. A long struggle ensues, captured in more detail than it is by Marx by E. P. Thompson, in a now-celebrated article, "Time, Work-Discipline, and Industrial Capitalism,"[3] in which he traces a gradual but by no means inevitable historical movement between preindustrial and industrial disciplines and internalizations of time. It is crucial to both Thompson and Marx that this process should not be seen as inevitable, because it is important for both that the institution of the working day as a broadly accepted aspect of a wage-labor economy is understood instead as the outcome of social and political struggle: only with this historicization of the seemingly "natural" order (as night follows day) might it be possible to imagine this order as susceptible to change through future political action. "The historical record," writes Thompson, "is not a simple one of neutral and inevitable technological change, but is also one of exploitation and of resistance to exploitation."[4]

The movement described by Thompson begins in ways of life in which "the day's tasks [. . .] seemed to disclose themselves, by the logic of need, before the crofter's eyes," an attitude toward the temporality of work that Thompson characterizes as "task-orientation" and that, he suggests, is "more humanly comprehensible"[5] than what is to follow. As work increasingly becomes a matter of waged employment (rather than devoted to, say, either the corvée or subsistence), "the shift from task-orientation to timed labour is marked."[6] Thompson's close attention to records of working-class life offers a picture of English capital experiencing, as part of the upheavals of early industrialization, major problems with the time-discipline of its workforce, so much so that as early as 1700 *The Law Book of the Crowley Iron Works* runs to more than one hundred thousand words and provides the basis for the imposition of similar private penal codes in the cotton mills seventy years later.[7] The development of machinery as part of the means of production contributes a further dimension to the time-regime: machines dictate rhythms to their operators on a minute-by-minute basis, as well as seeming (seeming, only seeming) to demand constant attention in order that they should never be left idle. During the course of the eighteenth century—in the period leading up to the more or less contemporary (that is, nineteenth-century) struggles that Marx will present in some detail—Thompson sees a capitalist organization of work and time achieving its "normalisation": "In all these ways—by the division of labour; the supervision of labour; bells and clocks; money incentives; preachings and schoolings; the suppression of fairs and sports—new labour habits were formed, and a new time discipline was imposed."[8]

Thompson's reference to "the suppression of fairs and sports" might lead one to suppose a simple inverse proportionality between work time and leisure time, in which the more work, the less leisure. But the process Thompson describes here is now widely understood as the basis for the "invention" of leisure, in which, to put it very schematically, sprawling and partly spontaneous festivities based on cyclical, seasonal time give way to the quick fixes of nightly entertainment (cyclical but not seasonal, except in the idea that a popular TV drama series like *The Wire* is packaged and sold in "seasons").[9] The predictable time schedule of the working day encourages a corresponding rationalization of play and recreation, and "leisure industries" develop accordingly.

This interdependence of work and leisure is a key insight of the "submerged" tradition in leisure studies excavated by Chris Rojek in *Capitalism and Leisure Theory*. Rojek notes the powerful appeal of the narrative established in Thompson's article (of leisure in its modern form as the creation of industrial capitalism) and sees it as part of a broader understanding within sociological thought (Veblen, Weber, Durkheim, Elias) that sees leisure not as free time, but as time always already conditioned by its dependence upon the established working day. Rojek suggests that a key element in this relationship is that disposable time is "subjectively experienced by the labourer as an alien force which he does not fully control."[10] In this respect the time of leisure is as unfree or as alienated as the time of work. Noting Marx's contribution to this tradition of thought, he observes that, in Marx's analysis, the "working class can have leisure only if it fulfils the production requirements of capital. The capitalist class can only maintain its leisure relations if it ensures that in the long run more surplus value is extracted at source, i.e. by intensifying the exploitation of labour."[11] The absence of any such thing as "free time" is vital to this understanding of leisure. As Rojek comments in introducing the topic of his study, in terms that will resonate with anyone working in the theatre (or other branches of the leisure industry), "the saying that work for some is leisure for others is not only a popular truism, it is also a vital analytical insight."[12]

It becomes clear that this interdependence is essential to capitalist production when one recognizes the key role of leisure time in Henry Ford's conception of the working day, which, as David Harvey explains, includes the idea that "the purpose of the five-dollar, eight hour day was only in part to secure worker compliance with the discipline required to work the highly productive assembly-line system. It was coincidentally meant to provide workers with sufficient income and leisure time to consume the mass-produced products the corporations were about to turn out in ever vaster quantities."[13] That leisure should become a form of productive consumption was a key element in the development and extension of the Fordist system in the twentieth century (we shall see, shortly, that aspects of this organizational form penetrated the theatre fairly early). That theatre, therefore, is becoming a site of productive consumption (in specifically capitalist terms) at around the time of the first production of *Uncle Vanya* is going to be an important element in the discussion that follows.

For now, though, we turn away, again, from leisure and back to Marx's "Working Day." Marx summarizes (anachronistically, of course) Thompson's account (which strangely, or accordingly, contains no reference whatsoever to Marx), in which a landowner state spends several centuries trying to compel its population to work enough, before, at last, the idea of a working day, in which one turns up at the beginning, works throughout, and only returns home at the end, is properly established and socially normalized: people accept waged labor. He then moves on to the struggles of the nineteenth century, which are fought not over the day as such, but over its length. Because capitalist enterprises aim to maximize their profit, they must maximize the surplus-value they generate. Since the surplus-value of any product is the result of the value transferred into it above and beyond that conferred by the socially necessary labor time taken to produce it (the amount of time the worker must work in order to make a living), the management of the workers' time becomes a key issue for the owners of capital. To use the formulation to which Marx repeatedly returns, if it takes six hours a day for a worker to make a living, but the worker works twelve hours every day, then the additional six hours translate directly into surplus-value and therefore profit for the owner. "Moments," writes Marx, "are the elements of profit."[14]

In this latest historical phase of the struggle over the working day, capital is seeking to maximize its returns by extending the working day for as long as possible, while the emergent industrial working class is seeking to secure the support of the state (a state of capitalists and land-owners) for the enforcing of legal limits. One key outcome of this phase of the struggle would be the Factory Act of 1850, which put an end to em-ployer abuses of the Ten Hours' Act of 1844 by outlawing relay systems, specifying that the working day (for young people and women) must fall between 6 a.m. and 6 p.m., and making two one-and-a-half-hour meal breaks mandatory. Marx notes with characteristic irony that the gains in productivity achieved in the period since this legislation, which the own-ers and representatives of capital had vehemently opposed, were hailed by classical political economists as "a characteristic achievement of their 'science.'"[15] He also observes that "the longer working day which capital tried to impose on adult workers by acts of state power from the middle of the fourteenth century to the end of the seventeenth century is approx-imately of the same length as the shorter working day which, in the sec-ond half of the nineteenth century, the state has here and there interposed as a barrier to the transformation of children's blood into capital."[16]

The partial victory chronicled here by Marx is secured by the indus-trial working class in concert with "allies in those social layers not directly interested in the question."[17] These allies are essentially bourgeois re-formers who increasingly come to serve as "moral obstacles"[18] to the lim-itless exploitation of workers. It is from this class that emerge the factory inspectors who witness the appalling conditions in which industrial labor performs its functions, and the doctors who recognize that some deaths, such as that of the millinery worker May Ann Wilkes, are the consequence of overwork; in Wilkes's case of "long hours of work in an overcrowded room, and a too small and badly ventilated bedroom."[19] In abstract terms, Marx argues, "Capital asks no questions about the length of life of labour-power. What interests it is purely and simply the maximum of labour-power that can be set in motion in a working day. It attains this objective by shortening the life of labour-power, in the same way as a greedy farmer snatches more produce from the soil by robbing it of its fertility."[20] This abstract conception of capital's view of labor leaves out politics (and this is precisely Marx's point in telling the story of the struggle over the work-ing day); it omits the possibility that, unlike capital in the abstract, capital-ists in the flesh might be capable of being persuaded or coerced by worker activism, bourgeois reformists, and even the state, into acting against their own (seeming, only seeming) interests in this sphere. Marx observes that the 1859 *Reports of the Inspectors of Factories* suggests—"with sup-pressed irony"—that the reform of the working day may have granted the capitalist some measure of freedom from the "brutality" of his role as the mere embodiment of capital, as the shorter working day "has given him time for a little 'culture.'"[21] For it is not simply the worker who must contribute productive consumption by way of the leisure industries but also the capitalist, who, after all, will have substantially more disposable income than the worker to expend on such things as opera and football.

If the regulation of the working day and subsequent victories for organized labor have contributed to an increase in both the quantity and the quality of life enjoyed by workers under capitalism, it may be the case that the next key phase of this struggle will be over the length of the working life, rather than the working day, as current political tensions over the retirement age and pension arrangements in Europe might suggest. This is a subject that will return in each of the following chapters.

WORK IN RUSSIA

The country estate of *Uncle Vanya* might not immediately conjure up images commensurate with the industrial urban setting for the exploitation unto death described by Marx. But the creative-destructive logic of industrialization nonetheless encircles the play. The encroachment of industry into the countryside is just offstage. It is made present in Astrov's passionate (but professional) account of the destruction of the forests. It is personified in the appearance near the end of Act One of a "workman" who comes to tell Astrov that "they" have come for him from "the factory."[22] At the very beginning of the play, as Astrov bemoans what has become of him over the preceding ten years—"I've worn myself out [. . .] I don't know the meaning of rest"—it is his recollection of the death of a "railway pointsman" on his operating table that provokes his agonized speculation about how "those for whom we are laying down the road to the future" might "remember us."[23] Work, toward a future, whether by "road" or "rail," is established from the outset as a central preoccupation of the play, and its cost, in terms of the loss of the living, be they railway workers or forests, is a recurrent question. Each "working day" is an exhausting step toward the construction of some better world. As Raymond Williams writes of Chekhov's plays in general, "the way to the future is seen, consistently, in work."[24] This work is always shadowed by fear: that exhaustion will tend to death; that progress will destroy what it feeds upon; or even, in Astrov's case, that the whole process will yield nothing in return for all this work and death:

ASTROV: If in place of all these destroyed forests they had laid
  highways and railroads, if we had here factories, mills,
  schools, the people would be healthier, richer, better
  educated—but there's nothing of the kind. [. . .] We have here
  a decline which is the consequence of an impossible struggle
  for existence.[25]

At the time of the writing and production of *Uncle Vanya* (1897–99),
these were pressing questions of government policy and everyday social
reality. In the decade following the 1892 appointment of Count Sergei
Witte as minister of finance (he had previously served as director of railway affairs within the same ministry), the industrial sector in Russia grew
by over 8 percent a year. While the urban population had grown rapidly
since the emancipation of the serfs (1861), it is crucial to recognize that
this growth also involved the urbanization and industrialization of the
countryside itself, with the railways as a crucial element in this process.
According to Neil B. Weissman's study of the social and economic reforms of the nineteenth century, the census of 1897 revealed that "over
half the empire's industry and sixty percent of its workers were located in
the country" and that "in the province of Moscow alone some two hundred villages had become commercial and industrial in nature."[26] Spencer
Golub points to just one way in which this rail-assisted industrialization,
whose consequences are rendered more explicitly by Chekhov in *The
Cherry Orchard* (1902–4), was changing the experience of work and time in
this now perhaps only partially rural Russia, noting that "the major temporal dialogue in *The Cherry Orchard* is between the urban timetable of the
railroad, which begins and ends the play, and the rural timetable of the
agrarian seasonal cycle, which gives the play its act structure." With an
eye on the future, in which Lenin's arrival by train will come to signify the
launch of a process of convulsive political change, with work—political,
ideological, "Taylorized"—at its heart, Golub suggests that "Lopakhin,
whom Richard Stites calls an 'ineffectual Taylorist' [. . .] cannot get the
characters in the play to conform to the new schedule."[27]

Not that the old schedule of the "agrarian season cycle" was a schedule without work: it was rather—as Thompson and others have described—an earlier way of organizing the time of work. In *Uncle Vanya* the
arrival of the Professor and his wife has disrupted this schedule:

VANYA: Ever since the Professor came to live here with his wife,
  my life has left its track. . . . I go to sleep at the wrong time, for

lunch and dinner I eat all kinds of rich dishes, I drink wine—
that's all unhealthy. I used not to have a spare minute, Sonya
and I worked—my goodness, how we worked, and now only
Sonya works and I sleep, eat and drink. . . . That's no good![28]

This life of consumption is not the opposite of the life of productive work,
even though it may be experienced as such by both Vanya and Sonya; it is
its counterpart. Until it arrived here, in person, on the estate, it could be
imagined as something distant and somehow unrelated. Now, perhaps
most vividly in the person of Yelena, it makes its relation to production
unavoidably, even radiantly visible, while simultaneously giving rise to a
suspicion that something might be wrong:

ASTROV: She just eats, sleeps, walks, enchants us all with her
beauty—and that's all. She has no responsibilities, others work
for her. . . . It's true, isn't it? And an idle life can't be a virtuous
one.[29]

It is not that work has ceased, then—Sonya, after all, keeps it going—
but rather that Vanya and Astrov have been seduced into the scene of
consumption, to letting "others work" for them. Their feelings (their
love?) for Yelena constitute a kind of becoming-Serebryakov, not only
through a desire to supplant the Professor in Yelena's affections but, crucially, by adopting his role as the consumer of the labor of others. Their
compromised and uneasy embrace of indolence—while they may experience it as the absence of work—is therefore only really its displacement.
The work goes somewhere else (Sonya does it)—a spatial fix—or it is de-
ferred, becomes mere aspiration, a vision for the future. This might be
conceived as a kind of temporal fix (the kind of thing that financialization
seeks to achieve, perhaps, by permitting speculators to be paid now for
work that will be done by future generations of workers). Thus the indolence on which the characters of the play repeatedly comment may be
seen as a product of new relations among work, time, and space, rather
than as the absence of work. It is not "free" time. Like the process of industrialization, which I have already suggested circles the play, encroach-
ing upon its space and its time, work itself lurks in the wings. The indolence on stage is the form in which it appears. It is, of course, an indolence
that the actors on stage must work to produce, for an audience of consumers. In the consumption of this indolence-work is it possible to be wholly

oblivious to the fact that, in the service industry of the theatre, as everywhere else, one person's leisure is always another's labor?

The idea that work might be the motor of social progress and a form of political activity ("the way to the future," to recall Williams's phrase) underpins Astrov's various speeches, and they are, at times, just that, speeches, as Yelena's apparent failure to concentrate rather sharply reveals ("I see by your expression this doesn't interest you"[30]). It will also become a central ideological motif of the Soviet Union, though Astrov is not to be confused with Stakhanov (even if we might see Lopakhin as an "ineffectual Taylorist" and Lenin as a rather more "effectual" one) any more than the "indolent" characters of any of Chekhov's plays can really be wholly identified with the justly doomed aristocracy whose rule will end in 1917. John Tulloch identifies the embodiment and articulation of this idea, in Chekhov's plays, with the emergence of the medical profession as a key element in the *zemstvo* system of rural self-governing bodies in which Chekhov himself was an active participant.[31]

The establishment of the *zemstvos* formed part of the attempt at reform initiated after Russia's defeat in the Crimean War. The *zemstvos* consisted of elected local assemblies, each of which appointed an executive board to take responsibility for the organization and delivery of elementary education, public health, and charity in the local area.[32] In the context of the industrialization process accelerated in the 1890s, state support for the *zemstvos* was intensified, with annual increases in expenditure on *zemstvo* activity of up to 18 percent. It was also at this time that the so-called third element within the *zemstvos*—doctors, teachers, agronomists, and statisticians—gained ground relative to the gentry and the peasantry, while they also consolidated (not without struggle) their relative autonomy from the state bureaucracy. During the 1890s, therefore, the *zemstvos* became channels through which an emergent professional class could exercise social influence and develop some measure of political agency.

While Tulloch does not suggest that Astrov in *Uncle Vanya* stands in for Chekhov himself in any straightforward way, he does demonstrate how Chekhov's experience with and commitment to the practice of *zemstvo* medicine shaped his own social position and sense of self. While he may not represent Chekhov, Astrov most certainly does stand for and articulate social and professional values and aspirations associated with this emergent class of practitioners, of which Chekhov himself was one, and their conception of working toward the future. He is, in a sense, the representative within the play of the English "factory inspectors" whose alliance with the industrial working class helped secure the regulation of the working day in the story of political struggle recounted by Marx in *Capital*. Astrov represents—in compromised and damaged form, of course—a powerful idea of professional expertise at the service of the people and of human social progress.

This conception of professional expertise and the specific historical situation in which it emerges has two significant related consequences. First, it enables doctors to carve out a new social position for themselves as autonomous professionals. As Stanley C. Kramer notes, writing on public health in the *zemstvo* system, the new framework

> created ever greater numbers of salaried positions outside the state bureaucracy in which the enthusiastic members of a populist intelligentsia could serve the people. By transforming the physician's identity from state servant to servant of society, it also enhanced the potential authority of modern medicine among the peasantry.[33]

Second, as Tulloch points out, this autonomous role, increasingly understood in terms of public service, permits doctors to articulate a political project expressive of this revised social position, articulating a universalizing movement away from a narrow and élite class ideology:

> The new zemstvo service role was clearly an environment of great public need where universalistic ideals could be directed to practical tasks. If, as MacIver suggests, one sign of professionalization is "when activity of service replaces passivity of station," and when educated men move from a culture of patronage to one of functional specificity of competence, then this was certainly taking place among Russian zemstvo doctors who, by a conscious decision, rejected the class nature of "city medicine."[34]

Work thus becomes a way of doing politics. It is no longer simply the necessary tasks of production and reproduction, which Hannah Arendt placed in the category of "labor"[35] and which Marx regarded as "eternal."[36] Nor is it even just what Arendt would categorize as work—namely the fabrication of things in the world, such as art, buildings, railroads. Instead, in this vision, work begins to transcend the category of work itself and becomes a form of what Arendt calls action: the relational activity that constitutes politics. Work as political action is what will carry human society forward into a future in which we might one day experience freedom, including, perhaps paradoxically, the freedom from the "eternal" necessity of work: "We shall rest! We shall rest!"

THE PROFESSIONAL IS/AS THE PASSIONATE AMATEUR

This development of the medical profession in late nineteenth-century industrializing Russia was part of a broader set of developments across capitalist Europe during the nineteenth century. The consolidation of "the professions," as a way of conceiving and organizing such practices as medicine and the law, led to the emergence of the distinctive and ambiguous ideologeme of "professionalism." This was deeply rooted in industrial capitalism and in many respects reflected its practitioners' dependency upon both capital and the state, but it also carried forward certain antimarket principles that, as I aim to show in this brief digression on the subject of the professional, means that it bears striking resemblances to what I have called the romantic anti-capitalism of the passionate amateur.[37] Indeed, the central theme of the ideology of professionalism may be summarized as work for work's sake. The professional turns out to be the amateur. Or at least, that is how things are made to appear. Under certain circumstances, in the right light perhaps, the professional appears as the passionate amateur.

Magali Sarfatti Larson identifies this idea of the "intrinsic value of work" as one of a number of "residues" of pre-capitalist conceptions of such service labor, along with the idea that service is universally available in the interests of protecting the social fabric or community and the tradition of "noblesse oblige" in which social status confers social responsibilities (which, in turn, of course, confer social status).[38] But, while these residues help legitimate the ideology of professionalism, they do so in spite (or perhaps precisely because) of the fact that professions "are, in fact, one of the distinctive features of industrial capitalism, even though they claim to renounce the profit motive."[39] What the organization of services into professions actually seeks, she argues, "is a monopoly over the provision of specialist services, frequently secured by means of the control and regulation of training and education (access), assisted by state power which outlaws non-qualified practitioners (who become 'quacks'), and consolidated by means of professional 'associations' rather than unionisation." As the beneficiaries of state-protected monopolies the members of professions can accentuate their difference from wage labor within capital by abstaining from its most public organizational form in the market (the union) while regulating their own rights to set levels of remuneration by operating as cartels.

Although dependent upon capital for their income and upon the state for their legal protection, professionals are able to imagine themselves as somehow independent of both. Thus, as Sarfatti Larson observes, "at the centre of the ideology of profession we find, necessarily, the general postulates of bourgeois ideology":[40] the professional is, above all, a free and autonomous individual and thus claims for herself, in the conduct of her work, certain inalienable privileges associated with this status, paramount among which is the right to control her own time. Private offices and secretarial support are also important, but nothing more distinguishes the professional from the wage-laborer than the freedom to set her own working hours. To charge by the hour rather than be paid by it might be another way of articulating this distinction. Of course many professionals internalize the time-disciplines of industrial capitalism with great ferocity and, under certain economic circumstances, may need to do so simply in order to make a living. Many professionals justify this self-imposed discipline by insisting on just how much they love their work. I work eighteen hours a day, six days a week, because I am a "passionate amateur."

There is not necessarily anything disingenuous here. While the principles that appear to be antimarket are in reality nothing of the sort, the structural inaccuracy of the claim to autonomy should not obscure the fact that it is subjectively sincere. Many professionals are indeed, to some degree or another, opponents of capital (or wish to see its powers limited), even while being among its most privileged structural beneficiaries. This is perhaps why, in its positive aspect, professionalism is a socially progressive or reformist element within industrial capitalism. The ideology has organizational force and can be mobilized in support of a wide range of social and political goals, as in the contribution of the medical profession to the struggle over the length of the working day narrated by Marx in *Capital* or, more broadly, as Harold Perkin notes in his work on the professions, again in England, in "the special role of the professional idea in the rise of the welfare state."[41] Because this apparent "third space" between the state and the market is largely imaginary, however, the professional classes tend to be quite vulnerable to political co-optation by either or both (the New Labour "Third Way" associated with the lawyer Blair and the academic Giddens is just one example of this tendency). In formations of this kind the professional ideology becomes, as Larson argues, simply a way of "justifying inequality of status and closure of access in the occupational order."[42]

The "Third Way" may best be regarded as a device for packaging professional capitulation to neoliberalism, which, as an approach to the relationship between an individual worker and the market, might be regarded as intrinsically hostile to the maintenance of the social and economic privileges of the professions. In practice the emergence of a full-fledged neoliberalism in late twentieth-century capital has tended to enrich and empower those members of the professions most able to make their services indispensible to business (those most dependent upon capital, such as corporate lawyers, for example) and to impoverish and disempower those whose services tend to rely more heavily on the state (teachers, for example).

Herein lies the political ambiguity of the ideology of professionalism—an ambiguity in which it again resembles the position of the passionate amateur. On the one hand the professional, or the passionate amateur, "with its persistent antibureaucratic appearances [. . .] deflects the comprehensive and critical vision of society [. . .] functions as a means for controlling large sectors of educated labor, and for co-opting its elites,"[43] as Sarfatti Larson writes.[44] Professionalization, she argues, by protecting educated elites from certain market exigencies (allowing them to set their own time-discipline, for instance), has "functioned as an effective form of social and ideological control" and thus as a defense for capital against "elite dissatisfaction."[45] On the other hand, however, and it is interesting that Sarfatti Larson saw this trend emerging in the late 1960s and early 1970s in France and then Italy, there are within neoliberal structures "increasing tendencies" toward the "proletarianization of educated labour," which, she notes, "[have], potentially, great political consequences."[46] In this context, as professionals (or, increasingly, former professionals[47]) find themselves exposed to the exigencies of the market in new ways, often in ways that effectively convert their autonomy into precarity, the professional as passionate amateur reappears as a figure both subjectively *and* structurally hostile to the interests of capital and thus as a potential participant in a political coalition organized around the solidarity of "immaterial labour." I will take up this theme at greater length in subsequent chapters.

WORK ON THE MOSCOW STAGE

Uncle Vanya appears on stage just seven years after the abolition of the Imperial monopoly. Not that Russia had lacked for theatre beyond the Imperial stages: all kinds of theatre and performance had circulated beyond the legitimized locations, including a substantial amateur theatre movement, in which Stanislavski participated and which gave Chekhov himself his earliest experiences of theatre. The significance of the abolition of the monopoly is rather to be found in its facilitation of a professional theatre, in which the burden of patronage fell on investors, shareholders, and subscribers, rather than upon the budget of the Court. It is also a professional theatre built, as it were, in the first instance, by amateurs-turning-professional. This is the theatre in whose formation Chekhov's work participated and in which the role of the director, as industrial manager, was to become increasingly significant. The role of the director is, of course, not entirely new—Stanislavski's own practice was strongly influenced by the example of Georg von Saxe-Meiningen, to name but one obvious antecedent—but the coincidence of company management, artistic vision, and day-to-day organization of the work of the actors is a decisive consolidation of the role. Nor are all directors industrial managers, even today. Many share the freelance precarity enjoyed by the actors whose work they direct. Nonetheless, even when the director is not the "chief executive" of a building-based theatre, or in some other way part of the "management" of a permanent or semipermanent company, her role tends toward management functions and appropriates certain management prerogatives (even if these sometimes take only illusory form). Actors seeking employment at a major theatre will often imagine that it is the director, rather than the organization, that hires them. The power of the director over the employment prospects of actors is far from entirely illusory, even here: it is, after all, the director who constantly evaluates the employee's performance and who, in the workplace, appears to determine the rhythm and direction of work. It may even be that the director represents the actor's best chance of being employed again. Even where the director is employed on similar freelance contracts to those given to actors, and where it is the permanent stage staff of the theatre itself who keep time in the rehearsal room, the director is still subjectively experienced by the actors (and perhaps even by the permanent stage staff) as the representative of management. The director herself, in this situation, however, is still likely to experience her own role as that of an employee, in a somewhat compromised position between the "real" management and the "real" employees. In this ambiguity of economic and even class position, she resembles, of course, the figure of the "professional," negotiating between a commitment to the work for its own sake and the fact that this work is in fact the management of the work of others. The basis for this generalized experience of workplace relations is the position of the director as manager consolidated in the emergent professional theatres of the late nineteenth and early twentieth centuries, including, of course, the Moscow Art Theatre.

The requirement that a theatrical production should be under the overall control of a director is usually understood in aesthetic terms. Laurence Senelick, for example, accounts for the development of a director's theatre, with specific reference to the productions of Chekhov's plays at the Moscow Art Theatre, as follows:

> Chekhov's plays were written at a time when the stage director was becoming a paramount factor in the theatre. [. . .] The technical innovations of the modern stage, including electric lighting and *mises-en-scène* intent on reproducing "real life," required expert handling to blend and harmonize the various elements. Chekhov's development as a playwright from 1888 to 1904 coincides with this move from a stage governed by histrionic and spectacular display to one in which ensemble effect and the creation of "mood" reigned supreme. [. . .] But Chekhov's "Big Four" can succeed on stage only with strong and coordinated ensemble playing, best achieved under the baton of a single "conductor."[48]

But, as Senelick is clearly aware, this is not simply a question of a new kind of play requiring a new kind of production process. The coincidence of Chekhov's development as a playwright with the emergence of the director as "paramount factor" in the theatre involves reciprocal causality: the reorganization of the production process shapes the kind of plays that get written within it. Indeed, as Nick Worrall suggests in his study of the Moscow Art Theatre, it is partly the emergent understanding of the making of a theatrical performance as a production process that characterizes this reorganization. It was Stanislavski, as director of what was initially called the Moscow Public-Accessible Art Theatre's first production, *Tsar Fedor Ioannovich,* who "staked a claim for the importance of the role of the director as overall organiser of the production." Previously, Worrall writes, "Russian critics and commentators invariably spoke of 'performances'; henceforth they would speak of 'productions,' with all the implications this had for ensemble, unity of intellectual conception and aesthetically effective *mise-en-scène.*"[49] One key feature of this production process was the extent to which performances would now be made by way of rehearsal. While rehearsals in the Imperial Theatres would typically number no more than around twelve per production,

Stanislavski's production of *Tsar Fedor* had seventy-four. This move toward extensive rehearsal, and the more or less simultaneous development of a formal training regime for actors as part of the Moscow Art Theatre project, marks therefore a transition between two conceptions of theatrical work. In the first the objective is to get as quickly as possible to the "real" work, conceived as the performance on stage. In the second the "real" work is what is done in the rehearsal room. This logic will find its almost paradoxical realization in the paratheatrical work of Grotowski, in which the work of the theatreomaker is carried out entirely for its own sake. But it underlies nearly all modern conceptions of the work of the theatre, from the development of extensive and departmentalized work facilities backstage (from design to marketing) to the process orientation of much experimental practice in the twentieth century, for both of which the term *workshop* reveals the presence of an industrial model. It also generates the conditions in which actors' demands to be paid for rehearsals could no longer be effectively resisted by theatrical managements. The actor's job in the modern theatre is to rehearse, rather than simply to perform, and rehearsal is no longer understood as a kind of informal personal preparation (for hourly paid teachers in UK higher education this preindustrial attitude to preparation still prevails, however).

The director's job is to organize this work process—management is the organization of work—and implicitly, therefore, to ensure that sufficient use of the rehearsal period leads to a successful (and even profitable) production. Thus the work of the actor becomes subject to the general conditions of the working day in industrial capitalism, and the director has charge, on behalf of capital, of the labor time of the actor. This incipient Taylorization of the theatrical production process makes itself most visible, at least to those whose focus is what happens on stage rather than backstage, in aesthetic principles such as unified vision, ensemble playing, "complicité," and the like. The industrial and aesthetic aspects of this "moment" in the development of the theatre most obviously coincide on stage in the subordination of character (and actor) to dramatic function encouraged in Stanislavski's theatre and carried forward (alongside Lenin's enthusiasm for Taylor) in the work of Meyerhold.

WORK AND REST

In the dramatic fiction presented onstage in *Uncle Vanya,* the estate turns out to be a workplace, perhaps even a kind of factory, in which it only looks as though work is not there. The theatre in which this dramatic fiction is presented turns out to be the same kind of place. To return, then, to the questions posed at the start of this chapter: what kind of work? what kind of rest? Sonya and Vanya are going to work. But, Sonya promises, they will eventually rest. The actors presenting this work in which they are about to work are working but will soon rest, when "the curtain slowly falls." The spectator is not working now, not yet, having paid from her waged labor for this very particular kind of rest: "recreation." But she will soon have to work again (and if she doesn't she won't be buying any more theatre tickets).

Work, then, first of all, is the labor of self-reproduction. We all have to make a living somehow. There is a certain resignation to this: "we shall patiently bear the trials that life sends us"; we will all go home, get up in the morning, and go to work. "Labour," claims Marx, "is a condition of human existence which is independent of all forms of society; it is an eternal natural necessity which mediates the metabolism between man and nature, and therefore human life itself."[50] So even if someone were successfully to overthrow capitalism overnight, they would still have to go to work in the morning. So, if there is to be rest, it cannot be rest *from* work.

Work is also the basis for certain ideologies. In all their various versions these tend to involve claims that work has intrinsic, often moral merits, beyond the production of surplus value. Stakhanovism and the so-called Protestant work ethic are examples of this, but the most pertinent here is "professionalism," in which work, even when waged, is ostensibly conducted for its own sake and directed toward the common good. A certain restlessness comes as part of this ideological formation, making its adherents a slightly unpredictable bunch, as will become clear when the events of May 1968 take center stage in chapter 4.

Work is also the production of leisure, a form of rest (amid rather than beyond work). The work of the actors—their professional work—is organized as part of a set of interlocking industries that produce the recreation that is an essential aspect of the worker's self-reproduction. For workers outside the "leisure industries" work is what permits the leisure in which the work of the "leisure industries," like the theatre, may be consumed. The intensification of this interrelation finds its zenith in Theodor Adorno's and Max Horkheimer's vision of the culture industry, in which

> amusement under late capitalism is the prolongation of work. It is sought after as an escape from the mechanized work process, and to recruit strength in order to be able to cope with it again. But at

the same time mechanization has such power over a man's leisure and happiness, and so profoundly determines the manufacture of amusement goods, that his experiences are inevitably after-images of the work process itself.[51]

No real rest, then, for the wicked, even in the "little culture" secured by the capitalist in his acquiescence in the reduction of the working day.

Work, at last, is how we will make the world a better place. This is, in a sense, an extension of the ideology of the professional—who is of course a close relation to the passionate amateur—in which the intrinsic merit and the common good combine to underwrite political work, revolutionary work even. This kind of work can sometimes be done in theatres, too, by professionals and passionate amateurs alike and sometimes together. It is the work is that Astrov talks about in *Uncle Vanya,* even if we don't see him actually doing it. Other figures in other Chekhov plays talk this way too, carrying varying degrees of conviction, in *Three Sisters,* for example:

> TUZENBACH: In many years' time, you say, life on the earth will be beautiful and amazing. That's true. But in order to take part in that life now, even if at a remove, one must prepare for it, one must work.[52]

And in The Cherry Orchard, too:

> TROFIMOV: Man goes forward, perfecting his skills. Everything that is now beyond his reach will one day become near and comprehensible, only we must work, we must help with all our strength those who are seeking the truth. In Russia as yet we have very few who do work.[53]

The fact that as they say these things neither Trofimov nor Tuzenbach, nor even Astrov, is actually doing any work is not simply a way of holding up either these figures or what they say to the play of irony. Or rather, it is the kind of irony upon irony of which theatrical production is especially capable, particularly on the subject of work. Raymond Williams sees the recourse to mere irony as typical of what he calls "English Chekhov," in which

> the dominant tone is pathetic charm. The call to work is ironically displaced, by the undoubted fact that it is made by those who do

not work, and apparently will never work (as Trofimov, the "eternal student," in the speeches just quoted). Thus the aspiration is converted into just another idiosyncrasy. [. . .]The aspiration is genuine. To deflect it ironically is to cheapen and sentimentalise the whole feeling.[54]

After all, if they (Trofimov, Tuzenbach, Astrov) were just "doing it," we wouldn't be hearing them talk about it. Their talk, produced by way of the work of the actor, is, rather, like the indolence that constitutes the appearance of work in *Uncle Vanya*: the only way the idea of work (rather than just the fact of it) can make an appearance on stage.[55] This is the irony of irony. Conversation is the medium in which such realities move in this theatre. Even less than leisure, then, is it the opposite of work. Indeed, as will become more apparent later, in consideration of the place of conversation in the work of the Nature Theatre of Oklahoma and of communication, including even "idle chatter" in the political thought of Paolo Virno, conversation is itself a form of work, with emancipatory potential.

Work finally, then, is the motor of historical change, at least in the vision articulated by Astrov, Trofimov, and Tuzenbach. In one or two or three hundred years' time this work will perhaps be done. Then "we shall rest." But how can this be the case if work is "an eternal natural necessity"? The answer lies in a rejection of the very teleology in which Chekhov's characters seem to invest their hope. The realm of freedom (freedom from work, rest) is not to be found on the far side of the realm of necessity in some future beyond work. When Marx writes, in volume 3 of *Capital*, about the realm of freedom, he insists that, although it does constitute a kind of "beyond," it is nevertheless grounded in the continuing realm of necessity. Freedom from work can be maximized under conditions of "common control" over production, enabling "that development of human energy which is an end in itself," but this "can blossom forth only with this realm of necessity as its basis." That is to say that there is not a process through which we may pass from the realm of necessity to the realm of freedom, but that we are engaged, instead, in a constant struggle to build the realm of freedom within the realm of necessity. In a production of *Uncle Vanya* in the theatre today, at least one hundred years after the moment in which a spectator might imagine Sonya's words to have been spoken, there is a double contemporaneity at work that undoes or loops back the implicit teleology. The spectator *is* the future in whom Sonya's hopes rested. Now is *still* the moment in which such hopes may be entertained. The prerequisite, Marx says, for the realization of such hopes—that "we shall rest"—is "the shortening of the working day." So, rather than working now in order to build the freedom of the future, political struggle over work might be about reducing the part it plays in life. This is an interesting idea to consider when leaving a theatre of an evening, as the curtain comes down on this encounter between her work and our entertainment.

This moment or encounter in the theatre also constitutes an instance of the production of social relations. This is not simply another version of the largely empty claim in which the theatrical event is said to create sociality or even community in general by means of its mere gathering together of people in one place. A swimming competition would do this just as well. This theatrical encounter is rather the production of social relations with specific content: social relations whose content is social relations, as it were, and precisely those social relations that are organized and understood by way of work. And they are also social relations that cross historical time: if I am the future in whom Sonya placed her hope, then I recognize both a social relation between myself and a social situation of a hundred or so years ago, and the historicity of my own social relations. In both recognitions there is a most definite lack of inevitability. And a social relation that implies, even demands, a measure of reflection upon social relation, inviting a cross-temporal conversation.

The moment in which these social relations are produced does not posit a position on the outside of contemporary regimes of production; there is no clear exterior space of opposition available either in the theatre or in the play, let alone a utopia. Instead, whatever social relations with content might be produced in this encounter are produced from within the very core of production itself: in the characters' resignation to their work as a kind of destiny, as well as in theatrical production's own knowing participation in precisely those structures of capital that determine the difference between work and play, between necessity and freedom. For theatrical production, far from being an instance of the heterogeneous exteriority to capitalist production that might be claimed by and for aesthetic subjectivity, is of course a nest in which the logics of that production assert themselves with insidious and delightful force, even as they seem to produce, or perhaps to promise, at the very same time, that "rest" that for Vanya and Sonya, at least, comes only beyond the grave, but that might, in some other world, such as this one, be possible in life. The promise of performance, here, turns out to depend, for its very possibility, on the fact that it is production—production rather than performance, as the Russian commentators so rightly noted—and not, as has been claimed elsewhere, something to be valued precisely because it is unproductive.

Miranda Joseph develops a critique of claims that performance is unproductive, shaped by a reading of Marx alongside Judith Butler. In Joseph's reading of Marx, she emphasizes the idea, most strongly present, she suggests, in his early texts, that all human work, not simply that which is normally understood as economically productive (like making things in factories), might be understood as production. This enables her to include "the production of all sorts of things beyond traditional material objects" as production and to graft onto Marx's theory of value the vital contribution of feminist thought to the "recognition of values other than monetary exchange as the measure of productivity."[56] For Joseph, then, diverse production thus produces a "diversity of subjects."[57] Following Raymond Williams (in his late, Marxist vein), Joseph argues that these subjects participate in (are produced by and themselves produce) material significations that may include "subjectivity, social relations, and consciousness,"[58] as well as more obviously material products in the form of commodities. Joseph then adds to this reading of Marx's materialism Butler's suggestion that, although "highly constrained,"[59] consumption is also a site for the production of both individual and collective subjectivities.

Taken together, then, it is from these linked ideas that production may be capable of more than just commodities, that consumption itself is a form of production, and that this form of production may be more than simply the reproduction of the status quo ante, or what Peggy Phelan calls "the Same,"[60] that Joseph derives an account of the moment of performance that she distinguishes from that offered by Phelan:

> The notion that performance is unproductive because it is live, because it is produced and consumed in the same moment, because it is not a material commodity [. . .] is, as I think I've made clear by now, simply wrong.[61]

This is because Phelan "cannot recognize the audience's consumption as production" and because, in thus "losing the audience" she "loses the theatrical aspect of the artwork's performativity," which Joseph defines as "both its reiterative and witnessed, and therefore social, aspects."[62] For Joseph this leaves Phelan with only the narrow performativity, that the work "enacts that which it names,"[63] a performativity that would elude the economy of production by unnaming itself in the moment of bringing its enactment to an end: "performance becomes itself through its disappearance."[64]

In a performance of *Uncle Vanya*, then, the simultaneous commitment

to both work and rest constitutes a kind of promise to any or every spectator that they might constitute themselves in some new orientation toward
work and its time. That this is the promise is evident only from a recognition of the structure of theatrical production, and not merely from the
content of the drama: that the actors are working to produce something;
that they are about to stop doing so, and indeed to rest, in the instant of
their rededication to work and their longing for rest; and that this call is
addressed to a presumed (even if largely fictive) set of social relations in
which the addressee might, as an act of productive consumption, choose
to constitute some aspect of their subjectivity. Thus a productive performativity is in play, in which this subjective orientation, or orientation of
subjectivity, is on both the affective and the interpretative horizon. There
is, of course, only very limited efficacy in all this: there is no telling what
any particular spectator at any specific production might actually do or
feel within such horizons; what they might make of this promise. We
should not imagine anyone leaving the theatre and immediately dedicating themselves to their own version of Astrov's vision nor yet forming a
revolutionary party that might soon overthrow the Tsarist regime and
install a dictatorship of the proletariat.

What we might imagine, more modestly, though, is a suspension and
a fold. The time of the play suspends the work of history. In that suspension a subjectivity takes shape. That subjectivity is an imaginative self-
projection through the moment from which the play "speaks"—the moment that awaits, unwittingly, the Russian Revolution—into a future that
was the promise of that Revolution. This projection, or subjective self-
orientation in the moment of suspension, is toward at least two simultaneously possible futures, two destinies of the promise. Imagining forward, through the moment that is the play, makes visible both the
historical failure of one particular attempt at redeeming the promise that
"we shall rest" and the still-present possibility that such redemption
might be achieved. This subjective self-orientation constitutes a recognition that its own historical situation and social relations are not inevitable.
It brings into momentary being the subject of a history that has not happened yet or of a twentieth century that might have been otherwise. But,
nothing being inevitable, there is no teleology here. The structure of this
subjectivity might seem romantic in its desire to produce the future out of
an imaginary past. But in the theatre the past in question is as here now as
the future it imagines. It performs a temporal collapse or fold. An alternative future of the past is momentarily seized in the present. It is precisely

in this present that the promise has its time of redemption. Work really is suspended. We could rest. Right now.

Thus it becomes possible to experience, at the end of *Uncle Vanya*, not simply the bittersweet cradling of a loss, so often attributed to Chekhov's plays. It is instead a rather stranger sensation, of mourning the loss of a future that has not been possible while still believing fervently in its continuing possibility. Perhaps it is in an attempt to convey this strange feeling that Masha, in *The Seagull*, famously announces, "I am in mourning for my life":[65] she is in mourning for a life that, not being over, cannot yet be mourned and that is renewed in every production of the play. This double feeling, in *Uncle Vanya*, is mapped onto what we might have cared to call "love," which, as so often in Chekhov, seems to be a matter of being in the wrong time.

> VANYA: I used to meet her ten years ago at my sister's. She was seventeen then and I was thirty seven. Why didn't I fall in love with her then and propose to her? I could have—quite easily! And she would now be my wife . . . Yes . . . We would both now have been woken by the storm, she would be frightened by the thunder and I would hold her in my arms and whisper, "Don't be afraid, I'm here."[66]

For a moment the present—the present of the stage representation of a rainy night—is the result of a past in which the future was different. Of course the vicissitudes of love frequently deflect and almost wholly absorb directorly, actorly, and critical attention, not without some assistance from the text. It is nearly always easier to speak of love than it is to talk about communism. The trick, here, is almost to do both, somewhat amateurishly.

THREE

All Theatre, All the Time

In the autumn of 1928 the Latvian theatre director Asja Lacis visited Berlin as part of her work for Narkompros, the culture and education department of the government of the Soviet Union.[1] Among her priorities for this visit, undertaken as a member of the film section of the Soviet trade mission, was to make contact, on behalf of the "Proletarian Theatre" group within Narkompros, with the German Union of Proletarian Revolutionary Playwrights. She also gave lectures on film, based on recent work developing a children's cinema in Moscow. During the course of conversations in Berlin with two leading members of the German Communist Party (KPD), Gerhard Eisler (brother of the composer Hanns) and Johannes Becher, Lacis described some of the work she had done in the early years of the Soviet revolution, making theatre with children in the Russian town of Orel in 1918. Becher and Eisler were sufficiently interested in what she told them to imagine that her work might provide them with a model for the development of a children's theatre at the KPD headquarters, the Liebknechthaus. They asked Lacis to work out a program for them. Her friend Walter Benjamin, with whom she had discussed this work before, when they first met on the island of Capri in 1924, and who had been very interested in it, now volunteered to help her with the program: "'Ich werde das Programm schreiben,' sagte er, 'und deine praktische Arbeit theoretisch darlegen und begründen.'"[2] Lacis recalls that Benjamin's first draft was "monstruously complicated" and that when Becher and Eisler read it, they laughed and recognized immediately that Benjamin must have written it.[3] She took it back to Benjamin to be rewritten more clearly, and it is his second draft that exists today as "Program for a Proletarian Children's Theater," the text to which this chapter is devoted.[4]

1. READING "THE PROGRAM"

This short text is a kind of manifesto for the work of the passionate amateur. Or, to put it another way, it is a claim staked on the revolutionary value of play and an amateur's vision of a world in which work under capitalism is suspended or even abolished. It challenges four very powerful and widely held ideas: that work is inevitable, that work is good, that work might lead to a better world (the consolation offered, perhaps, by Chekhov's *Uncle Vanya*), and that a better world is something toward which anything might or ought to lead. As this chapter will seek to show, it holds out the prospect of a complete reorganization of work and time in relation to theatre; suggests a radical attempt to undo precisely the capitalist professionalism that had been establishing its hold over theatrical production; and, at the same time, proposes an alternative to the cult of work itself. This vision is articulated through the figure of the child-as-amateur, who finds her fulfilment in the now of her beautiful childhood rather than in the development of her skills in the service of capitalist development or even in the teleology of the revolutionary project. It is articulated, however, in a context—political and cultural collaboration within the Second International—where the teleology of revolution and the moral value of work were both hegemonic.[5] Once again, the professional and the amateur live in a paradoxical relation with one another, in Benjamin's text, in the text's own relationship to Lacis's practice, and in the various contexts—which this chapter will explore—from which both the text and the practice it accounts for and imagines arose. Within the broader logic of this book, Benjamin's "Program" warns that as long as passionate amateurs continue to work according to the logics of industrial capitalism, the radical potential of their activity will be continually suppressed.

Benjamin's "Program for a Proletarian Children's Theater" starts right in the grip of its own paradoxical position, claiming that while this "proletarian education must be based on the party program," the party program itself "is no instrument of a class-conscious education" (201). The party program itself, because it is ideology, will only ever reach the child as a "catchphrase," and while it would be easy enough to have children across the country "parroting" catchphrases, this will do nothing to ensure that the party program is acted upon once these proletarian children have become adults. Thus the program of which Benjamin's "Program" will form a part is of no use for the purposes it seeks to realize by including Benjamin's "Program." Benjamin's "Program" is, in effect, an attempt to insert a form of antiprogrammatic thought into the party program. Its "de-schooling" requires, more or less a priori, the abandonment of "program." While Benjamin's text might be said to observe the letter of the party program, its underlying logic suggests an ironic radicalization of that very program. He must both mean and not mean what he says when he writes that "proletarian education must be based on the party program." In this irony lies its own "secret signal" that the "party program" itself, if it is to be the basis for proletarian education, must change, and change to such an extent that it somehow ceases to be a program.

The "Program" is here already showing signs of Benjamin's familiar tendency (which will be examined in a little more detail below) to think against the logic of a unidirectional linear time, associated with both the relentless forward march of capitalist progress and the redemptive horizon of revolutionary teleology implied by an overdeterministic reading of Marx. Less familiar, however, is the possibility that such disruptions to historical time might also be performed at the level of the everyday. But that is precisely what is suggested in the "Program." Benjamin proposes that "the framework of proletarian education from the fourth to the fourteenth year should be the proletarian children's theatre" (202). The logic of the "Program" suggests, furthermore, that when this theatre has ceased to be the "entire life" of the proletarian child, once the child has passed the age of fourteen, it may have no further role to play. Since Benjamin declares his "Program," and, by implication, the theatre that he values, to "have nothing to do with that of the modern bourgeoisie" (202), we might reasonably conclude that in the society formed by graduates of the proletarian children's theatre, theatre will no longer take its place within the structure of life determined by the administrated alternation between work and leisure. Theatre will cease to be a place where people come to sit in the dark in their leisure time to watch people at work in the light. Its place in the composition of a lifetime will change. Now it is something people either do for a living or attend occasionally in the evening after work. In the future (which must also be, of course, for Benjamin, now) theatre is something you do for ten years as a child but that you may never do again. To think in Brecht's terms, this constitutes an *Umfunktionierung* (repurposing) of the theatre, far more comprehensive even than the *Lehrstück*, whose theoretical proposal, in its emphasis on continual rehearsal rather than an orientation toward performance, was frequently evaded in practice, including by Brecht himself.[6] Benjamin's *Umfunktionierung* of theatre is a redistribution of activity in time that detaches itself from the patterns of life imposed by the working day, including those that involve working during the day and going to the theatre in the evening.

This interruption of temporal logic, at the levels of both history and the life of the individual, is therefore a direct challenge to the normalization or naturalization of work as the purpose or meaning of a life. All the

more so, in the case of the "Program," because Benjamin does not con-
ceive of this proletarian education in terms of preparation for work. Instead it must precede "the teaching curriculum as such," in which specific
skills and knowledge might be acquired. It serves as "an objective space
within which education can be located," while a bourgeois education
needs "an idea toward which education leads." Lacis makes a similar distinction in her own account of the work on which the "Program" was
based:

> Bourgeois education was based on the development of a special
> capacity, a special talent. To speak with Brecht: it seeks to make
> sausages of the individual and her capacities. Bourgeois society re-
> quires that its members produce things as soon as possible. This
> principle is obvious from every aspect of a child's education. When
> such children play theatre, they always have the result in mind—
> the performance, their appearance before the audience. That's how
> the joy of playful production is lost. The director is the pedagogue
> in the background, drilling the children. [. . .] It is the goal of com-
> munist education, on the basis of a high general level of prepara-
> tion, to set productivity free.[7]

Lacis here clearly sees the activity of making or "playing" (she uses the
German verb *spielen*) as productive, however, whereas the rather more
paradoxical logic of Benjamin's text tends to suspend the idea of productivity as such, through its interruption of the temporality with which it is
normally associated. This suspension—of production and of teleology—is
incomplete, of course (either partial or temporary), in that the ultimate
purpose of his antiprogrammatic program is to ensure that "the party
program is acted on in ten or twenty years" (201). Productivity and program are suspended in order that the program's objectives may be produced. Things to be achieved at a future time depend upon the suspension of all movement toward that time, a suspension that takes place
through the conception of education as the fulfillment of activity in a defined "space" rather than as progress through time: "It is only in the theater that the whole of life can appear in a defined space, framed in all its
plenitude; and this is why proletarian children's theater is the dialectical
site of education" (202).[8]

This interruption of a unidirectional temporality in which education is
understood as training for productive work is repeated in the uncoupling
of the idea of making theatre from the presentation of professional theat-

rical productions. The idea that a performance, as such, is only likely to emerge as a kind of by-product of playfulness, as a kind of "mistake" or "prank," as Benjamin puts it,[9] means that there is no place in this theatre for the "bourgeoise Regisseur" (765), a term that is translated into English as "manager" but that in a theatrical context also, of course, refers to the "director."[10] That the theatre director is an industrial "manager" was a central claim of the preceding chapter. But the productive forces at play in the proletarian children's theatre do not need to be marshaled and coordinated into a repeatable production designed to enter the repertoire of a theatre company. The "Program" proposes an alternative to the industrialization of theatre. It unseats the recently appointed "Regisseur" who, as we have seen in chapter 2, had taken managerial control not just of the process of production but also of the education of the theatrical workforce. This is not simply a repudiation of a bourgeois logic. While Stanislavski's initial practice takes shape in a decidedly bourgeois context—and might even be understood as part of a systematic bourgeoisification of the theatre in Russia—its insistence on work, training, and the production by such means of a "character" proved substantially consistent with the ostensibly antibourgeois production priorities of the early Soviet period, which saw work as the means by which a "new man" might be produced. Although Benjamin did not know Russian—as the linguistic misfortunes detailed in *Moscow Diary* clearly show[11]—and is therefore unlikely to have studied Stanislavski's account of his work as a director and teacher, first published in Russian in 1926, it is still tempting to interpret his insistence in the "Program" that the leader of the proletarian children's theatre should not be a "moral personality" as a criticism of the figure of the director exemplified by Stanislavski, whose work as the director of Rimsky-Korsakov's *The Czar's Bride* he had seen in Moscow in 1927.

Of course Benjamin's ideas here are also in sharp distinction with what I have earlier called the "incipient Taylorization" of theatre carried forward in the work of Meyerhold. I shall develop further the implications of this contradiction between Benjamin's "Program" and Soviet communism's glorification of work in the section that follows. What matters here is the task Benjamin's "Program" assigns to the leader, who, far from being a Taylorist manager driving his charges forward toward defined future production, offers, in an attitude of "unsentimental . . . pedagogic love" (203), his or her observation of what the children are doing and making. It is this abstention from productivist goal setting, in which the future is crafted by work in the present, which allows the leader of the theatre to become a receiver of the "signal from another world, in which the child lives and commands" (204). This "world" is a future, too, but very different from a future whose outlines and contents have been planned in advance and then realized through the industrial production process of rehearsal. It is a future that, in its reception in the present, takes place now; it is a fold or rupture in the progressive historical continuum. What Benjamin's text suggests, then, is that the role of the manager in the process of production is, at least in part, to look after that continuum. Professionals keep history on track by keeping the workers in line. The unsentimental love of the passionate amateur derails it. Instead of leading the children forward, away from childhood itself, and toward the adult responsibilities of productive work, the "Program" claims to offer its young participants "the fulfilment of their childhood" (205), while its adult facilitators are privileged with a glimpse of an unplanned-for future in the "secret signal of what is to come that speaks from the gesture of the child" (206). The signals are coming back down the yet-to-be constructed line to the future, reversing the normal direction of pedagogy repudiated at the start of Benjamin's text: "the propaganda of ideas" that seeks to make the future in its own image is jammed by what the future has to say back to the present.

The "Program" that turns out to be so antiprogrammatic is therefore one of those moments in Benjamin's writing where his thinking about theatre appears as part of a theorization of history or rather, in this case, perhaps, where a theory of history underpins a theorization of theatre. The outlines of Benjamin's theorization of history are visible in his 1919 doctoral dissertation, "The Concept of Art Criticism in German Romanticism," where he links a critique of the ideology of progress, as articulated by Friedrich Schegel in particular, with the idea of messianism, which, he suggests in a letter to Ernst Schoen, constitutes the "centre of romanticism," even if, as he claims to Schoen, he is unable fully to explore this improperly mystical concept in the context of a text composed for academic examination. It is realized rather more substantively, if only in typically and appropriately fragmentary form, in his 1940 text, "On the Concept of History." Benjamin's history is a crucial concept for this book's attempt to explore distinctions between the practices of the passionate amateur and those of the "professional"—either bourgeois-capitalist, reformist, or revolutionary—for whom working toward the future construction of the ideal community is the dominant mode in which history might be experienced or enacted. Werner Hamacher, in the very act of drawing attention to the persistence of the motif of the "critique of progress" from Benjamin's early work on romanticism to his later historical materialist reflections of history, also cautions that "one should not identify the configuration of messianism and critique of the ideology of progress in this very early work with his later outlines on the philosophy of history."[12] Nor, perhaps, is the conception of history underlying the "Program for a Proletarian Children's Theater" of 1928 strictly identical with those in play in either the earlier or the later texts. All the same, there is at the very least an inclination in all three moments toward an understanding of history in terms of rupture and possibility, rather than continuity and progress. It is in its interruption of continuity and the possibilities that might thereby be realized that the practice of theatre proposed in the "Program"—nonprofessional, antiprofessional, amateur theatre—attains its particular significance, for Benjamin and for the present project. Hence, and taking the form of a momentary digression from the forward movement of this chapter, in which a historical account of the practice (Lacis's) on and for which the "Program" came to be based lies in the imminent future, the time has come for a brief account of how this particular text takes center stage in the conception of the "passionate amateur."

Let us think first of the "secret signal" from the future, in relation to the "weak messianic force" with which, according to Thesis II of "On the Concept of History," we have been "endowed" on the basis of "a secret agreement between past generations and the present one."[13] One might imagine, then, that it is the "weak messianic force" carried by the adults of the present generation that solicits the "secret signal" from the children. The "signal" comes as a kind of recognition that the "weak messianic force" is still, or rather, will continue to be, alive. It is a testimony that the "secret agreement" is still in place. The agreement is "secret" inasmuch as neither generation knows its content; what it is that is agreed can only be known in the moment in which the signal is received and recognized. The arrangement is a little like an encryption software program, in which both sender and receiver possess private keys that the other cannot know, but where the interaction of one's private key with the other's public key (or vice versa) allows the file or message to be decoded. It takes both parties, both generations, for the signal to appear or to appear meaningful. It cannot simply be projected from the present, intentionally and knowingly, into the future, to be redeemed there, without already being there. As Hamacher writes, this "weak messianic force" is

> never messianic in the sense that we ourselves are enabled by it to
> direct the hope for our own redemption towards the future or, to

be more precise, to future generations, but only in the entirely different sense that we have been "endowed with" it by former generations, even by all former generations, as the compliance with their expectations.[14]

In the present, it is an endowment through which "the past has a claim" upon us. The "secret signal" from the future is a recognition of the persistence of this claim. In other words, our capacity to recognize in the gesture of the child a secret signal from the future is the evidence for the existence of the "weak messianic force," that our own claim upon the future might be recognized, even if the content of the claim we might be making cannot be specified in advance (now) but is only realized or redeemed in its relation to the specific historical situation of a future we cannot know.

This messianic force is weak, Hamacher suggests, because it is always susceptible to failure, open to the possibility that possibilities (for happiness, justice) might be missed. If they are not grasped by someone capable of rising above the lethargy produced by the "automatism of the actualities unfolding homogeneously out of possibilities,"[15] the future will conform with the present, in a reproduction of the same oppressions, over and over again:

> A historian and a politician takes a stand for the historically possible and for happiness only if he does not see history as a linear and homogeneous process whose form always remains the same and whose contents, assimilated to the persistent form, are indifferent.[16]

The problem is not just the urgency with which industrial capitalism asserts its claim upon the future—with its relentless expansionist drive—but also, and perhaps most disastrously, the conformity of anti-capitalist political movements in the very same historico-temporal logic. As Benjamin writes in his "Paralipomena to 'On the Concept of History'":

> In the idea of the classless society, Marx secularized the idea of messianic time. And that was a good thing. It was only when the Social Democrats elevated this idea to an "ideal" that the trouble began. The ideal was defined in Neo-Kantian doctrine as an "infinite [unendlich] task." And this doctrine was the school philosophy of the Social Democratic party—from Schmidt and Stadler through Natorp and Vorländer. Once the classless society had been defined

as an infinite task the empty and homogenous time was transformed into an anteroom, so to speak, in which one could wait for the emergence of the revolutionary situation with more or less equanimity. In reality, there is not a moment that would not carry with it *its* revolutionary chance, provided only that it is defined in a specific way, namely as the chance of a completely new resolution of a completely new problem.[17]

There is a possible paradox here, which the "Program" exposes rather clearly. Once political opposition to capitalism comes to regard itself in terms of the "*infinite* task," it seems to abandon itself to doing nothing, in sure and certain expectation that the revolution will just turn up. At the same time, in regarding its opposition to capitalism as an "infinite task," it aligns itself with precisely that historically specific logic of capitalism itself—that value is derived from work—from which it might, more radically, choose to dissociate itself. Thus in Benjamin's uncoupling of play from productivity, and in his extraction of theatre from the leisure (or culture) industry, there is also a possibility that the progress of capitalism's "empty and homogenous time" might be interrupted. It is no longer a matter of either waiting or working one's way through that expanse of time in order to build something for the future. In place of more of the same of this homogenous time of capitalism, then, there might come some "flash" of a possibility not to be missed, a constellation of two different but related "Nows" in which true historical time—the time of politics and of happiness—might appear. Hamacher writes that, in Benjamin's concept of history, "there is historical time only insofar as there is an excess of the unactualised, the unfinished, failed, thwarted, which leaps beyond its particular Now and demands from another Now its settlement, correction and fulfilment."[18] The "Program," in its rejection of the very logic of program, insists upon the constant generation of the "unactualised, the unfinished" in its refusal to finish either an education or a piece of theatrical performance. This is a refusal that does not content itself with waiting, either: it must be active in its interruption of the logic in which history is progress made by work. It is not a matter of replacing work with doing nothing. What is crucial is that a determinate "nonwork" must substitute for work and thus, in a sense, negate it.[19]

Theatre—if it can be taken out of its place in the culture industry, stripped of its professionalism, and radically repurposed—seems like a loophole through which the passionate amateur might exit from the "conformism" defined by the "illusion that the factory work ostensibly furthering technological progress constituted a political achievement."[20] As a "defined space" in which "the whole of life" can "appear," it constitutes the stage upon which an image of missed possibilities, overlooked in the submission to work and progress and flashing into visibility in the coincidence of two different "Nows," might appear: "It is not that what is past casts its light on what is present, or what is present its light on what is past; rather, image is that wherein what has been comes together in a flash with the now to form a constellation. In other words: image is dialectics at a standstill."[21] Perhaps that is precisely what becomes visible, as the latent possibility of even the industrial theatre, at the end of Chekhov's *Uncle Vanya* and, in chapters yet to come, in the revolutionary school-holiday school of Godard's *La chinoise* and the "romantic" evocation of "exodus" in the work of the theorists of post-Operaismo: the passionate amateur's determinate negation of work as dialectical image.

> Over and over again, in Shakespeare, in Calderón, battles fill the last act and kings, princes, lords, and attendants "enter in flight." The moment when they become visible to the audience stops them in their tracks. The stage calls a halt to the flight of the dramatis personae. Entering the sight of non-combatants and true superiors allows the victims to draw breath as fresh air takes them in its embrace. That is what gives the stage appearance of these "fleeing" entrances their hidden significance. Implicit in the reading of this form of words is the expectation of a place, a light (daylight or footlights) in which our own flight through life might be safe in the presence of watching strangers.[22]

2. PRACTICE BEFORE THE "PROGRAM"

Perhaps it is appropriate that the idea that Asja Lacis might develop a "Proletarian Childrens' Theater" based upon this "Program" was never realized—not because its realization would represent some betrayal of the text's antiprogrammatic character, but rather because the practice to which it gestures had already taken place ten years earlier. In October 1918, Lacis was asked to take up a position as a director in the theatre in Orel, a city about three hundred miles south west of Moscow and two hundred miles east of the border of Belarus. On arrival in Orel (Oryol), Lacis was immediately struck by the presence of large numbers of homeless children on the streets. Such children—widely known in Russian as the *besprizorniki*—had become a feature of city life before the Revolution of 1917. As Alan Ball explains, the phenomenon of *besprizornost*—not by any means new—had been amplified and intensified by the impact of World War One.[23] In the first place mass mobilization from 1914 deprived families of their main breadwinners, forcing women to work long hours outside the home and children, too, to find ways of earning money simply to survive. Many children moved between homes that could no longer support them and streets where they could improvise a precarious life out of "begging, peddling, prostitution and theft."[24] Then, as the war progressed and German forces pushed eastward into Russian territory, mass evacuations eastward from Ukraine and Belarus resulted in the separation of families from one another, as well creating conditions in which many adults died, leaving their children both orphaned and displaced. In the immediate post-revolutionary years the care and education of children were identified by the new Soviet government as key priorities, and radical proposals were developed in which both care and education might be provided by the state rather than by the family. By 1918 at least three new government agencies were claiming responsibility for making and implementing policy: in addition to the commissariats for Health and Social Security, Narkompros, the Commissariat for Education (which also oversaw artistic production), saw child welfare as part of its sphere of operation.[25]

The idea that a theatre director—and one who already had experience working with children, as Lacis had—should see the welfare of such children as something to which she might contribute is thus entirely consistent with both artistic and social policy in the first years of the Soviet Union, a clear expression of revolutionary ambitions for the transformation of social relations. In Orel, some of the *besprizorniki* had been accommodated in an orphanage where, Lacis reports, they received food and shelter but, as their "tired, sad eyes" showed, "nothing interested them": they had become "children without childhood."[26] Lacis herself was living in an old aristocratic house, in which the characters of Turgenev's novel *A Nest of Nobles* were supposed to have lived, and she proposed to the head of city education that she should transform it into a space for children's theatre rather than direct conventional productions for the city theatre. Her proposal was approved, and the rooms of the house were opened up for Lacis and the homeless children. In Lacis's account she was aware from the very beginning that in order to liberate the creative faculties of these traumatized children, it would be necessary to abandon any idea of working toward specific goals such as the performance of a play under the guidance of the "director's will" (*Willen des Regisseurs*).[27] The rejection of the manager-production complex as it is articulated in Benjamin's "Program" thus represents both a theoretical position derived from a critique of bourgeois education (which is how Lacis herself frames it, in the passage already cited, on the "goal of communist education") and a practical response to a specific historical situation. Lacis is proposing to "re-purpose" (*umfunktionieren*) her own role as both teacher and director. She is doing so, as we shall see, at a moment of historical possibility in which all prior assumptions as to how basic social functions should be organized are in flux. In undoing recently consolidated bourgeois assumptions—that the care of children should be undertaken in the home of the "nuclear" family and that activities like education, welfare, and theatre should be guided by appropriately qualified "professionals"—the Bolshevik revolution's moment of historical possibility also threatens the Platonic foundations of propriety upon which, at least in the political sphere, the distinction between professionals and amateurs (workers and rulers) depends. Jacques Rancière's critique of Plato,[28] in which he advances the idea that only those with no qualification to govern are qualified to govern, might indeed be said to have found concrete expression in this immediate post-revolutionary moment, in which, as Sheila Fitzpatrick observes in her account of the first years of Narkompros, "almost nobody [. . .] had any administrative or organizational experience outside the sphere of emigré revolutionary politics."[29] In this moment, then, the revolutionaries, Lacis among them, are "passionate amateurs," undertaking an experimental practice of individual and collective *Umfunktionierung,* before circumstances seem to require that they should settle down into becoming "revolutionary by profession."[30] However, rather than merely recapitulating a familiar narrative of the revolutionary potentiality of the "amateur" giving way to the bureaucratic totalitarianism of the Soviet "professional," this observation serves to unsettle another familiar conceptualization, in which Lacis the "professional revolutionary" repurposes or "turns" Benjamin, the dreamily romantic amateur.

In Lacis's own account of the origins of the "Program" itself, it seems as though this strongly gendered articulation of people to their work is already in play. Benjamin is reported as announcing that, in writing the "Program," he will turn Lacis's practice into theory. In his first attempt to do so, he fails to be sufficiently practical as an author of a proposal for action, and the "professionals" in the Communist Party leadership laugh at what he has produced. Here Benjamin the amateur, a figure that seems to have contributed substantially to the slightly cultish way in which his work has been received in some quarters, appears to be a distinctively male, almost gentlemanly role. Benjamin appears here as the gentleman whose dilettantish skills as a *feuillitoniste* license his self-nomination as the theorist-advocate of the professional woman, as though, to return to Hannah Arendt's distinctions, he alone has the time to write (to speak, to act), while Lacis, condemned to the sphere of mere labor, does not. In this scenario, the laughter of the "professionals" at the appearance of a theoretical text so clearly not "fit for purpose" serves only to reinforce this distinction. Benjamin is too naïve, too unworldly, to accommodate himself to the heteronomous demands of professional revolutionary practice, just as, in the broader narrative of Benjamin as heroic failure, the rejection of his *Habilitationschrift* marks his inassimilability to the limiting structures of the professional academy.

This dyad in which women's labor supports men's (political) action appears with varying degrees of stability throughout the material with which this book engages. In the Platonic conception the exclusion of women from Athenian citizenship rests upon a gendered division of labor; in Chekhov's *Uncle Vanya* it turns out to be Vanya (who imagines he could have been "a Schopenhauer, a Dostoevsky") who relapses into idleness during the visit of the Professor and his wife and Sonya who just keeps on quietly working; in Godard's *La chinoise,* as we shall see, it is Yvonne, the young woman from the countryside, who serves tea and polishes shoes for the young people playing at revolution; and, in a theoretical exposition of the gendered division of labor that makes capitalist (and orthodox revolutionary) production possible, it is Maria Rosa Dalla Costa who notes the fundamental significance of the work of women in the home for the conceptualization of post-Fordist "immaterial labour."

Benjamin's "Program for a Proletarian Children's Theater" has the potential to undo this dyadic figure of the female professional and the gentleman amateur by putting to one side the logic of work around which this gendered valorization takes shape, even as accounts of its conditions of production point to the extent to which that logic continued and continues to operate. This book's organizing figure of the passionate amateur always stands in an ambivalent place: if on the one hand, in its dependence upon conventional understandings of the "amateur," it might suggest a certain kind of male subjectivity, on the other it seeks, at least, a trajectory that might escape both gender distinctions grounded in work and the very professional-amateur distinction upon which its concept seems to rest. It does so acknowledging, all the same, that both such distinctions remain fully operational within capitalism. Like the related figure of Rei Terada's "phenomenophile"—who prefers to let his attention stray from the matter at hand toward the seemingly inconsequential and flickering detail—the passionate amateur will tend to appear more readily in male than in female form.[31] Recognizing Lacis's children's theatre in Orel as the work of a passionate amateur, however, rather than as a practice to be elevated into action by a subsequent theorization by someone with time on his hands, represents, then, an attempt to hold on to the historical contingency of the category itself and of the construction of gender involved in capitalism's labor theory of value. It also points to the passionate amateur's inherent potential for self-dissolution in the resistance to work itself. Historical circumstances, foremost among them the new state's need to compete economically with its capitalist antagonists, meant that the potential for repurposing that the Soviet Union seemed in its early years to offer would never reach so far as to question the purpose of work itself. As the revolutionary project of communism came increasingly to identify itself, in Lenin's terms, as "soviets, plus electricity," and to promote figures such as Stakhanov as its ideological heroes, the self-dissolution of the passionate amateur would become one of the movement's unattempted trajectories—"unactualised . . . unfinished . . . failed . . . thwarted"—but returning, in the "Program," ten years later, as a potentiality that had yet to expire.

At the heart of Lacis's account of her work in Orel is a story that seems to value precisely the kind of potentiality with which an aprogrammatic and nonprofessional radicalism might wish to affiliate itself. Although she had decided not to work in a conventional way, directing the children in a production of a play, Lacis and her coworkers had chosen, as the basis for improvisational work by the children, a play by Meyerhold (*Al-inur*) based on a story by Oscar Wilde (*The Star Child*), although they had not told the children that this text was determining the improvisational scenarios they were invited to play. Lacis had successfully engaged children from the orphanage, and work was proceeding very well with them, but she had yet to persuade the street children to take part. One day the children are improvising a scene suggested to them by Lacis, in which a group of robbers are sitting around a fire in the forest, boasting about their exploits. It was during the playing of this scene that the street children decide to pay their first visit to the "Turgenev house." At first the children from the orphanage are frightened of the intruders, but Lacis urges them to continue with their scene and to pay no attention to the intruders. After a while the "leader" of the street children signals to his fellows, and the group invades the scene, forcing its players to one side and improvising their own far more ambitious boasts of murders, arson, and robbery, trumping the imaginations of the original improvisation. At the conclusion of this performance they turn on the other children and announce, "So sind Räuber!!"[32] For Lacis, the moral of the story lies in the interruption or suspension of all pedagogical rules into which this intervention has forced her. In its way this is a classic anecdote of radical and child-centered pedagogy, in which the unschooled and fully embodied imagination of the streets offers more to the theatre than the tamer confections of the more docile participants. It is a story in which the pedagogue confronts the limits of her pedagogy, "tears up the rulebook" in the face of "real creativity." But it is not just a story about spontaneous creativity. Its alternative moral is a deeply Platonic one, in which the theatre is interrupted by the real, in the form of those who don't have to pretend to be "robbers." The street children's claim is that they know better. They are, as it were, professionals, and this qualifies them for the role of theatrical robbers in preference to the supposedly less convincing efforts of the children from the orphanage. At the conclusion of the story, in which Lacis chooses to emphasize an anarchic overturning of professional regulation ("I had to interrupt all pedagogical rules"), there's a dynamic counter-interruption staged on behalf of a theatre based paradoxically on specialist expertise, rather than on the mere imitation of something the actors know nothing about. The passion of the street children expresses the craft pride of a labor aristocracy.

3. WORK, EDUCATION, COMMUNISM

The story of the robbers in the forest is for children and romantics and above all for those romantics who, like Benjamin himself (his doctoral dissertation, "The Concept of Art Criticism in German Romanticism," recalls the significant place of the Jena *Frühromantiker* in the formation of his thought), return again and again to the memory or the imagination of childhood. It is a story for Jean Paul, one of only two writers mentioned in the "Program" (the other is Konrad Fiedler, a nineteenth-century art theorist who emphasized the artist's capacity to see "with his hand"), of whom Benjamin notes that he was one of only "a few unusually perceptive men" to have glimpsed the world from which the "secret signal" of the child is sent. And it is a story for Friedrich Schiller, the hero of whose *Robbers*, Karl Moor, is a dramatic prototype for leaders of revolutionary movements. In the contradictory figure of the "robbers" of Lacis's anecdote lies a tension between two potentialities of the child, a tension that Benjamin's text also expresses: between children as fairy-tale romantics or as revolutionaries in the making, between pure amateurs or professionals in training. This tension might also be understood in terms of a historical relationship between bourgeois and proletarian conceptions of education and its function. This relationship is largely one of contradiction, a contradiction that is to be found within the emergent communist discourse, seeking an alternative to bourgeois education, as much as in the differences between that discourse and either conservative or liberal approaches to bourgeois education. In terms of both the structure for education and the conception of history implicit in Benjamin's "Program," this contradiction opposes Marxist-Leninist work for a communist future to a romantic-utopian attempt to produce the future within the present by drawing upon the forces of the past (what Benjamin earlier conceptualized by way of his notion of "origin as the goal")[33] "The Program for a Proletarian Children's Theater" does not just look back ten years to Lacis's work in Orel; it also recalls some of Benjamin's own first intellectual and activist engagements, in the youth and student movement of the final years before World War One.[34]

Benjamin was one of the leading members of a relatively short-lived left-leaning youth movement operating in both Vienna and Berlin called Anfang. Among its fellow members were Siegfried Bernfeld from Vienna, who later became a psychoanalyst, and Gerhard Eisler, who, as we have already seen, would become a leading member of the KPD. The leadership of the movement also included one exceptionally influential older "mentor" figure, Gustav Wyneken. Wyneken was already well known as a theorist and practitioner of radical education. Benjamin had spent three years at a rural school at Haubinda in Thüringen, directed by Wyneken, apparently as an alternative to the Kaiser Friedrich Gymnasium in Berlin, which he hated, and had subsequently joined a movement for school reform in Freiburg, formed in response to a public appeal for collective action by Wyneken.[35] In a statement in the inaugural issue of the movement's journal, also named *Anfang*, published in May 1913, Wyneken, Benjamin, Bernfeld, and Georges Barbizon (a leading Berlin member of the group) established its main principles, conceived as a direct attack on the mainstream education of the time. As Philip Lee Utley notes:

> In most members' experience, the school employed curricular and noncurricular practices that made it the adult world's worst offender against five values. The values were major tenets of the

movement's program: social justice, universalist national neutrality, individual freedom, communitarianism and sexual liberation.[36]

A crucial "framework of unifying ideas"[37] for Anfang was Wyneken's concept of *Jugendkultur* (youth culture), which affirmed that, far from being a mere transition of the infant toward adult maturity (a transition for which formal education was conventionally assumed to be necessary), childhood was a distinctive moral or spiritual condition:

> Autonomous youth were morally superior—more spiritual (geistig) in a Hegelian sense than any other age-group. Youth's spiritual character (Eigenart) meant that youth were idealistic rather than materialist, the theory ran; therefore they adhered to absolute values and were inclined to realize them without compromise. Inherent in their spiritual character was also a need to be exposed to humanistic culture—art and the humanistic and scientific disciplines—and absorb what was consonant with absolute values in the material learned. If given autonomy, youth would select spiritual teachers who would aid in this task. Thus armed with absolute values and spiritual culture, youth were considered the dialectical antithesis of the material, philistine adult world, which they struggled to modify.[38]

Rather than seeking to acquire the skills and behavior necessary for her incorporation into the adult world, the child has a spiritual mission (in this extremely Hegelian formulation) to transform the adult world itself into one in which the values of the child could find full realization (as absolute spirit, presumably); or, in a more Benjaminian formulation, the child's mission is to blast open the continuum of successive homogenous time in which she moves automatically along the path to adulthood, thereby collapsing industrial modernity back into an idealized, romantic vision of its own past (of childhood, or of the medieval forest). This means, as Benjamin explains in an essay published in *Anfang* in 1913, that the adult cannot look back at the child from a standpoint of superiority, based on knowing what it is that the child will become. To do so would be to fail to recognize the child as the condition in which the adult might wish to ground her own social or political reorientation, toward an "origin as a goal." Benjamin writes that the adult who claims to have "experienced" things and to know more than the young person smiles in a superior fashion: this will also happen to us—in advance he devalues the years we will live, making them into a time of sweet youthful pranks, of childish rapture, before the long sobriety of serious life. Thus the well-meaning, the enlightened. We know other pedagogues whose bitterness will not even concede to us the brief years of youth; serious and grim, they want to push us directly into life's drudgery. Both attitudes devalue and destroy our years.[39]

It is not hard to discern in this early text, and in another that appeared a year later as a published version of a speech given by Benjamin as president of the Berlin Free Student Group, the emergence of Benjamin's distinctive conception of history as a necessary corollary of this valorization of childhood. The two ideas appear linked to one another in these early texts just as they are in the "Program." In his "presidential" speech, given first in Berlin at the start of the 1914 summer semester and then again in June of that year in Weimar, at a meeting of all the Free Student Groups, Benjamin announces that his aim is, in effect, to do precisely what he will later propose as the goal of the Proletarian Children's Theater:

> There is a view of history that puts its faith in the infinite extent of time and thus concerns itself only with the speed, or lack of it, with which people and epochs advance along the path of progress. [. . .] The following remarks, in contrast, delineate a particular condition in which history appears to be concentrated in a single point. Like those that have traditionally been found in the utopian images of the philosophers. [. . .] The historical task is to disclose this immanent state of perfection and make it absolute. [. . .] the contemporary significance of students and the university [. . .] as an image of the highest metaphysical state of history.[40]

What follows is a critique of the instrumentalization of knowledge and scholarship in the university that sounds very much like later critiques of higher education such as the famous 1965 text produced by members of the Situationist International—On the Poverty of Student Life:

> Being a student is a form of initiation. An initiation which echoes the rites of more primitive societies with bizarre precision. It goes on outside of history, cut off from social reality. The student leads

a double life, poised between his present status and his future role. The two are absolutely separate, and the journey from one to the other is a mechanical event "in the future." Meanwhile, he basks in a schizophrenic consciousness, withdrawing into his initiation group to hide from that future. Protected from history, the present is a mystic trance.[41]

While one might readily imagine that the militants of Strasbourg would view Wyneken's notion of *Jugendkultur,* and its development by Benjamin into the idea of a childhood that finds its own fulfillment, as just another "mystical trance," there is an insistence in both texts, over fifty years apart (at the beginning and at the end of the period of the Fordist exception), upon the relationship among history, education, and work. Both texts share a desire to interrupt the process by which education prepares its subject for the work that will ensure the continuation of the very historical sequence in which education leads to work. In his 1914 speech Benjamin writes:

It leads to no good if institutes that grant titles, qualifications, and other prerequisites for life or a profession are permitted to call themselves seats of learning. The objection that the modern state cannot otherwise produce the doctors, lawyers and teachers it needs is irrelevant. It only illustrates the magnitude of the task entailed in creating a community of learning, as opposed to a body of officials and academically qualified people. It only shows how far the development of the professional apparatuses (through knowledge and skill) have forced the modern disciplines to abandon their original unity in the idea of knowledge, a unity which in their eyes has now become a mystery, if not a fiction.[42]

The simultaneous subject and object of the historical sequence that Benjamin wishes to interrupt is, of course, the bourgeois professional: the "doctors, lawyers and teachers" among whom Benjamin himself was supposedly destined to take his place but from whom he was soon decisively to separate himself, first by refusing to assimilate his "knowledge" to the institutional demands of the "modern disciplines" and then by orienting himself toward a radically different "community of learning" from that envisaged by the romanticism on which his rhetoric here seems to draw: the proletariat.[43]

Benjamin's views are not simply a restatement of romantic Humboldtian ideals, however, but may also be understood in their own particular historical context. Despite the lip service paid to such ideals in the often self-authored historiography of the modern German university, the real transformation achieved during the nineteenth century was the simultaneous expansion and diversification of university studies in order to facilitate the development of an increasingly bourgeois cadre of professionals in administration; law; and, crucially, industry. This process, implicit in the establishment, by the Prussian state, of Berlin University in 1810, accelerated and intensified at the end of the nineteenth century.[44] Now universities faced competition from the Technische Hochschulen, specialist training institutions that were adapting themselves more readily than the universities to the demands of new industrial processes and forms of industrial organization. Universities were accused of being out of touch and unsuited to modern economic conditions.[45] Between 1890 and 1914, however, the universities not only expanded (from twenty-eight thousand students to sixty thousand) but also diversified and professionalized, in what Konrad Jarausch describes as a "transition from the traditional elite to a modern middle-class university."[46] Geoff Eley summarizes the findings of Jarausch's extensive research, which shows that this diversification and professionalization had two dimensions. The first, Eley writes, was "the upgrading of commercial, technical, and pedagogical institutions, the proliferation of teaching and research fields, and the reconfiguration of the academic career structure into an elite of senior professors and a new subordinate category of Assistenten."[47] Previously lower-status institutions of higher education (including the Technische Hochschulen) acquired new status because they could meet the needs of an industrializing nation, and higher-education institutions in general started to adopt organizational forms derived from commerce and industry. The second dimension of this process "concerned the societal dynamic of professionalization and the growing imbrication of professional, managerial, and administrative careers with a system of regulated higher educational qualification."[48] Thus the professionalization of the university itself became integrated with the industrial world of work in which university graduates were increasingly seeking employment, and their university qualifications became an increasingly standardized requirement for finding such work.

As Jarausch notes, therefore, this expansion was more than just a matter of quantity: it would transform the very nature of the university. Conservative defenders of the existing elitism, in which the *Bildungsbürgertum,* or academic bourgeoisie, who were at least rhetorically committed to the supposedly Humboldtian ideals of scholarship as vocation, held themselves apart, like gentlemen, from the "arrivistes" of the petty-bourgeoisie and feared that the traditional experience of the university life (much romanticized in memoirs) would be contaminated. But optimistic advocates of the integration of university study with the demands of an industrializing economy sought to imagine the university itself as a kind of factory. Jarausch cites the celebrated historian of Rome, Theodor Mommsen, who, in 1890, had "coined the term Grosswissenschaft as a scientific counterpart to big government and big industry."[49] In 1905 Mommsen's friend, the liberal theologian Adolf von Harnack, director-general of the Royal Library, published an article, "Vom Großbetrieb der Wissenschaft," in which he explicitly compares even the most apparently arcane scholarly labor of philology—its editions, its accumulation of knowledge about sources—to the factories of industry, arguing that scholarship was now becoming a process of industrial knowledge production.[50] Jarausch sees this conception of collaborative research—which extends, as Harnack is keen to emphasize, to formal international partnerships and exchange—as "signalling the arrival of the mass research university."[51] Harnack is fully aware of the objections that might be raised against this terminology and the practice it names:

> So whoever speaks against the large-scale industry of scholarship— the word is not beautiful, but I can find no better one—does not know what he is doing, and whoever seeks to inhibit the progressive extension of this method of global conquest is damaging the common good. Of course we know the dangers of this industry— the mechanization of work, the valuation of collecting and refining material over intellectual insight, and even the genuine stupefaction of workers—but we can protect ourselves and our collaborators against these dangers.[52]

The emergence of the idea that the highest form of education and the scholarly inquiry with which it has become associated in the German university during the nineteenth century is now best understood as a large-scale industry, contributing to the general good by means of its participation in a global network of production, signals a key moment in the professionalization of thought. It was not simply that the university was losing touch with its supposed mission to cultivate a unified knowledge, as Benjamin seems to claim, a mission betrayed by means of specialization and subservience to the demands of the profession. The transformation is much more foundational. The structures and ideologies developed for the purposes of industrial production have come to determine how knowledge itself is understood. The emergent epistemology of the professional understands the production of knowledge according to a newly dominant ideology of work, which consigns the amateurism of the old *Bildungsbürgertum* to an increasingly residual position. Such residues can become resources for subsequent emergent forms, however. Benjamin's defense in his 1914 speech of the "original unity" of academic disciplines in the "unity of knowledge" need not be seen as a gesture of elitist nostalgia. Instead it might be viewed as an attempt to reach toward a new unification of faculties that would resist the division of labor in the large-scale industries of modern capitalism. Only a few years later the educational reformers of revolutionary Russia would seek to realize such a vision through either the "polytechnic" or the "united labour school";[53] reformers in Germany would pursue similar projects;[54] and, Benjamin himself, following his own encounter with communist thought, would develop ideas about education radically different from any that might once have been associated with the *Bildungsbürgertum*. In the "Program for a Proletarian Children's Theater" these ideas take their most "amateurish" form, whereas in another text of the same year, a review of the communist educational theorist Edwin Hoernle's *Grundfragen der Proletarischen Erziehung*, they seem to acquire a "professional" orientation.[55] This tension between "free" work and productive work in these two texts of 1929 is evidence of two very different critical responses to the ideology of work that had taken a very firm hold in both Soviet Russia and the major industrial economies of capitalist Europe and North America and of Benjamin's interest in both.

The establishment of an ideology of work (many of whose proponents saw it as a science, of course) derived initially from mid-nineteenth-century developments in physics that supported the conceptualization of the human body as the medium through which labor could be applied to nature in order to produce the materials necessary for human progress. Anson Rabinbach, who traces this development in some detail, suggests that this ideology—and the scientific practices in which it was instantiated—led to a major shift in how labor was generally conceived. Where once it might have moral value, either positive, as in Christian ideas of work as a spiritual mission, or negative, as in the aristocratic Greek view of work as a degrading activity, it came, during the nineteenth century, to be regarded as a neutral (even natural) foundation for human existence, without specific purpose or teleology but capable of being directed toward one. This, Rabinbach argues, helped the ideologists of the science of work to claim, after 1900, that their ideas transcended politics. In Germany, the idea of a science of work (*Arbeitswissenschaft*) was developed by the psychologists Emil Kraepelin and Hugo Münsterberg, with a view to placing the insights of the scientific study of human behavior at the service of industrial production.[56]

Critics of their work, including the sociologist Max Weber, complained that their theorizations were remote from industrial application and responded by developing an alternative and empirical approach that would be pursued through the participation of the Verein für Sozialpolitik. This was a professional organization, originally founded in 1873 and composed of academics, civil servants, and a few industrialists, that concerned itself with applying the achievements of social science to central issues in German social policy. In 1908–9 the Verein für Sozialpolitik conducted a survey of the "impact of industrial work on workers' attitudes and circumstances" directed by Alfred Weber, Heinrich Herkner, and Gustav Schmoller, on the basis of a theoretical blueprint mapped out by Max Weber. This example of "the new empirical social science" was, Rabinbach notes, "primarily concerned with determining the optimum yield of labor power conceived as a social phenomenon."[57] Frederick Taylor's *Principles of Scientific Management* was published in a German translation in 1912, arousing criticism from advocates of the "science of work," who feared that Taylorism's explicit drive toward maximizing the productivity of workers at the expense of their well-being would undo scientific claims to political neutrality. So although Taylorism was far from universally accepted, a broad consensus took shape around the belief that work was central to social and economic progress and that its productivity could be enhanced through the application of scientific research to industrial processes, including, of course, to the training and education that was to prepare children and students for participation in the economy. This consensus included significant sectors of the German left: "In the early phase of the Weimar Republic, industrialists, experts in fatigue, and Social Democratic trade unionists generally shared a positive view of the science of work as compensation for the negative effects of Taylorism."[58] Few voices seem to have been raised in resistance to what we might call the *Großbetrieb der Arbeitswissenschaft* (the large-scale industry of the science of work and its application to everything that moves) and its ambition to ground and justify the whole of social life in terms of work. Even the leading educational theorist of the German Communist Party, Edwin Hoernle, envisages "large-scale industry" as the basis, the location, and the purpose of a "new pedagogy" for "mass" or "proletarian education."[59] Walter Benjamin concurs, affirming that Hoernle's book is "at its best" when it offers a "program" of "revolutionary education for work."[60]

The immediate inspiration for Hoernle's program lay in the radical proposals for the transformation of education adopted in Soviet Russia in the first decade of the revolution. The "communist pedagogy" so enthusiastically welcomed by Benjamin in his review of Hoernle's work thus took programmatic form in precisely the historical circumstances in which Asja Lacis developed the theatrical practice upon which Benjamin's "Program" is based. One of the central elements of Narkompros education policy from 1917 was the idea that all children should be educated through the United Labour School, which, as Sheila Fitzpatrick explains, "according to the Narkompros programme, was 'polytechnical' but not 'professional': it taught a variety of labour skills without specializing in any one of them or providing a professional or trade qualification."[61] There were two competing versions of the United Labour School. One, advocated by the commissar himself, Lunacharsky, and his colleagues in Petrograd, was largely based on the "orthodox progressive" position of antiauthoritarian, nonscholastic education and the full development of the child's individuality, using Dewey's activity school approach as the basis for a polytechnical education.[62] The other, advanced by leading figures in Moscow, emphasized the school-commune, in which children would live seven days a week and where labor skills would be acquired by taking part in "life itself" in the organization and maintenance of the commune.[63] While both visions decisively rejected the idea that education should be organized in order to facilitate the specialization upon which the division of labor in industrial capitalism is organized, the Petrograd version seems, on the face of it, to offer education a greater measure of autonomy from the workplace, since the Moscow version effectively turns the workplace into the site of education, or vice versa. However, the Moscow version, with its idea that the "school is a school-commune closely and organically linked through the labour process with its environment,"[64] offers a vision of childhood as a complete way of life ("life itself") with its own intrinsic value (achieved through its own labor), rather than as a transitional phase through which children pass on their way to productive labor. In this respect, its relation to work—and, indeed, to historical progress—is utopian in character and resembles more closely than the Petrograd version the proletarian education envisaged in Benjamin's "Program." It seeks its own realization (the fulfillment of childhood) here and now rather than by way of an orientation to a future still to be produced by the full development of adult capacities by the maturing child.[65]

Hoernle's *Grundfragen* specifically credits Lunacharsky and Narkompros with providing a blueprint for the development of a new pedagogy suitable for a proletarian education and refers, in particular, to an exhibition presented in Berlin titled "Labour Schools in Soviet Russia."[66] His own proposals seem to echo the Moscow approach, rather than that of Lunacharsky and the Petrograd vision of the United Labour School, however. In repudiating the associated "orthodox progressive" approach, he is also distinguishing the communist approach from that adopted by German social-democratic school reformers who, like Lunacharsky, drew on a liberal tradition encompassing Pestalozzi, Froebel, Dewey, and others.[67] But one cannot read his text without also noticing the extent to which it seems, simultaneously and paradoxically, to subscribe to the ideology of work in terms that suggest a clear affinity with the goals of "global conquest" through professional work as articulated by Adolf von Harnack:

> The proletarian school will not only, as the pedagogical reformers demand, be "loosened up," it will not just be "rationalized" in terms of performance by new teaching and learning methods (Montessori methods, Dalton plan), it will become ever more closely connected to the public life of the proletariat and the industrial and agricultural operations, it will become an important link between economic production and public administration. Large-scale industry has created all the material, social and psychological prerequisites for this new pedagogy. Large-scale industry brings the child into the factory, albeit in the evil and murderous context of capitalist exploitation. It creates the possibility for the application of the hands of children to the machines, it places the creative child alongside the creative mother, alongside grown-up men and women. It creates thereby the new social role, the *new social function of the child*. But thereby it creates the possibility for a new, higher stage of children's education.[68]

In approving the idea of a "revolutionary education for work" Benjamin appears to respond to this idea of the potential of human creativity, developed holistically rather than in order to reproduce the division of labor in capitalist specialization, as the key contribution of a communist pedagogy. This communist pedagogy perhaps enables him now to imagine the replacement of the nostalgic attachment he expressed in 1914 to an "original unity in the idea of knowledge," with a commitment to "universal labor" in which polytechnical education is the lever for the *Aufhebung* of a principle formerly negated by industrial capitalism:

> The immeasurable versatility of raw human manpower, which capital constantly brings to the consciousness of the exploited, re- turns at the highest level as the polytechnical—as opposed to the specialized—education of man. These are basic principles of mass education—principles whose seminal importance for young peo- ple growing up is utterly obvious.[69]

The apparent contradiction between the "amateur" impulse articu- lated so forcefully in the "Program for a Proletarian Children's Theater," on the one hand, and the pedagogy of a "revolutionary education for work" celebrated in the review of Hoernle, on the other, is one in which any romantic anti-capitalist sensibility seeking to move toward a commu- nist politics is very likely to find itself. In theoretical terms, the only way of moving beyond this contradiction would be to undo the ideology of work itself and to detach value from labor. The "labor theory of value" is not a universal or transhistorical constant; it is a regime of value specific to capitalism. To move beyond the contradiction, then, would require nothing short of the abolition of wage labor (which Soviet Russia, over ten years after the revolution, had not even yet attempted). Or, to put it in more practical terms, until an alternative is found to a form of life in which the adult human works for a living, it is likely that education will continue to focus on preparing her to do so, however the division of labor is organized. Any program of education that seeks to exit this logic is likely to be compelled to return to it in some form or other: either by ac- cepting that education is preparation for work or by making work and education one and the same. Benjamin's "Program for a Proletarian Chil- dren's Theater" lingers much more insistently in this contradiction than does "A Communist Pedagogy," as though Benjamin wished to continue to make available, to thought at least, the possibility that it might be oth- erwise and as though Lacis's theatre practice had shown that it might.

In the absence of a truly communist society in which a communist pedagogy might indeed be emancipated from its subjugation to wage la- bor and the labor theory of value, the virtue of a polytechnical education lies in its potential to release human creativity from the restraints of the division of labor. The virtue of theatre, as a mode of polytechnical educa- tion, is that it is an artistic practice that can be practiced, collectively, by amateurs, rather than produced by professionals for the consumption of others. In "The Storyteller" Benjamin suggests that the oral transmission of stories has been largely superseded in industrial capitalism by the novel, a literary form in which the professional establishes herself as both author and principal subject matter of the story. The kind of theatre that Benjamin and Lacis have in mind—a theatre in which children enact stories that exist in a collective repertoire, rather than in the commodity form of the book—might be precisely the performance form in which the tradition of the "storyteller" might return and the experience of experience be restored. Edwin Hoernle, too, like Benjamin and Lacis, grasps this possibility and desires its realization within industrial capitalism (rather than in a romantic retreat to the pre-capitalist forest). For Hoernle, like a number of other German socialist and communist writers and artists of the early 1920s, saw a proletarianized fairy tale, stripped of its conformist moralism, as precisely such a new form of collective artistic production, crucial to the education of proletarian children:

> The proletariat will create new fairy tales in which workers' struggles, their lives and their ideas are reflected and correspond to the degree which they demonstrate how they can continually become human, and how they can build up new educational societies in place of the old decrepit ones. It makes no sense to complain that we do not have suitable fairy tales for our children. Professional writers will not produce them. Fairy tales do not originate at the desk. [. . .] The new proletarian and industrial fairy tale will come as soon as the proletariat has created a place in which fairy tales are not read aloud but told, not repeated according to a text, but created in the process of telling.[70]

Benjamin, Lacis, and Hoernle are all, then, insisting upon the value of a kind of theatrical improvisation, which they all view as an artistic practice that might allow one to "continually become human" (Hoernle), that might "set productivity free" (Lacis) and receive "a secret signal" that would "blast open the continuum of history" (Benjamin). This theatre is one of those artistic practices that Susan Buck-Morss suggests might, at the beginning of the revolution in Russia, have been the basis for an "ungoverned cultural revolution"[71] but that was eventually unable to do so because

> it could not challenge the temporality of the political revolution which, as the locomotive of history's progress, invested the party

with the sovereign power to force mass compliance in history's name. Hence the lost opportunity: the temporal interruption of avant-garde practice *might have continued* to function as a criticism of history's progression *after* the Revolution.[72]

Such practices look, she writes, like "one of the dead ends of history" but "still merit consideration"[73]—not simply as historical curiosities but as possibilities that, "unactualised, . . . unfinished, failed, thwarted," might yet leap into a new now and demand "fulfilment."[74]

FOUR

Of Work, Time, and Revolution

The theatre is about to open. Someone is speaking across the end of the opening titles: "Un film en train de se faire."[1] As the titles give way to the film they authorize—"Visa de contrôle numéro 32862"—the lights, if you like, come up on a forestage, a kind of balcony or terrace, it seems, upon which a young man holding a book is pacing, reading aloud from his book, in front of a set of three windows, all behind shutters that look like they have recently been painted a casual but meaningful red. He does not seem to be addressing anyone in particular, either within the frame or beyond it. Nor is he speaking to camera. This reading, speaking, thinking person is observing a theatrical convention instead—one that might authorize the reading aloud of the letter or, perhaps more appropriately, the setting down of observations in "my tables"[2]—for this fretful intellectual-as-actor makes notes, too, as he reads. Quoting, thus, the behavior of the stage, this actor also quotes his text, of course: "La classe ouvrière française ne fera pas son unité et ne montera pas sur les barricades pour obtenir douze pour cent d'augmentation des salaires."[3] The author cited here is André Gorz, who would later come to bid farewell to the working class[4] altogether, but who was at this moment—this is 1967—one of the most prominent intellectuals articulating revolutionary demands on their behalf in France, in the pages of Sartre's journal *Les Temps Modernes,* as well as in his own books, including *Le socialisme difficile,*[5] from which this opening text for Jean-Luc Godard's film *La chinoise* is taken.[6]

Throughout this most theatrical of films (as I shall hope to show that it is) its characters will address one another, in lectures and performances as well as in conversations, and they will speak to camera in response to more or less inaudible questions posed to them from the film's invisible director, but they will also declaim, as it were, into the air, making their speech itself (very often speech citing other speech or writing) the stuff of the film. "Nous sommes le discours des autres,"[7] as Guillaume and Véronique will shortly announce, to no one in particular. "Words, words, words."[8] Or, as they say in the movies, "Action."

SPEECH AND ACTION

The commonplace that "actions speak louder than words" is normally taken to mean that the truth about a person may more readily be inferred from what they do than from what they say. Various associated more-or-less-commonplaces, such as the claim that "a picture is worth a thousand words," or the accusation that someone may be "all mouth and no trousers," point similarly to the idea that what counts is action, while speech may be discounted. This cluster of attitudes can also shade into a posture of anti-intellectualism, particularly in political contexts where direct action assumes the aura of revolutionary virtue, while reading, writing, and speaking are regarded as markers of indecision, weakness, and, in some versions of the prejudice against words, class privilege.[9] The idea that actions might speak louder than words has been perhaps nowhere more politically charged than it was during the Chinese Cultural Revolution, from which the protagonists of Godard's film take their inspiration. It is an idea that calls into question the relations between theory and practice, between workers and intellectuals, relations that had already become central to political debate on the French left by 1967 and that would be a predominant theme in retrospective analyses of the thought and action of May '68. It is also, of course, an idea that bears directly on the questions of work, leisure, and professionalism explored in the preceding chapter, as well as on the idea of the passionate amateur itself.

In *La chinoise*, there are thousands upon thousands of words—spoken, printed, quoted, scrawled, painted, flashed on screen—and perhaps only one action, and a singularly unconvincing and bungled one at that. In both speech and action, then, it resembles Chekhov's *Uncle Vanya*. In *La chinoise* a neophyte intellectual and self-appointed representative of "the workers" attempts the assassination of a visiting Russian apparatchik (the "intellectual" minister of culture of a "worker's state"). In *Uncle Vanya* a frustrated intellectual who "might have been a Schopenhauer, a Dostoevsky,"[10] had he not been condemned to work for "a beggar's wage,"[11] attempts the assassination of a visiting Russian apparatchik (the "intellectual" Professor Serebryakov). Both would-be perpetrators of action— Véronique Supervieille and Ivan Voinitsky—turn out, on the face of it at least, to have been much better at speech than they are at action. Their bungled shootings might perhaps be taken as comic hints as to the inadequacy of action or, at least, as pointing to some kind of discrepancy between what can be said and what is to be done. That is, unless the commonplace, as many commonplaces do, conceals within itself evidence of some secret measure of untruth; unless speech is action, theory is practical and the intellectual is indeed a worker.

For Hannah Arendt speech and action are the conjoined modes in which humans (or "man" in Arendt's own text) reveal themselves to one another: "Action and speech are so closely related because the primordial and specifically human act must at the same time contain the answer to the question asked of every newcomer: 'Who are you?'"[12] One cannot do without the other because without speech (to claim, announce) action would lack an "actor," without whom it would merely be the function of "performing robots." One model for such an actor might be the hero of a dramatic narrative, whose identity is disclosed to an audience by way of speech that claims responsibility for action, who names (and eventually perhaps, immortalizes) himself, as it were, by means of the enunciation of his own deeds: "In acting and speaking, men show who they are, reveal actively their unique personal identities and thus make their appearance in the human world."[13] Thus actions only speak louder than words when there is speech to go with them. Arendt's conjunction of speech and action is significant here, not for the conjunction alone, but for the role it plays in her conception of politics. This is of particular relevance, not simply for this chapter but for the book as a whole, as we have already seen (see chap. 1), because it is perhaps the clearest and most influential twentieth-century articulation of an old Greek idea: that politics is for those who are free from the burden of work. First of all, the space of politics is constituted through the speech and action of its participants and nothing else. "The *polis*, properly speaking," argues Arendt, "is not the city-state in its physical location; it is the organization of the people as it arises out of acting and speaking together, and its true space lies between people living together for this purpose."[14] Second, this space is only fleetingly inhabited, and many "men" are excluded from it: "This space does not always exist, and although all men are capable of deed and word, most of them — like the slave, the foreigner, and the barbarian in antiquity, like the laborer or craftsman prior to the modern age, the jobholder or businessman in our world — do not live in it."[15] Objections to this position (which might rightly be described as an antidemocratic ideological stance adopted primarily by representatives of the Greek aristocracy[16]) might focus on its explicit exclusion of "workers" from political activity, especially, as we shall see, in the context of 1967 and after, where the formation of a political alliance between students and workers, based on genuine class solidarity rather than assumed class difference, was a real political possibility.

In the suspension of work (the fleeting habitat of a summer vacation) that enfolds the action of Godard's *La chinoise* (just as it does the action of Chekhov's *Uncle Vanya*), speech and action constitute for the film's characters their very own brief "polis" in the form of a fictional Marxist-Leninist cell, which they name "Aden-Arabie." The hunch of this chapter is that *La chinoise* is an experiment in the possibilities of theatricality as a mode of being political situated somewhere between Arendt's categories of work and action, a zone, that is to say, in which "actors," uncertain of their place in an emergent new economic order (what will come to be known as post-Fordism), take advantage of the statutory summer holiday to talk themselves into becoming passionate amateurs.

WHAT HAPPENS

Here's what happens. Five young people have moved into the Paris apartment of Véronique's bourgeois relatives ("Ils ont des usines ou quoi"[17]) for the summer and formed themselves into a Marxist-Leninist cell. Véronique, a student of philosophy at the newly created University of Paris-Nanterre, appears to be the leader of the group. Her boyfriend, Guillaume, is an actor. Yvonne is a young woman from the countryside who seems to belong to the group by way of her relationship with Henri. Henri has trained and worked as a chemist (and it is he whom we see first, speaking, on the balcony). Serge Kirilov is a painter, his name a reminder that the film is very loosely derived from Dostoevsky's novel *The Possessed*. During the course of the film members of the group educate one another in the theories of Marxism-Leninism, taking Mao's *Little Red Book*, of which the apartment has hundreds of identical copies, as their primary text. Prompted by Véronique, the group votes to carry out an act of political violence. Henri, who had voted against this suggestion, is expelled from the group. Serge agrees to commit suicide and leave a note claiming responsibility for the assassination of the visiting Soviet minister of culture, but it is Véronique herself who attempts the action and then bungles it by misreading her target's room number from a register and shooting someone else by mistake. As the "cell" breaks up, Guillaume pursues his search for a true socialist theatre, and Véronique's cousins return to find, to their annoyance, that their apartment has been redecorated in Godardian primary colours and Maoist slogans.

As James S. Williams notes in a recent essay on the film, *La chinoise* has been generally considered a uniquely prescient film forecasting the events of May '68."[18] On its release it met critical hostility from both of the main French Maoist political publications, the *Cahiers Marxistes-Leninistes* and *Nouvelle Humanité*, with the latter describing the film as a "fascist provocation"[19] and both claiming that it misrepresented the nature of their political struggle. Much subsequent critical reaction has, quite naturally, viewed the film in the light of May '68 (and, of course, Godard's subsequent artistic trajectory in the Dziga Vertov Group), with Pauline Kael, in an assessment that is used to blurb the Optimum DVD release of the film, describing it, somewhat bafflingly, as being "like a speed-freak's anticipatory vision of the political horrors to come."[20] The twenty-first-century viewer might therefore enjoy something of the same historical relation to the film as that of the contemporary spectator at a production of Chekhov's *Uncle Vanya:* looking back in order to look ahead, with the 1917 revolutions and the events of May '68 asserting themselves simultaneously as the tangible futures of the represented presents and as the noninevitable sequels to the fictional events. But Godard does not really predict or anticipate. On the one hand, the intellectual experiment of thinking Maoism in relation to late-1960s France was well under way at the time the film was being made: inasmuch as Godard is engaging with a historical reality, he is filming an immediate present, in which both Anne Wiazemsky and his future collaborator in the Dziga Vertov Group, Jean-Paul Gorin, are actively involved at Nanterre. On the other, there is nothing whatsoever in Godard's film to suggest the activism on the streets that would characterize May '68. That Nanterre should have come retrospectively to be seen as the catalyst for the events of May '68 may lend a fortuitous sense of pertinence to Godard's film, but it does not make Godard in any way prescient. Nor yet does it make the film an anticipation of "political horrors," by which one can only assume Pauline Kael is referring to the political violence that followed '68, in actions undertaken by groups such as the Red Army Fraction, the Red Brigades, and the Weather Underground. While the question of the role of violence in political struggle is engaged in the latter part of the film—most extensively in the long dialogue between Wiazemsky's Véronique and the philosopher Francis Jeanson—the argument in favor of violence, as James S. Williams notes, "never translated itself into reality in France."[21] Nor does it even begin to resemble reality in Godard's film.

For, although the conversation about violence between Véronique and Jeanson stands out in relation to the rest of the film for its "reality effect"—it's shot in a "real" train rather than the stagey location of the apartment, and sound and vision are edited unobtrusively in accordance with tacit realist conventions—the scene of the bungled assassination, even if it is at odds with the overtly theatrical conventions of much of the film, suggests a daydream as much as reality, perhaps most strongly because of its complete absence of consequences. Véronique arrives at the building in which her target, Soviet minister of culture Sholokov, is supposedly located, in a car driven by an apparent collaborator who has never appeared in the film before. It is as though we are suddenly in some entirely other film. The building has the appearance of an office but seems to function rather like a hotel (perhaps a symptomatic architectural conflation of work and leisure that reveals incidentally both superficial and structural characteristics of the hotel itself). A single receptionist or clerk sits at a table in the foyer. An automatically controlled sliding gate allows the car to be driven into the forecourt. We watch from outside, through the vertical bars of the gate and the glass wall of the foyer, as Véronique enters the building and speaks to the receptionist so that she can obtain the minister's room number by reading it from a register on the table. As Véronique disappears momentarily from view through a door inside the foyer, a cartoon frame shows a man being blown up ("AAAAH!"). The next shot is of Véronique's colleague sitting in the car smoking and Véronique herself getting into the car, to report that she has done the deed, only to realize—"merde, merde, arrête"[22]—that in reading the room number upside down she has shot the wrong man. Her return to the building through a previously unnoticed door is accompanied by much maneuvering of the get-away car, the sliding of the gate, and, in response to the movements of the car, the opening and closing of automatic glass doors, as well as some very self-conscious "waiting" behavior on the part of the driver, before Véronique appears on a balcony and makes an ambiguous signal that could mean either that she has accomplished the assassination or that she has not.

No bodies, no blood, no "red,"[23] no gunshots, even. The episode is barely spoken of again, and there is no sign of any police response. The receptionist, like the rest of the film, acts as though nothing has happened. While the preceding scene—the conversation with Jeanson—is presented as anchored in a "real world," not least of course by the device of using a "real" person in conversation with an actor, and nearly the whole of the rest of the film has until this point been contained within the aesthetically coherent and thus similarly anchored setting of the apartment, this scene feels curiously implausible and fictional. That the Soviet minister of culture, who may or may not have been assassinated in this fiction, bears the name of the author of the novel *And Quiet Flows the Don*, who had been awarded the Nobel Prize for Literature in 1965, rather than that of the actual minister of culture,[24] and that in an earlier conversation members of the cell were unsure whether he was called Sholokov or Shokolov (chocolate, anybody?), only add to the sense of fiction within fiction. As far as we can tell, the receptionist appears to have been right. Nothing happened. In several reasonably convincing accounts of this film, including an extensive conversation between Godard himself and a group of writers from *Cahiers du cinéma*, the dialogue on violence between Véronique and Jeanson is taken to be the moral or intellectual crux of the film, as a scene in which it apparently matters who the audience concludes has had the better of the argument (most interpretations favor Jeanson, although Godard, in this interview, says that he thinks Véronique prevailed). In light of the metafictional character of the "violence" that follows, it bears recalling that the "reality effect" of the dialogue scene disguises, at least to some extent, the nature of the conversation and, indeed, the scene: namely, that it is a scene and a conversation that takes place between a real person and a fictional character. It might be naïve, then, to suppose that, following such a conversation, a fictional character could go out and commit a real action, rather than perpetrating a further fiction. Perhaps, here, actions simply don't speak louder than words.

WHAT *REALLY* HAPPENS: THEATRE

"I guess I didn't make it clear enough that the characters aren't members of a real Marxist Leninist cell," says Godard in his interview with *Cahiers*. Perhaps not, but not, it would seem to a twenty-first-century spectator, for want of trying. At the time of its initial reception several factors may have contributed to obscure what looks today like a pervasive and unmistakeable theatricality. In spite of the fact that the film was first shown publicly as part of the Avignon Festival of 1967, in a screening in the Cour d'Honneur at the Palais des Papes (the theatre festival's most prestigious location), critical reception appears to have been shaped by a combination of factors that have directed attention away from its concern with theatre. There is, of course, the film's self-evident topicality and the fact that it was clearly derived from Godard's own developing association with students at Nanterre in general and the radical left organizations taking shape there. There is also the apparent trajectory of Godard's work at the time: *Masculin-féminin* (1966) and, especially, *Deux ou trois choses que je sais d'elle* (released earlier in 1967) could be taken to indicate an increasing interest on Godard's part in the politics of the student generation and the social and political state of Paris, France, and indeed the world under capitalism. His participation in the making of *Loin de Viétnam* (1967), a film commentary on the war in Vietnam, along with directors such as Marker, Resnais, and Varda, traditionally associated with the political left, in distinction to Godard and his familiar *Cahiers* associates, would have contributed further to the perception that Godard himself was increasingly politicized. Clearly this was not entirely a misperception. Despite Godard's later claim[25] never to have read Marx, after 1967 he devoted himself almost completely to the exploration of what it might mean to "make films politically," first under his own name, then with Jean-Pierre Gorin and others[26] as the Dziga Vertov Group, and then again with Gorin as codirector—from *Un Film Comme les Autres* (1968) to *Letter to Jane* (1972)—and subsequently in video and television projects with Anne-Marie Miéville—from *Ici et Ailleurs* (1974) to *France/tour/détour/deux/enfants* (1978), before his so-called return to commercial film production with *Sauve qui peut (la vie)* (1979). As critical responses to this growing body of work sought to establish the kind of narrative that might make sense of a filmmaker's "career," it is perhaps inevitable that the "political" content of *La chinoise* should have attracted more attention than its formal theatricality, as it took its place in the critical narrative as a key precursor to the Dziga Vertov work. However, this emphasis to some extent misses the point of Godard's own conception of what it means to "make films politically": for Godard, at least when he articulated this distinction, the political is not a question of content, but rather a matter of how and why a film is composed. While the question of why would seem to drive much of the Dziga Vertov Group work, in that it appears motivated by a sense of historical urgency and by a desire to develop a meaningful purpose for the filmmaker, in *La chinoise* it is more a matter of how. How, that is, the ostensibly "political" content of the film is shaped, or produced, even, by the formal choices made in its composition. So, having earlier offered a brief account of "what happens" in *La chinoise,* I now present a brief account of "how it happens," which will highlight—in keeping with the analysis already offered of the "fictional assassination"—the theatre that constitutes, I will suggest, the actual politics of the film, in which there is clearly "no real Marxist Leninist cell."

That it is a question of theatre is because it is also a holiday. The film takes place in the summer vacation (between the end of classes and their resumption). As Véronique reports at the end of the film—in words and in a manner that can only corroborate the idea that there has been no assassination—"Avec l'été qui finissait pour moi c'était la rentrée des classes."[27] The film ends with the bourgeois "cousins" returning to their apartment and preparing to make good whatever damage has been done by its summer residents: in this the narrative resembles that of Ben Jonson's *The Alchemist*,[28] in which homeowner Lovewit returns from a sojourn in the country at the end of the play to expel the fraudster Subtle and his coconspirators, making for a conclusion that is both comic and conservative, in Jonson and perhaps, too, in Godard. It also begins and ends with "curtains," in the form of the red-painted shutters in front of which Henri delivers his opening text and through which the cousins and Véronique make their exit from view in the final shot of the film. Between the opening and the closing of the "curtains," then, a theatrical holiday—a suspension in the time of work, not unlike that imposed upon the estate in *Uncle Vanya* through the visit of the Professor and his wife. But, as the discussion of work and leisure in the preceding chapter has shown, one person's holiday is always someone else's work. In *Uncle Vanya*, although Vanya himself condemns the visit of the Professor and his wife for having forced him to suspend his labor, it is simultaneously clear that, however great the disruption, Sonya has been working throughout. In *La chinoise* a similar presentation of gendered labor is in play: while the bourgeois bohemians like Véronique and Guillaume develop their political sensibilities, it is Yvonne who brings them tea, cleans their windows, and polishes their shoes.

Godard's use of the holiday as the frame for cinematic narrative in *La chinoise* is not new, and it will return, too. In *Pierrot le fou* (1965)[29] Belmondo and Karina take off together, abandoning Paris for a romantic-picaresque holiday-adventure in the Midi, escaping their daily worlds of advertising and babysitting for beaches, a parrot, boats, and, eventually, torture and death (a holiday gone wrong). *La chinoise* is a holiday-adventure of a different kind, but both seem linked to a highly specific French appreciation of the *vacances payés*. It was as a result of widespread labor unrest in the period between the election of 1936 and the eventual formation of the Front Populaire government that employers were obliged, by law, to permit their employees two weeks paid holiday a year. The same legislation also effectively installed the weekend as part of the structure of everyday work-leisure life. Godard's second film of 1967, *Weekend*,[30] combines elements of both *Pierrot le fou* and *La chinoise*, presenting the weekend itself as a Fordist nightmare—almost literally in the form of its famous tracking shot of a traffic jam of Parisians in exodus—as well as the precursor to an extended season in hell, as its bourgeois protagonists murder a parent to secure an inheritance before falling into the hands of the cannibalistic Front de Libération Seine et Oise. The Front Populaire government may be said to have inaugurated Fordism in France in legislation that resembled, in its social and economic effects, the innovation of the "five-dollar day" by the Ford Motor Company in the United States in 1914: setting in place a system in which the workers' wages enabled them to consume enough in their leisure time to provide capital with the profits needed for its continued expansion. If these films contain an intuition that there is a crisis taking shape around the relationships between work and leisure or production and consumption in France at the end of the 1960s, perhaps Godard is indeed "prescient": what he sees, though, is not so much the immediate future of May '68, but rather the longer underlying process in which a Fordist accommodation between labor and capital is coming apart and will eventually give way to what is now widely understood as a post-Fordist regime. But post-Fordism still lies in the future, for France and for this chapter. For now we are still in the summer holiday of 1967, and there is theatre to be made.

So Henri steps off the balcony, through one of the three windows, and into the apartment, where Véronique and Guillaume will very soon and almost casually name the cell, once again adopting the "speech of others." Their choice, "Aden-Arabie," suggested by Guillaume, refers explicitly to a short novel of that name, written in 1931 by a school friend of Jean-Paul Sartre's, Paul Nizan. The novel depicts its narrator's disgust at the conditions of life in 1920s Paris, his flight to Aden, and his politicized return to Paris. It had been republished in France in 1960 with a substantial foreword by Sartre. In having the cell named after a novel, rather than after a "real" revolutionary figure, and presenting this decision as a casual act of playfulness, the not-"real" condition of the "cell" seems to be accentuated. Of course the name carries an additional contemporary resonance, to which Godard could have chosen to allude more explicitly had he wanted the cell to be understood as "real": in 1967 Aden was the center of an armed uprising by leftist and nationalist Yemenis, which would result, in November 1967, in the hasty withdrawal of British troops and the establishment of the People's Republic of South Yemen. The affiliation with Nizan, in a way that overshadows a relationship with a contemporary revolution, becomes part of the citational playfulness of the cell's formation.

While there may be a kind of "reality effect" associated with the casting of Anne Wiazemsky as Véronique (even though she had previously appeared, as an actor, in Bresson's *Au hasard Balthasar*, she *was* studying at Nanterre), the figure of Guillaume, by contrast, is already embedded in citational networks that only enhance his theatrical character. First, as Guillaume Meister he is Goethe's Wilhelm Meister, hero of the Romantic *Bildungsroman Willhelm Meisters Lehrjahre,* a young man who leaves his comfortable bourgeois life for a journey, through the theatre, to self-realization. Second, he is played by Jean-Pierre Léaud, the instantly recognizable poster boy for *nouvelle vague* cinema, teenage star of François Truffaut's *Les quatre cents coups,* who had recently taken a central role in Godard's *Masculin-féminin.* Inasmuch as Léaud is "real," he is real as an actor. As he explains in his interview within the film: "Je suis un acteur [. . .] je suis sincère."[31] The sincerity of the film, then, might be understood to reside in its confession of theatre and, indeed, in its insistence upon theatre as one of the courses of "action" that its central characters might choose to take. The search for a "théâtre socialiste veritable"[32] is sustained throughout by Guillaume and includes readings from Althusser's essay on Strehler's production of Bertolazzi's *El Nost Milan*[33] and a presentation using a blackboard from which the names of celebrated playwrights are erased one by one to leave just "Brecht" still visible.

Guillaume's sense of theatre seems to infect the cell more generally, most notably when his lecture about the Vietnam War turns into a performance in which Serge (Lex de Bruijn), wearing a plastic tiger mask, stands in for President Johnson, as Yvonne (Juliet Berto), made up to look stereotypically Vietnamese, is first harassed by toy US warplanes and calls out desperately for the Soviet prime minister to help her ("Au secours, M. Kosygin!") and then turns a toy radio into a toy machine gun that she fires repeatedly from behind a defensive shelter composed of Little Red Books. For Manny Farber, this sequence introduces an unwelcome "amateur" and theatrical element into the film; he describes the "playacting" as "rawly, offensively puerile" and claims that "the use of amateurs who play their ineptness to death is a deliberate, effectively gutsy move, but it can make your skin crawl."[34] For me, the escalation of theatricality within the film at this point is consistent with the strange "deanchoring" effect achieved both by the dreamlike assassination and by the most uncinematic practice of declaiming into thin air with which the film begins. This is because it is entirely unclear (and purposefully so, I think) who is doing the play-acting here: Yvonne and Serge or Berto and de Bruijn? To explore this ambiguity a little, it is worth comparing this sequence with a similar one in *Pierrot le fou,* in which Marianne (Anna Karina) and Ferdinand (Jean-Paul Belmondo) play out little puppet-theatre-style scenes of the war in Vietnam as a way of earning money to finance their adventure. Here it is clear that it is Marianne and Ferdinand who are performing. But in *La chinoise* there is no diegetic clue as to whether what we are seeing is a scene staged by Berto and de Bruijn for the camera or by Yvonne and Serge for the presumed spectators in the apartment. The actors and the characters come apart, at least slightly and momentarily, from one another, in an experience of uncertainty far more familiar from the theatre than it is in the cinema.

Guillaume's search for a "théatre socialiste veritable" extends past the end of the "assassination" narrative and the apparent dissolution of the cell, into the concluding scenes of the film, in which are shown brief snapshots of what appears to be an attempt to approach "théatre année zero" (via an installation with women behind Plexiglass and some take-the-culture-to-the-people activity involving an attempt to console a lovesick woman with doorstep Racine). That the film is interested in showing this, while on the other hand it abandons the narrative of the "assassination" as if it never took place (which, of course, it didn't), further suggests that it is at least as interested in the questions of theatre as it is in the supposedly political questions it appears to address (such as the role of the working class in class struggle). The balance of real and not-real in the actions pursued by the other characters also tends toward the not-real, or at least the representational. By the end of the film Yvonne seems to have entered the "real" world (she is last seen selling copies of *Nouvelle Humanité*, which suggests either a need to earn money or a genuine engagement with the Maoist left, or both), and Henri plans to find himself a "real" job and perhaps join the "normal" Communist Party (the very "revisionists" who beat him up early in the film). Kirilov chooses suicide (which might, perhaps, like Vanya's bungled shooting, be seen as a "theatrical" gesture). Veronique's "action" is even more ambivalent.

Indeed, it is by no means entirely fanciful to understand Véronique's action as theatrical too, on two levels. First, her conception of political violence, as outlined in her dialogue with Jeanson, is demonstrative: she imagines actions of the kind that would come to be known as "propaganda" warfare in the 1970s, where targets are symbolic (such as the Louvre) and actions effectively performative rather than instrumental (they accomplish their purpose by way of their intervention in a system of representation rather than by weakening a material enemy). Second, her leadership of the cell, including its installation for the holiday in her cousins' apartment, her role in its naming, and the literal-minded but somehow oddly playful sincerity with which she seems to infuse its activities in the apartment all suggest an interest in the observation of forms and conventions that, coupled with the decoration of the apartment (in colors, images, and texts), might more readily suggest the work of mise en scène than that of political militancy. Like Guillaume's explicit interest in theatre, Véronique's influence over the group's mise en scène of itself is pervasive, with her playful sincerity becoming a predominant tone. Renata Adler characterizes this tone in terms of a look: "the look of these young who are so caught up in the vocabulary of the class struggle of a class to which they do not belong—the look of hurt and intelligence and gentleness quite at odds with what they are saying."[35] Adler also suggests that it is the relationship between politics and theatre that generates this tension or contradiction in their playing: "all the characters seem more or less on the verge of playing themselves—very much preoccupied with another problem at the heart of the new radicalism: the relation between politics and theater."[36] The revolutionary attitude here expressed is both literal and ironic, sincere and playing at sincerity. As Véronique acknowledges at the end of the film, in a remark that may be taken to refer to the whole summer vacation and to the "assassination" that did not take place, "Oui, d'accord c'est de la fiction, mais ça m'approchait du réel."[37]

In short, not only is the film long on words and short on action (all mouth and no trousers), but it seems to insist, again and again and at multiple levels, that the action that it depicts is theatre. The theatre of what Paul de Man, writing on irony in the wake of Friedrich Schlegel, would call "perpetual parabasis,"[38] for its insistence upon negating or confusing its own truth claims in the moment of their utterance. Indeed, it turns out that Henri's rejection of the group stems not so much from his opposition to its decision to act violently, which, in any case, he says, was "complêtement irréel,"[39] but from its confusion of Marxism with theatre, of politics with art, a confusion that he denounces in his interview within the film as "romanticism." He attributes this "romanticism" to the influence of Guillaume, whom he describes as a fanatic, whose father had worked with Artaud (even if, as Guillaume has revealed in his own interview earlier in the film, he now runs a Club Med, which, he claims, anticipating Giorgio Agamben while reaffirming the inherent industrial character of twentieth-century leisure, resembles a concentration camp).

Henri, perhaps too straightforward to appreciate the kind of irony that interests Paul de Man, sees the theatre perpetrated by the "Aden-Arabie" cell as "merely theatrical," in the pejorative sense that it is superficial and lacks purchase on the "real" world. But as Guillaume/Léaud has already pointed out, to be an actor is to be sincere. The problem, he explains, as he acts out his story of the journalists who complain that the Chinese militant who unwraps his bandages while speaking of the wounds he has sustained in the struggle has no wounds on his face to show, is that "ils n'avaient pas compris que c'était du théatre, du vrai théatre."[40] As James S. Williams observes, drawing heavily on Jacques Rancière's essay on the film, it is in the accumulation of moments of this kind that *La chinoise* "could be said to reveal itself finally as a meditation on the theatre, as it had always, in fact, promised to be [. . .] an actor, like a political militant, aims to show what cannot be seen."[41] The point, in both the story of the bandaged militant and in *La chinoise* more broadly, is that there is not some simple opposition to be made between theatre and politics (or, for that matter, between speech and action), because theatre, made politically (like film), can make visible political possibilities not otherwise available to view. Here, the political possibilities seem to lie more in the mise en scène of a holiday play-revolution than they do in such more obviously political actions such as assassinations. And since neither film nor theatre is capable of carrying out an assassination, might it not make more sense to make the making of either political-in-itself than attempt to make either act outside-itself? The proposition of the film—inasmuch as it has one, and to be fair, it is probably far too playful and ironic truly to sustain such a burden—might then be that there is political value in the formation of a revolutionary cell as an end in itself, rather than as a means toward revolution as such. *La chinoise* as a "program for a proletarian children's theatre" for "the children of Marx and Coca-Cola"?

If so, then this value must derive from something other than work, for, as we have seen in chapter 2, the theatre proposed by Lacis and Benjamin constitutes an attempt to unravel the logic and the temporality of work under capitalism. The proletarian children's theater only produces (a performance) as a "prank"[42] or an inadvertent by-product of its activity and bears no relation to the theatre in which performance is the work of an evening's leisure ("nothing at all in common with that of the modern bourgeoisie"[43]). Likewise the homemade theatre of the cellule Aden-Arabie, whose members are filling the time of Véronique's holiday from school at Nanterre to make a school of their own, to interrupt the work-time rhythm of the Fordist economy by working on holiday time, and to produce precisely nothing, neither cars nor a new social order. To make of work something other than what it appears to be under capitalism, then, and to do so right now, is the program for Godard's passionate amateurs. It is a program that arises directly from the conditions of life, work, and study encountered, in what would become their historically iconic form, at Nanterre.

NANTERRE

The Nanterre campus opened in 1964. It had been built to deal with expanding student numbers at the University of Paris, which had led to facilities in the Quartier Latin becoming seriously overcrowded. Henri Lefebvre, who joined the faculty at Nanterre in 1965, wrote of the new facility that "it contains misery, shantytowns, excavations for an express subway line, low-income housing projects for workers, industrial enterprises. This is a desolate and strange landscape. [. . .] it might be described as a place of damnation."[44] In its proximity to the shantytowns (bidonvilles) it brought students from relatively privileged backgrounds not only into contact with a mode of French life far removed from their own but also into an encounter with the presence of the Third World within the First (an interpenetration that would come to be characteristic of life in the post-Fordist and globalizing phase of capitalism): "No need to go to Algeria, to Vietnam, to India, to discover the Third World [. . .] the Third World was living at the gates of the Nanterre Faculty."[45]

This is what Godard has Véronique describe, in her interview sequence midway through *La chinoise*, as her encounter with Marxism. Intercut with the well-known drawing of Alice pulling aside a curtain, she speaks of how at first Nanterre had bored her, because it was a factory inside a slum, but that gradually she realized that the same rain fell on her, on the Algerian children, and on the Simca workers; that they are at the train stations at the same time; they are in the same bistros and do more or less the same work. From this experience, she says, she comes to an understanding of three "inequalities" or false divisions in "Gaullist France": between manual and intellectual labor, between the city and the country, between agriculture and industry. Nanterre is here a "wonderland" behind curtains (a sort of theatre?) in which the emergent transformation of French education at the service of a reorganized capitalism reveals something of what is at stake in that very process: what Véronique takes as an education in Marxist critique, the planners and managers of the transformation will characterize as a step toward a modernization of capitalism—variously understood as the transition to post-Fordism, the end of organized capitalism (Lash and Urry), the emergence of neocapitalism (Lefebvre), of neoliberalism (Harvey), and of neomanagement (Boltanski and Chiapello).[46] It is Lefebvre who names the Nanterre contribution to this project:

> The buildings and the environment reflect the real nature of the
> intended project. It is an enterprise designed to produce mediocre

intellectuals and "junior executives" for the management of this society [neocapitalist society], and transmit a body of specialized knowledge determined and limited by the social division of labour.[47]

Here Lefebvre is articulating a critique that coincides, unsurprisingly, with the analysis offered just a few years earlier by five students at Lefebvre's previous institution, the University of Strasbourg, in a now famous pamphlet entitled *De la misère de la vie étudiante,* in which Lefebvre himself is briefly mentioned, alongside Althusser and other prominent "stars in the vacuous heaven" of the contemporary professoriat. The student's predicament is to be in "rehearsal" for a social and cultural role for which neocapitalism has no place:

By the logic of modern capitalism, most students can only become mere *petits cadres* (with the same function in neo-capitalism as the skilled worker had in the nineteenth-century economy). The student really knows how miserable will be that golden future which is supposed to make up for the shameful poverty of the present.[48]

They inhabit an increasingly precarious social position in which the class privilege of which a university education forms part comes into conflict with the reality that their university education may not lead directly to the kinds of élite social positions it might once have done. This tension is also experienced within the day-to-day operations of the university itself. The expansion of the university and its transformation from a site of scholarly privilege into the edu-factory[49] entails the introduction of new kinds of teaching, in terms of both method and matter. This means that students drawn into protest within the university—against both scholastic arcana and associated hierarchies, as well as against infantilizing social conditions—become active agents for the development of a "modernizing" view of the function of the university. They thus become the structural engineers of their own subjugation to the emerging logic of the edu-factory. Such an analysis, both inspired and directly informed by thought developed within the Internationale Situationniste, prefigures to a substantial extent subsequent critical accounts of what was to take place in May '68.

Danielle Rancière and Jacques Rancière, in their coauthored contribution to a special issue of the journal *Révoltes logiques* devoted to a theoretical and historical consideration of May '68, argue that the transformation of the university was a contradictory process. Before '68, "life was cut off from the School," and while there is no place for "tender feelings for the old forms of oppression," the opening up of "School" to "life" (including the introduction of Althusser, psychoanalysis, semiology, and Foucault to the curriculum, alongside more "modern" modes of teaching and assessment) has led, they argue, to the subjugation of university teaching and research to powerful external forces (of cultural production and consumption):

> Pendant que les militants de la Gauche prolétarienne proclamaient la révolte contre le savoir bourgeois et l'autorité académique, c'est un nouveau type de savoir qui se mettait en place dans la dissemination des universités et dans la spécialisation des filières, un système moderne de développement des forces productive théoriques qui **socialisait** le pouvoir des professeurs. Le système des unités de valeur, du contrôle continu et des mini-mémoires marquait l'entrée de l'apprentissage universitaire dans l'âge de la rationalisation tayloriste. A l'artisanat du cours magistral et de l'examen annuel succédait une demande de production continue aussi bien pour les enseignés que pour les enseignants, déterminant un besoin d'aide extérieure.[50]

To cast this development in terms familiar from the last chapter, the French university system had been an institution characterized by strong residual elements of a pre-Fordist conception of the relationship between education and work (that is to say, a relationship in which the relationship is neither necessary nor self-evident), in which the ideology of the disinterested professional could be nurtured in isolation from the demands of the factory and the market. It is now on the way to becoming something very different: it is no longer to be a mechanism by which a distinction between the professional and the worker is inscribed and sustained, precisely because the production system of "neocapitalism" has no particular use for such distinctions. The contradictory nature of this development may be considered from two perspectives. On the one hand it involves students studying Althusser but being encouraged to instrumentalize such study toward the demands of the very ideological state apparatuses that Althusser depicts. On the other it opens up possibilities for new kinds of class solidarity and alliances—between the traditional proletariat of the car factory and the partially proletarianized young bourgeoisie of the edu-factory. Of course it was precisely such an alliance that momentarily raised the possibility of revolution in France in 1968, and it is toward the dissolution of the supposed distinction between worker and intellectual that much of Jacques Rancière's subsequent writing has been directed. In the last chapter the passionate amateur turned out to be the figure under which the professional went to work at the beginning of the Fordist phase of capitalism; here in post-Fordist or neo-capitalism the passionate amateur has no profession to pursue any longer and must instead invent for herself new modes of living and working, either within or against the logics of capitalist production. This is the predicament and the possibility that Godard's *La chinoise* presents.

The authors of *De la misère de la vie étudiante* take a largely pessimistic view of the situation in the French universities before '68, emphasizing predicament rather than possibility but noting, as it were, the possibility of possibility in light of the actions of students at Berkeley, of whom they write:

> From the start they have seen their revolt against the university hierarchy as a revolt against *the whole hierarchical system,* the dictatorship of the economy and the State. Their refusal to become an integrated part of the commodity economy, to put their specialized studies to their obvious and inevitable use, is a revolutionary gesture. It puts in doubt that whole system of production which alienates activity and its products from their creators.[51]

It is precisely this possibility that the events of May '68 were to instantiate. For Kristin Ross, in an analysis that builds on that offered by Danielle Rancière and Jacques Rancière in the piece already cited, and in subsequent writings by Jacques Rancière, the significance of the events of May '68 lay in their being a "revolt against function";[52] not just against the increasing specialization of both work and study but against the very idea of work itself. In the present context such tendencies take shape in the idea that the passionate amateur of late Fordism is in flight from social location and that this flight might be achieved by way of theatre, a nonlocation where there is scope for pretending to be, and perhaps actually becoming, someone else and in the process moving beyond given identities of class or occupation.

For Jacques Rancière, this "refusal of work" is not a new phenomenon, however. Indeed, in Rancière's own work on nineteenth-century labor, leisure, and education, he identifies in the French working class an attitude that resembles a recalcitrance regarding wage labor very similar to that which E. P. Thompson records in the English working class's resistance to the very process that "made" them into the working class. Rancière identifies the theatre-going habits and aspirations to make theatre among the nineteenth-century Parisian working class as an important instance of this resistance to work and to social location. He suggests that workers attending *goguettes*[53] attend as spectators who frequently entertain the fantasy of becoming performers themselves and then devote work time to teaching themselves music and versification with this aim in mind. For Rancière, this movement of working-class people into a cultural sphere supposedly beyond that to which their formal education had prepared them "was perhaps more of a danger to the prevailing ideological order than a worker who performed revolutionary songs,"[54] on the basis that it destabilized deeply held notions of class identity and behavior (or, in Rancière's more recent terminology, disrupted the distribution of the sensible), producing "fissures" in which "a minority might see a line of escape from work which had become unbearable, but also from the language and behaviour of the workshop, in a word from the unbearable role of the worker-as-such," because they thereby "develop capacities within themselves which are useless for the improvement of their material lives and which in fact are liable to make them despise material concerns."[55] The theatre is a particularly fertile location for this dislocation for Rancière, for precisely the same reasons for which Plato feared it: it cultivates "the habit of always being somewhere where there is nothing to do but concern oneself with matters which are not one's own business."[56]

This constitutes, argues Rancière, "a spontaneous movement of deprofessionalisation [. . .] abolishing the distance between specialist knowledge and amateur culture."[57] *La chinoise*—with its playful-serious autodidacts (or passionate amateurs) making theatre with apparent disregard for "material concerns"—looks like a revival of such practice in a new historical conjunction.

The revolt of 1968, as understood by Rancière, Rancière, and Ross, is more than a resistance to the terms under which labor is sold, then; it is a renewed expression of a fundamental objection to the very fact of wage labor, on the one hand, and to the agonizing distribution of the sensible that it imposes upon human life under capitalism:

> What if the hazards of selling one's labor power day after day, which elevated the worker above the domestic who had sold it once and for all and thereby alienated his life, was the very source and wellspring of an unremitting anguish associated not with working conditions and pay but with the very necessity of working itself?[58]

It is this sentiment that also lies behind Godard's citation of André Gorz at the very start of *La chinoise:* no revolution is going to be staged for the sake of pay rises or better working conditions. Revolution, or something resembling it, will only take place by way of a far more radical conflict, which Gorz himself was later to identify as characterizing the moment of '68 and the most energetic socialist movements of the 1970s. Gorz describes this tendency as a "refusal of work," which gave rise, in turn, in the early 1970s, in all the major capitalist economies of the West, to a "crisis of governability." Nowhere was this crisis more evident than in Italy, where, as Gorz writes, it took

> the form of industrial action radically different from the customary strikes: rejection of imposed work-rhythms; rejection of wage differentials; refusal to kow-tow to bullying foremen; self-ordained reductions in the pace of work; lengthy occupations in which bosses or trade-union leaders were held against their will; refusal to delegate negotiating power to the legal representatives of the workforce; refusal to compromise over grassroots demand; and, quite simply, refusal to work.[59]

As we shall see in the next chapter, some of the most influential current theorizations of the changing nature of work in "neocapitalism," or under post-Fordism, may be traced to this "refusal to work" in Italy in the 1970s: the thought of Antonio Negri, Paolo Virno, and Maurizio Lazzarato, to name just three of the writers most commonly associated with the theorization of "immaterial labor," was shaped by the politics of this moment. While the next chapter will deal with the predicament of the passionate amateur as immaterial laborer in the first decade of the twenty-first century, this one moves toward its concluding stages by identifying Godard's passionate amateurs as predecessors of today's precarious collectives and individuals and theatre as a way of holding in tension the only seeming contradictions between action and speech, work and play.

NOT NOT WORKING (A STRUGGLE ON TWO FRONTS)

Although it is only Yvonne who works in *La chinoise,* work is what everyone talks about, perhaps partly in order not to be doing it. Although, of course, with each character in turn giving an interview to camera that is largely devoted to the topic of work, the not-work in which they participate here visibly becomes a kind of work: the work of the making of this film "en train de se faire." Only Henri, who imagines that he will return to the "normal" Communist Party once he has found himself a job—either in Besançon or in East Germany—seems to see his future in terms of work. For the others, work—whether it be the political work of the organized party or the wage labor of Fordism (and the two of course go hand in hand, with the latter being a key location for the formation of the former)—is no longer central to their conception of life. This, rather than the pseudo-dispute over the place of (theatrical) violence in the political struggle, is the real distinction between Henri and the rest of the cell. Not between work and nonwork, however, because the making of the film and its fictional analogue in Guillaume's socialist theatre instead constitutes a kind of not-not work. To make a film; to make theatre; to educate oneself; to make revolution is no longer work but nor is it not work. Here then is another way of describing the position of the amateur within capitalism, in terms that suggest a particular relationship with theatre (the realm of the not-not). The amateur does for pleasure (or some other personal or collective purpose) something that others do for wages. One cannot practice, as an amateur, something for which there is no corresponding professional or "work" version. To be an amateur, then, is to not-not work. The Aden-Arabie cell is thus composed of amateur revolutionaries, a new social category emerging in the context of the decline of Fordism and the concomitant decline in the organizational forms of professional politics (most particularly the trade unions and the communist parties). Inasmuch as such amateurs—lovers of the not-not—might seek to come together, to make common cause, to act collectively, they might be understood as seeking to do so as what Jean-Luc Nancy calls a "communauté désoeuvrée" or inoperative community. Nancy, writing some time after the historical moment of *La chinoise* (which might be understood, after the fact, as at least the beginning of the end for a certain kind of communism) but before the more widely publicized "collapse" of 1989, claims that

> there is [. . .] no form of communist opposition—or let us say rather "communitarian opposition," in order to emphasise that the word should not be restricted in this context to strictly *political* references—that has not been or is not still profoundly subjugated to the goal of a *human* community, that is, to the goal of achieving a community of beings producing in essence their own essence as their work, and furthermore producing precisely this essence *as community.* An absolute immanence of man to man—a humanism— and of community to community—a communism—obstinately

OF WORK, TIME, AND REVOLUTION 107

subtends, whatever be their merits or strengths, all forms of oppositional communism, all leftist and ultraleftist models, and all models based on the workers' council.[60]

If Nancy's critique of community is not to be neutralized as a call for an abandonment of political action in favor of a melancholy reflection upon the conditions of subjectivity, it might best be taken as a challenge to animate alternate forms of politicized sociality, such as for example the school—a kind of transient collective circumscribed in both place and time, through which one passes rather than making one's lifework there—or even a kind of theatre company. To hold the analysis within the moment of *La chinoise*, however, is to suggest that the cellule Aden-Arabie is precisely not a community nor yet a revolutionary movement, but rather a temporary association formed with its dissolution preordained (by the end of the vacation and the return of the cousins) whose purpose is not to make a "project" but to engage temporarily in an action composed mainly of speech, to produce a way of being in conversation (at school) with one another but not fully to orient this conversation toward a concrete common goal or to subsume its potentiality to the working out or working up of action. Or, to take this a step further, it seeks to avoid the collapse of the field of aesthetic play wholly into the work of either capitalism or community or revolutionary struggle. So, at precisely the moment at which a political alliance between artists/intellectuals and workers seems to become possible and even necessary, *La chinoise* seems to articulate the idea that such an alliance should not involve the subsumption of one to the other. It insists, rather, that there is a struggle to be conducted on two fronts, a phrase Godard takes from Mao himself:

> Works of art which lack artistic quality have no force, however progressive they are politically. Therefore, we oppose both works of art with a wrong political viewpoint and the tendency toward the "posters and slogan style" which is correct in political viewpoint but lacking in artistic power. On questions of literature and art we must carry on a struggle on two fronts.[61]

This is the text from which Serge is reading aloud in a scene in *La chinoise*, in which Guillaume and Veronique sit opposite each other, absorbed in their work (reading and writing, I mean). There's a record player on the table beyond them. Serge is walking around the apartment reading from the Mao text. "Fighting on two fronts," muses Guillaume, that's too complicated, and as he speaks the music from the record player cuts in over his voice. "I don't understand how you can do two things at once, write and listen to music," he tells Veronique, who, after a while, stops the music and tells Guillaume, "I don't love you any more. I no longer like your face, eyes, mouth. Nor your sweaters. And you bore me terribly." "What's happening. I don't understand," says Guillaume. "You will," promises Véronique and puts on another record. As it plays—it sounds like Schubert this time, in a longing and melancholy register—she tells him again, "I no longer love you." She elaborates, slowly, sadly, as the Schubert plays: "I hate the way you discuss things you know nothing about." She seems to be taking Socrates's view of the actor here, by the way, the actor as the worker who knows no real craft, one who concerns himself with "matters which are not one's own business."[62] "Do you understand now?" she asks. He says he does. "Je suis vachement triste." And then she explains: see, he can do two things at once, and he has understood it by doing it, listening to her and to the music. "Music and language." Véronique has said that she no longer loves him, and she has not said that she no longer loves him. What's not clear is whether this apparently infelicitous performative—an utterance that supposedly doesn't work—has worked or not. Or what has worked, exactly. What does Guillaume now understand? He still seems "vachement triste," and Véronique sounded ever so sincere (just like Guillaume himself, the actor, and especially with the Schubert), and now she's said it, even if she didn't mean it, she's said it, and language may have done its work. In just the same unsettling way, the film's depiction of the "revolutionaries" throughout is radically ambiguous. They mean it, and they don't mean it. It's theatre, and it's for real. Or it's not, and it's not. What I'm suggesting, in highlighting this persistent and theatrical ambiguity at the heart of the film, is that in *La chinoise* it is now possible to see not some politically confused depiction of nascent revolutionary struggle and its tendencies toward violence, but instead a film that captures a moment in which it was becoming fascinatingly unclear whether revolution (and the liberation of human desire and potential that it ought to entail) would be achieved by means of proper work (in the factories, with 12 percent pay rises, or through the labor of a revolutionary party) or instead by way of an intervention on the aesthetic "front" mounted on the peculiar wager that the nonwork of theatrical work might actually work.

This is a wager that Godard's work after 1967 suggests he was not inclined to take up. After *Weekend*, made in the months following production of *La chinoise*, and in which he (seriously?) announces the "end of cinema" with this "film thrown on the scrap-heap," Godard was to turn away from the mode of filmmaking whose potential he seems to have exhausted. As Colin MacCabe argues, in his biography of Godard: *La chinoise*, pilloried on its release in the autumn of 1967 as wildly unrealistic, has come in retrospect to foreshadow the events of the following year. Even more significantly, 1968 marked Godard's definitive break with his previous methods of production and ushered in four years of political experimentation with film.[63] The key point here is that the significance of *La chinoise* lies less in its depiction of the seeds of '68 than in its near exhaustion of the mode of production and techniques of cinematic representation to which it still, precariously, adheres.

Until 1968 Godard had operated within what I am inclined to call the Fordian-Keynesian economy of French film production, in which subsidies against box office receipts for producers are available and in which "professional" legitimacy is a prerequisite for participation. To some extent Godard and other *nouvelle vague* directors constituted a reaction against aspects of this system, which they condemned for the conservative tendencies it encouraged: "cinéma de qualité," which emphasized literary values and historical subject matter to the exclusion, for example, of nearly all contemporary social or political content, was a frequent target for the critics of *Cahiers du cinéma*. The work of directors such as Truffaut (the selection of whose *Les quatres cent coups* for the Cannes Film Festival in 1958 is often cited as the breakthrough moment for the *nouvelle vague*) and subsequently Godard, while made on more modest resources (the production budget for Godard's first feature, *A bout de souffle*, was reported as having been about one-third of the normal production budget at the time), nevertheless depended upon the investment of producers and upon distribution through established theatres. However radical in either content or form their work may have been, it was produced and consumed like other cultural commodities—alongside the work of the Hollywood auteurs whom the *nouvelle vague* lionized (Ford, Hawks, Hitchcock, etc.), as well as that of the "cinéma de qualité" they so vehemently disparaged. And, as Godard was clearly coming to believe by 1967, there were, as a result, limits not only to what could be made and shown within this industrial system but also to who could make and see, and how.

His post-1968 films—first under his own name (*Le gai savoir, One Plus One*) and subsequently as projects of the Dziga Vertov Group (*British Sounds, Pravda, Vent d'Est, Lotte in Italia, Jusque à la victoire, Vladimir and Rosa*)—thus constituted an attempt, or a series of attempts, to make cinema differently, to make cinema outside the established structures for "professional" filmmaking within the Fordian-Keynesian economy or, as Godard himself puts it in his 1970 manifesto "What Is To Be Done?", to "make films politically."[64] They amount to "a voyage to the other side" comparable to that of Maoist intellectuals in France who immersed themselves in factory labor as part of their political struggle. It is notable, however, that none of these films take the actual political situation in France as their subject matter, addressing instead political struggles in locations such as Britain, Czechoslovakia, Italy, and Palestine: in opting out of the French system of subsidies and theatrical release, Godard and then the Dziga Vertov Group made what we might see as a paradoxical move characteristic of politically engaged artists of the neoliberal or neocapitalist society that is taking shape around them. That is, they make radical socialist cinema that depends for its production upon new entrepreneurial possibilities in a globalizing economy, such as the emergence of independent television and its franchising in the United Kingdom, for example, which created the conditions for the commissioning of *British Sounds*. But in a further paradox, made apparent by the perspective of the passionate amateur, these films, made "politically," seem to reinscribe the very suture of work, collectivity, and political action that *La chinoise* has, as I have argued here, unpicked. The passionate amateur gives way, as the felt urgency of the political situation hails the artist to a seductive new role, that of the "professional" revolutionary, who is no longer not not working. The next chapter restores the paradoxical, in its consideration of the precarious labor of the artist in the more thoroughly developed post-Fordist economy of the early twenty-first century.

| Of Work, Time, and
(Telephone) Conversation

Once upon a time, back in the second decade of neocapitalism, or, as it is
now more familiarly known, post-Fordism, a telecommunications monopoly, still quite recently released into the private sector, numbered
among its subsidiaries a market research company that employed a shift-
ing population of mostly young theatre professionals to conduct telephone interviews. This arrangement was far from unusual at the time.
State-funded university programs in the arts and humanities and vocational training programs at a range of state-accredited drama schools
were generating a reliable supply of potential and occasional actors, writers, and directors to carry out such work in the lengthy gaps between
voiceover auditions and self-funded theatrical productions presented in
small theatres above pubs. Personable, overconfident, and hyper-
exploitable, these mostly young employees earned just enough money to
keep going and enjoyed just enough social interaction with one another to
sustain their desire to be or become theatre professionals. By keeping the
dream alive they made sure that they stayed in the "phone room" (the
term "call center" was not yet ubiquitous) for rather longer than any of
them had imagined they ever would. There were moments when they
would even start to take pride in their work, almost as though they considered themselves "professionals."

The bulk of this work was to cold-call from a "list" of contacts, in the
hope of persuading whoever answered to participate in a market research
survey and, in the event of securing this participation, to conduct a
scripted interview designed to produce market data for "the client." In
many cases "the client" was the recently privatized telecommunications
company itself, which was just starting to feel the effects of market de-
regulation with the emergence of its first competitors for wired telephony.
Occasionally a business-oriented project related to the future of telecommunications would be undertaken, a process that involved the mostly
young theatre professionals having to give the impression they were *au
fait* with such terms as "electronic mail" and "packet switching," which

would mean nothing to any of them for at least another six or seven years. But far more often the projects undertaken were consumer related, dealing with supermarket locations, malt-based drinks, and domestic telephone services.

Some of the mostly young theatre professionals chose to conduct these scripted conversations using pseudonyms, partly because their own names, when spoken as part of an introductory script for a telephone conversation, would be likely to make a baffled interlocutor hold up the whole business by asking "Who?" but also, perhaps, in order ironically to underscore their own alienation in the workplace, to insist, against all the evidence, that they weren't actually doing this, not really, that their true self was the one going to voiceover auditions and mounting self-financed theatrical productions in rooms above pubs. These "Potemkin" subjectivities were not the only ones being manufactured here in the "phone room." Like all such polling and surveillance of the population the surveys initiated here involved the manufacture of wholly fictional subjects to be counted as having responded to, rather than having been produced by, the so-called research. These subjectivities were produced using a range of techniques, from demographic classification—"male, head of household, university education"—and linguistic approximation, involving ingenious attempts to make the answers given by actual people on the telephone tally with the range of possible answers accommodated by the form of the survey—"slightly interested, not very interested, not interested at all." Occasionally there were fatal flaws in project design that made it nearly impossible to produce the subjectivities needed.

Take, for example, the survey about malt-based drinks. The "client," so the briefing went, was concerned about a declining consumer base, largely composed of "older" people, who, it was assumed, although this was not actually articulated within the briefing, might not have a great deal of diposable income. The client wanted to reach a "younger demographic" perhaps not currently attracted to the product because of its strong association with the elderly. A special "mixer"—a kind of glass cylinder in which the powder used to make the drink in question could be excitingly combined with warm liquid—had been designed with a view to enticing these potential new customers. The task of the survey was to find out how "interested" these potential new consumers might be in the product if it came accompanied by this "mixer." The "list" of contacts provided for the purposes of this survey was entirely derived from contact details given by people who had entered a "competition" by peeling off and sending in labels from jars of the product. Yes, the potential new consumers were all selected from a list of people almost certain already to be consumers. In this theatre of bafflement no amount of vocal training, schooled extroversion, script-delivery skill, or even improvisation could produce the necessary subjectivities.

Similar if less completely circular exercises involved interviewing people in Leicestershire about a supermarket that didn't yet exist ("No, love, sorry, I've not been there") and a project about telecommunications itself that was almost poststructuralist in its self-reflexivity. In this latter case the "list" was constituted by people who had, in the first place, reported a fault with their telephone service and had subsequently received a kind of customer survey call designed to evaluate their level of satisfaction with the fault-repair service they had received. Most of these people were therefore utterly bewildered (and occasionally a little irritated) to receive, some months later, a further telephone call from a bright and breezy and mostly young theatre professional using a pseudonym asking them questions about how satisfied they had been with the way the previous survey of their customer satisfaction had been conducted. Other projects involved forays into the world of car repairs and international finance capital, in the form of "mystery shopper"—style call sequences, both of which involved entirely unconvincing acts of impersonation. In the first, in which a Scottish auto-repair service company had paid to give its employees telephone training, the task was to make a series of calls—perhaps one or two each every hour—to one of this company's outlets and present oneself according to a script in which one had broken down or punctured a tire near Aberdeen or Kilmarnock or wherever the outlet in question was located. Few mostly young theatre professionals actually owned cars at this period of neocapitalism, so most were as ignorant of tire brands as they were of "electronic mail." For some reason they were also encouraged to betray their identities in the most obvious (and offensive) way imaginable by putting on "Scottish" accents with which to make the calls—one of the more interesting uses for drama school "regional dialect" coaching—thereby compounding the public secret of the whole operation's theatricality with a good dose of class condescension (middle-class southern English luvvie types effectively taking the piss out of presumably working-class Scottish employees at auto-repair shops by producing bad imitations of their speech). The interactions with finance capital involved similar routines (although the impersonations did not involve simulated regional or national identities), in which calls were made to City of London finance houses to ask whoever answered what the LIBOR was.[1] It seems quite possible that the responses given in both these "mystery shopper" scenarios, by workers subject to the surveillance of "performance management" even more acutely than were the mostly young theatre professionals (whose calls were monitored for "quality control purposes"), were as fictional as the identities fabricated to pose the questions, since the aim of both surveys was to address the manner in which information was exchanged rather than to verify its accuracy. Thus both sides of the scripted conversation were completely fabricated. The data supposedly authenticated by being attached to these entirely fictional subjectivities, on either side of the telephone conversation, might be regarded as the pure product of the regime of performance management itself, which has nothing to manage until it performs its own object into being.

In some cases it was often difficult, no matter how hard anyone tried, to secure enough interviews (manufacture sufficient subjectivities) in the more extended surveys to meet the "quota" set for the time period allocated to the "project." In order that the company should not have to overspend on labor time, and therefore cut into whatever profit margin it had built into the contract with the client, blank questionnaire forms were completed without any further interviews actually being conducted, thereby generating an entirely fictitious (not distorted or dissembling or dissimulating but actually nonexistent) fraction of the UK population, whose randomly assigned preferences and desires, invented by mostly young theatre professionals, would now help guide the market planning of the businesses paying for this "research." Let no one ever claim that "immaterial labor" produces nothing. The occasional feeling among this workforce, that these scenarios gave them the last laugh, was of course just the kind of illusory compensation that was needed to guarantee their continuing hyper-exploitability. If you can serve the man while convincing yourself that you are really fucking with the man, then you can count yourself really fucked.

This chapter takes up the story of the passionate amateurs of post-Fordism. The mostly young theatre professionals conducting telephone market research are working a job they mostly hate in order to be able to make the work they say they love. They are using their communication skills—developed for the purpose of producing fictional representations on stage—to produce fictional subjectivities in a market economy. Theirs is what is often termed "immaterial labor": immaterial because it does not produce material goods, rather than because the labor itself is somehow accomplished without material. Michael Hardt and Antonio Negri's definition is clear: "immaterial labor" is "labor that produces an immaterial good, such as a service, a cultural product, knowledge, or commur tion."[2] One of the key theoretical contexts for this chapter is the widely held idea that the "artist" in general, and the performing artist in particular, is a paradigmatic example of the immaterial laborer in post-Fordist capitalism and that immaterial labor itself is now taken by some to be the paradigmatic form of labor in post-Fordist capitalism (even for those whose labor seems to remain stubbornly material). It is in this context that the final destination of this chapter—a consideration of the role of conversation, or "idle chatter" in Nature Theatre of Oklahoma's 2007 production, *No Dice*—is intended as itself exemplary of an identifiable tendency for contemporary theatre to explore the conditions of its own production. In *No Dice* a group of actors reperform telephone conversations about their daily struggles to do the work they need to do in order to get to do the work they are now doing—performing this very play. For example:

ANNE: Uh huh.
   So it's not that rewarding?
ZACK: No.
ANNE: I just . . .
ZACK: No. It's not. Not really.
ANNE: Did that first compliment make you feel like . . .
   "Hm! I'm good at something!"
ZACK: Yeah!
ANNE: Yeah?
ZACK: Yeah. I finally—
   I finally felt like I could really do something.
ANNE: Uh huh. Did it . . . for a while . . . trick you into thinking:
   "Hm! This might not be all that bad after all!"
ZACK: Yeah, like—
   if I—if I did this forever . . .
ANNE: Uh hum.
ZACK: . . . and uh . . .
   I—I think I'd go a little crazy.[3]

FROM MAY '68 TO POST-FORDIST PRECARITY

The year of the telephone market research surveys was 1988, twenty years after May '68, and the occasion for much retrospective analysis of the events in Paris twenty years earlier, analysis that, as we shall shortly see, had perhaps more to say about the circumstances of 1988 than it did about the historical events of 1968 and their significance. As Kristin Ross shows, by 1988 a fairly solid consensus had taken shape around what significance was to be attributed to what happened twenty years ago. To be recuperated from '68 were precisely those values most readily associated with the now dominant ideology of the 1980s—the neoliberalism championed by the governments led by Reagan in the United States and Thatcher in the United Kingdom and adopted somewhat more shamefacedly in France under Mitterand—the values of the autonomous, self-reliant individual, or the "entrepreneur of himself,"[4] happy to live in a world where "there is no such thing as society."[5] Some of the most powerful intellectual voices of this recuperation were former *gauchistes* now reinvented as media-friendly *nouveaux philosophes*: André Glucksmann, Bernard Henri-Lévy, Jean-Marie Benoist. They offered (and the French media eagerly consumed), writes Ross, an image of May as the point of origin of a purely spiritual or "cultural" revolution—a "cultural revolution" very distant from the Cultural Revolution in China that had once filled their thoughts.[6]

The "spiritual" content of this revolution was the liberation of the individual from the previously stultifying effects of Gaullist state conservatism on the one hand and the class politics of the socialist left on the other. This analysis depended upon emphasizing certain (television-friendly) aspects of May '68—young people, charismatic leaders, the idea of a "generation" in spontaneous revolt against an uncomprehending establishment—at the expense of others—rank-and-file militants from the working class, the general strike, political mobilizations away from the glamorous and symbolically charged locations of central Paris. In effect this constituted a refusal to engage with the more explicitly political dimensions of May '68, in favor of a sociological perspective in which participants were understood as motivated by psycho-social factors (generational rivalry, etc.), rather than acting with political intentions (we might note the influence of analyses such as that of Alain Touraine on this perspective).[7] Ross further demonstrates how the consensus was shaped by a presentation of recent French history in which present conditions effectively predicted the past:

> May now had to be proleptically fashioned into the harbinger of the 1980s—a present characterized by the return of the "individual," the triumph of market democracies, and an attendant logic linking democracy necessarily to the market, and the defense of human rights.[8]

Ross notes that Regis Debray had already, ten years earlier, written of how "the ruse of capital uses the aspirations and logics of militants against themselves, producing the exact result unwanted by the actors: opening up France to the American way and American-style consumption habits."[9] This logic lent itself readily to the political *volte-face* performed by the former leftists: in effect their position was to claim that what they had got (in the form of neoliberalism) was what they had wanted all along, even if, back then, they hadn't known that they wanted it.

Written at around the same time as Ross's book, and, like hers, clearly influenced by the events of 1995, in which a major social movement and a general strike against Alain Juppé's program of economic "reforms" returned protest to the streets of France, Luc Boltanski and Eve Chiapello's influential and much debated book *The New Spirit of Capitalism* represents a substantial new contribution to the discussion of the meaning of '68. It is of particular relevance to the present work because of the way it seeks to understand the relationships between work in general and cultural production in particular within the framework of post-Fordism. Originally published in France in 1999, and translated into English for publication in 2002, this work adds little to the chorus celebrating the triumph of the "spiritual" or "cultural" revolution of '68, adopting instead a critical perspective on the historical elision in which today's neoliberal capitalism constitutes the legacy of the revolt. As we shall see, Boltanski and Chiapello's analysis does depend, to some extent, upon precisely this historical elision, even if it takes a far dimmer view of its neoliberal destiny than that espoused by the *nouveaux philosophes*.

In Boltanski and Chiapello's analysis of France after 1968 the development of the post-Fordist economy in which we now live and work emerged as a response, on the part of capital, to the challenge of '68.[10] They track the emergence of this response through a survey of business and management theory and related literature through the 1970s and '80s, identifying the rise to hegemony of contemporary management theory, which they call "neo-management." They argue that "neo-management aims to respond to demands for authenticity and freedom which have historically been articulated in interrelated fashion, by what we have called the 'artistic critique,'"[11] and they cheekily supplement this argument with a lengthy footnote that shows the rhetorical similarities between contemporary management theory truisms and the personal and social values promoted by the Situationist Raoul Vaneigem in *The Revolution of Everyday Life*.[12] In this respect, Boltanski and Chiapello appear to reiterate the "ruse of capital" theory of May '68, which Ross finds in Regis

Debray's tenth-anniversary reflections, and in emphasizing the importance of the "artistic critique," they could also be said to be part of the consensus Ross critiques, in which the real struggle of May '68 was "cultural" or "spiritual," rather than social or political. More than simply noting these surprising yet somehow predictable continuities between tendencies in '68 thought and the texts of neo-management, they locate their cause in the transition of an influential generation of bourgeois intellectuals from *soixante-huitard* activists to *1980s* management consultants:

> In their formative years the *new consultants,* who in particular established local discussion mechanisms in the second half of the 1980s, had often participated very actively in the effervescence that followed May '68. [. . .] They had become experts in the Foucauldian critique of power, the denunciation of union usurpation and the rejection of authoritarianism in all its forms. [. . .] They specialized in humanist exaltation of the extraordinary potential secreted in each person [. . .]; in the supreme value of direct encounters, personal relations, particular exchanges; and in the proselytizing adoption of an attitude of openness, optimism and confidence.[13]

Thus, argue Boltanski and Chiapello, the values of '68 are carried from the streets into the new capitalist workplace, and the artistic critique is effectively answered: oppressive and hierarchical modes of work give way to teams and networks of professional partners; spontaneity and creativity become prized assets for corporations; work within capitalist production succeeds in satisfying the deep human needs that the revolt of '68 sought to articulate. Thus I come to love my job.

But this comes at a price, and this is where Boltanksi and Chiapello's account starts to diverge from that presented by the cheerleaders of French neoliberalism. Where the old form of capitalist production—what Boltanski and Chiapello call Taylorized work or Fordism—commanded and compelled the worker's body (and sometimes her mind) for the duration of the work shift, the new form subtly seduces but nonetheless compels the body and the mind of the worker in his or her every waking moment. If work is the sphere of creativity, what is left to the sphere of recreation, if not to dream solutions to the problems of work? Or, as Boltanski and Chiappello put it more sociologically:

> The Taylorization of work does indeed consist in treating human beings like machines. But precisely because they pertain to an auto-

mation of human beings, the rudimentary character of the methods employed does not allow for the more human properties of human beings [. . .] to be placed directly at the service of the pursuit of profit. Conversely, the new mechanisms, which demand greater commitment and rely on a more sophisticated ergonomics [. . .] precisely because they are more human in a way, also penetrate more deeply into people's inner selves—people are expected to "give" themselves to their work—and facilitate an instrumentalization of human beings in their most specifically human dimensions.[14]

The "artistic critique" of capitalism has been successfully answered, then, but in a manner that might remind us to beware what we wish for. However, it has a partner in anti-capitalist thought, which Boltanski and Chiapello call "the social critique," which "seeks above all to solve the problem of inequalities and poverty by breaking up the operation of individual interests."[15] Both were strongly present, they affirm, in the events of '68, when the "social critique" bore its familiar "Marxist stamp,"[16] but more recently, they write, referring to their book's genesis in 1995, "social critique has not seemed so helpless for a century as it has been for the last fifteen years."[17] Far from being answered, this critique has not even been fully articulated, and for Boltanski and Chiapello, as "sociologists," this commands attention, especially if, as we may suspect, the answer to the artistic critique has exacerbated the inequalities that the social critique seeks to contest: the freedom and creativity secured for some has been at the expense of others condemned to low pay, intensified and accelerating precarity, or long-term unemployment.

Boltanski and Chiapello's thesis of the two critiques is itself subject to a critique that returns us to the Rancièrian perspective articulated by Ross, in which the distinction between the social and the artistic critiques is seen as a production of bourgeois sociology that serves to obscure an underlying political continuity. As we have seen, Rancière suggests that the worker who aspires to participate in the artistic and intellectual activities usually assumed to be the preserve of the bourgeoisie poses perhaps a more fundamental challenge to the security of the bourgeois order than those who sing revolutionary songs and thus confirm their position. The unprecedented, even if not ultimately complete, let alone victorious, alliance between students and workers in May '68 revealed, as the analysis developed in *Révoltes logiques* suggests, a potential underlying class solidarity across sociological categories (students and workers) in a situation where the subsumption of the university under neocapitalism was creating conditions in which young would-be professionals from the bourgeoisie could start to recognize themselves as workers. Alberto Toscano, in a review essay that considers both Ross's book and Boltanksi and Chiapello's, suggests as much in arguing that

> to distinguish between social equality and cultural liberation is already to betray the paradoxical power of '68 as the attempt to abolish the functional distinction between these two facets of emancipation (and to preempt, one could argue, the recuperative attempts to play them off against one another).[18]

Sociological or market research approaches to the condition of the "cultural" or "artistic" worker might continue to insist that the "phone room worker" and the "actor," for example, constituted two separate identities, defined by their categories for distinction. A more political analysis would be able to understand how these two people (or statistical units) might be able to inhabit the same body. They do so as workers who sell their labor power, quantified in terms of time, to capital. This is true whether they are employed as actors or as telephone market research interviewers.

Maurzio Lazzarato presents a rather more polemical version of the same objection, informed by the emergence of "intermittent" theatre workers as a key element in the growing European anti-precarity movement:

> Les malheurs de la critique de la « critique artiste » conduite par Boltanski et Chiapello sont nombreux, mais le plus grand qui lui soit arrivé, est précisément le mouvement de résistance des « artistes » et des « techniciens » du spectacle et la naissance de la Coordination des intermittents et précaires, dont elle constitue l'expression la plus aboutie.
>
> Les six mots de l'un des slogans du mouvement des intermittents (« Pas de culture sans droits sociaux ») suffisent à faire vaciller toute la construction théorique de Boltanski et Chiapello et à faire ressortir les limites de leur analyse du capitalisme contemporain. Traduit dans leur langage, le slogan « Pas de culture sans droits sociaux » devient en effet « Pas de liberté, d'autonomie, d'authenticité, sans solidarité, égalité, sécurité ». Ce que Boltanski et Chiapello considèrent comme potentiellement « aristo-libéral », comme incompatible avec la justice sociale, devient un terrain de lutte: le seul,

peut-être, à partir duquel on puisse affronter et ruiner la logique néolibérale.[19]

Lazzarato, as we have seen, is the theorist of "immaterial labor" to whom Hardt and Negri direct the readers of *Empire* for a full definition of the concept. Toward the end of the previous chapter I promised that this one would consider the predicament of the passionate amateur of the early twenty-first century in terms of "immaterial labor," and so, before turning to a sustained engagement with the passionate amateurs of the Nature Theatre of Oklahoma's *No Dice*, I will conclude this discussion of the post-Fordist aftermath of '68 with an attempt to explain how the work of Lazzarato, and that of Paolo Virno, might illuminate the conditions in which *No Dice* was produced and of which it speaks.

Two ideas articulated in Lazzarato's "Immaterial Labor" essay are of particular relevance here. The first is that "immaterial labor" names all labor in post-Fordism, effectively eradicating distinctions between manual and intellectual labor. The second is that the communication now required of all labor is a manifestation of a "mass intellectuality" that poses a political challenge to the owners of capital. This second idea is a variant of one of the core claims of autonomist Marxism more generally, that the political action of workers is autonomous in the sense that it is not merely a response to the demands of capitalism. From this perspective, therefore, what Lazzarato sometimes calls the "great transformation" in capitalism since the early 1970s—the shift to post-Fordism—is a response on the part of capital to the revolt against work mounted in the late 1960s.

Lazzarato articulates the first of these ideas as follows:

> The concept of immaterial labor refers to *two different aspects* of labor. On the one hand, as regards the "informational content" of the commodity, it refers directly to the changes taking place in workers' labor processes in big companies in the industrial and tertiary sectors, where the skills involved in direct labor are increasingly skills involving cybernetics and computer control (and horizontal and vertical communication). On the other hand, as regards the activity that produces the "cultural content" of the commodity, immaterial labor involves a series of activities that are not normally recognized as "work"—in other words, the kinds of activities involved in defining and fixing cultural and artistic standards, fashions, tastes, consumer norms, and, more strategically, public opinion. Once the privileged domain of the bourgeoisie and its children,

these activities have since the end of the 1970s become the domain of what we have come to define as "mass intellectuality."[20]

Crucially, if a little confusingly, the concept of immaterial labor should not be understood as marking a distinction between material and immaterial labor. The point is rather to understand that the field of immaterial labor itself is highly differentiated and that it may include workers in all kind of employment, across all sectors of the economy, from the car factory to the fast-food restaurant, the university classroom and the theatrical stage. It is also to recognize as "work" all kinds of activities that are normally not understood as such, which might for our purposes here be considered to include the production of "amateur" theatre, as well as all acts of spectatorial consumption. Paolo Virno describes this reconstitution of the relation between "labor and non-labor" (or "work" and "life," as it is so often figured in mainstream discourse) in terms of a new distinction in a post-Fordist economy between "remunerated life and non-remunerated life."[21] He also suggests that this state of affairs amounts to an effective repudiation of the "proletarianization thesis," in which all labor, including the intellectual labor normally performed by the bourgeoisie (such as teaching in a university or working in the theatre), has been reduced to the form and status of manual labor and its workers socially declassed as a consequence. For Virno, whose account of "mass intellectuality" tends above all to emphasize "the generic linguistic-cognitive faculties of the human animal," the reverse is in fact the case in post-Fordism, when Marx's distinction between "complex" and "simple" labor comes undone:

> I hold that the intellectuality of the masses [. . .] in its totality is "complex" labor—but, note carefully, "complex" labor that is not reducible to "simple labor." [. . .] To say that all post-Ford era labor is complex labor, irreducible to simple labor, means also to confirm that the "theory of proletarianization" is completely out of the mix. This theory had its peak of honor in signaling the potential compatibility of intellectual to manual labor. [. . .] The theory of proletarianization fails when intellectual (or complex) labor cannot be equated with a network of speicalized knowledge, but becomes one with the use of the generic linguistic-cognitive faculties of the human animal.[22]

Rosalind Gill and Andy Pratt, in their review of recent theorizations of immaterial labor, affect, and precarity, point out that, while differentiated, this subsumption of all labor in post-Fordism under the heading of "immaterial labor" still risks obscuring precisely those distinctions between workers that might constitute profound differences in political interests:

> While it might be true that most work today is in some sense impacted by information and communications, the grandiosity of such a claim obscures profound differences between different groups of workers—between, for example, the fast food operative with a digital headset or electronic till in their minimum wage McJob, and the highly educated, well-paid cultural analyst.[23]

On the other hand it also provides at least a theoretical basis for the formation of the kind of "cross-class coalitions" that Andrew Ross identifies has having been produced, in the flesh, by the anti-precarity movement.[24] The emergence of such new formations is precisely the point of the second of Lazzarato's key claims that bears upon this discussion. That is that as capital comes to depend upon the "mass intellectuality" of its workforce, it becomes politically vulnerable to the powers of reciprocal communication and self-organization that it needs its workers to exercise:

> Work can thus be defined as the capacity to activate and manage productive cooperation. In this phase, workers are expected to become "active subjects" in the coordination of the various functions of production, instead of being subjected to it as simple command. We arrive at a point where a collective learning process becomes the heart of productivity, because it is no longer a matter of finding different ways of composing or organizing already existing job functions, but of looking for new ones.[25]

Workers who are "active subjects" involved in "collective learning" and "composing and organizing" in the workplace pose a potential threat to their employers because in acting upon their own autonomy they may come to insist upon and be able to force some reorganization of the terms on which they are employed, even when employers would wish to resist any such move:

> Employers are extremely worried by the double problem this creates: on one hand, they are forced to recognize the autonomy and freedom of labor as the only possible form of cooperation in production, but on the other hand, at the same time, they are obliged

(a life-and-death necessity for the capitalist) not to "redistribute" the power that the new quality of labor and its organization imply.

For Virno this means that labor itself becomes the site of political action, thus collapsing the distinction established by Hannah Arendt, upon whose thought Virno explicitly draws, between labor and work, on the one hand, and action (including, as we have seen in chap. 4, speech), on the other:

> My reasoning is opposite and symmetrical with respect to that of Arendt. I maintain that it is in the world of contemporary labor that we find the "being in the presence of others," the relationship with the presence of others, the beginning of new processes, and the constitutive familiarity with contingency, the unforeseen and the possible. I maintain that post-Fordist labor, the productive labor of surplus, subordinate labor, brings into play the talents and the qualifications which, according to a secular tradition, had more to do with political action.[26]

In the second half of this chapter the aim will be to explore what kind of communicative labor might constitute a mode of political action in the theatre. The crucial word here may be *in*. Just as the logic of Virno's argument might be that we should not be looking for political action outside the workplace, we might hold on to the possibility that the political action of the theatre will take place in the theatre, rather than seeking to extend itself into any other part of the so-called real world. This is to insist, once again, that the theatre does not stand to one side of the "real" world or offer an alternative to it: the theatre is a real place, where real people go to work, and where their work takes the form of "conversation."

NO DICE: "WE WANT TO ENJOY OURSELVES IN SOCIETY, RIGHT?"

The show is about four hours long, perhaps a little less. As the audience enters the theatre, the show's codirectors, Kelly Copper and Pavol Liška, prepare and distribute to everyone sandwiches (a choice of peanut butter and jelly or ham and cheese) along with a soda (a choice of Diet Coke or Dr. Pepper). Thus fortified for the long evening the public is then welcomed from the stage by Copper and Liška, who forewarn them of the length of the show but promise that there will be an intermission and that they have saved some of the best bits for the second half.[27] In the performance that follows three principal actors (Anne Gridley, Robert M. Johanson, and Zachary Oberzan), joined from time to time by Kristin Worrall (who also plays Erik Satie *Gnossiennes* on an electronic keyboard that rests on an ironing board) and by the directors, and accompanied on occasions by either Lumberob or Thomas Hummel, performing beatbox, play out scenes in which all the dialogue is fed to them as iPod recordings of telephone conversations that Liška previously conducted with "coconspirators, friends and relations."[28] Rather than imitate the voices and intonations of the recordings, however, Gridley, Johanson, and Oberzan present the script in assumed accents (French, Irish, Jamaican, and so forth) and with a gestural repertoire that seems to derive from both television melodrama and disco. The scenes consist mainly of conversations about boring clerical work; aspirations to write stories; the actors' own efforts to sustain an experimental theatre company; other actors they like; other performances (including a "Dinner Theater" event and the New York appearances of the Moscow Cats Theater); and relationships with food, drink, Radio Shack, and Philip Morris. In other words, the subject matter of this performance is the conditions in which it was made.

A sort of pendant to this performance may be found on the company's website, in the form of a video in which viewers are invited to "see Nature Theatre of Oklahoma get paid after a work-in-progress showing of *No Dice*. This is the first time we made any money at all."[29] The video shows Gridley, Johanson, Oberzan, Worrall, and Liška variously rolling around on the floor among dollar bills, performing fragments of musical theatre dance routines with fans of bills, covering one another with bills, and throwing bills in showers over one another, all to a soundtrack of Ginger Rogers singing "We're In the Money." Intercut with this material are intertitles with texts adapted from an essay by the artist Mike Kelley that discuss artworks as both commodities and gifts.[30] The end of the video informs viewers: "At the end of the work-in-progress run in July 2006 the box office was split among the performers. Each received $224.10 for over 115 hours of rehearsal. That's roughly $1.95 per hour."[31] This is a company that presents itself as being concerned with time and money. Just before the intermission the company discuss and perform a dance routine, which, they speculate, might serve as a commercial for cigarettes, thereby enabling them to "be the first theatre company that has found a way to—that goes CORPORATE!—that has SOLD OUT! . . . We do—ha!—we do our EPIC."[32] The "EPIC," we learn, will be eleven hours long and will require smoke breaks, so this dance-commercial will "be an invitation for an intermission!"[33] The published text indicates that during the intermission M&M candy will be sold to "MAKE MONEY FOR THE COMPANY."[34]

The video and the show itself foreground in one and the same gesture both a wholly "unprofessional" attitude to the relationship between time and money and a shamelessly "professional" one. A very long show, at least in theory, takes a long time to make and always takes a long time to perform. If the performers calculate their earnings by the hour, even though they are actually not hourly wages but a share of box office, it would make economic sense to make a much shorter show, since there is no indication that ticket prices are calculated in relation to the length of the performance. The audience is theoretically getting a good deal here then, even if, as the comically apologetic "warning" about duration at the beginning suggests, the actual economy of theatre-going works rather differently, and audiences tend to feel that since they are "giving" their time to the performance, it will have to be very good indeed to be worth four hours of it. The sandwiches and soda therefore seem to function as a kind of placatory countergift. There is a great deal of calculation devoted here to creating confusions around calculation. In getting more than they normally get (in terms of the calculable quantity of entertainment provided, plus snacks), the audience might be thought to be keeping the performers' wages unusually low, almost to a point at which the whole transaction seems to be threatening to depart from the logic of exchange and to participate entirely in an economy of the gift.[35]

But at the same time, by making these calculations visible as they do, the company insist upon their participation in an entirely rational market of commodity exchange, even if their own behavior within it might be experienced and understood as bordering on the irrational. The irony of exposing their own calculations (which may, of course, be entirely fictional, just like the eleven-hour version of the show, whose existence is nonetheless attested to in publicity materials[36]) is that the acts of calculation are simultaneously "naïve" (because sophisticated calculation would be far more discreet) and "calculated" (in that they are calculations and in that they seem to feign this naïveté). The idea of getting commercial sponsorship from Philip Morris by taking advantage of the fact that cigarette commercials are not, as far as they are aware, banned in the theatre is both devious and hopeless.[37] They come across as complete "amateurs" at being "professional" and highly "professional" in their calculating amateurism.

Another consequence of this attention to the economy of theatre production and consumption is that *No Dice* turns out to be a show performed by real people, rather than by actors pretending to be real people. It is not immediately apparent that this is the case, at least not in the way that it is immediately apparent in the work of Rimini Protokoll.[38] This is the collective "label" under which Helgard Haug, Stefan Kaegi, and Daniel Wetzel make a range of work, much of which, since 2000, has involved employing "experts" to make and perform theatrical projects with them. For example, *Karl Marx: Das Kapital, Erster Band* was a theatre piece in which people for whom Marx's text had played an important part in their lives appeared on stage to talk about it. In *Sabenation: Go Home and Follow the News* former employees of the Belgian state airline, Sabena, which went bust in 2001, devised and performed a piece that presented the stories of their lives as Sabena employees. In this last case the fact of theatre as a workplace was of course heightened by the fact that performing in *Sabenation* had become at least a temporary job for a group of people who had lost previous jobs as a result of Sabena's collapse. Just as the performers in *Sabenation* and other Rimini Protokoll shows were employed because of their prior expertise—work they had done or experiences they had had outside Rimini Protokoll—the "employees" in Nature Theatre of Oklahoma's *No Dice* may be understood as being employed because of their expertise in being members of a theatre company that doesn't pay them enough to live on. That this means that as a result of "being" actors they might be "good" at "acting" may be said to be incidental, particularly in light of a show that has deliberately worked so strongly against the grain of what might normally be thought to constitute "good acting" or acting defined according to "professional" norms ("lines" not being memorized, silly accents, clichéd gestures, incoherent costumes). This is a show about actors as workers, rather than one in which actors, who always are workers (except, of course, when they are amateurs, in which case they are workers elsewhere), pretend that they are anything else. In this respect, whatever its studied amateurism, it is a show about theatre as a professional activity. That is to say that it has questions to ask about what it means for theatre to be so, questions rather like those thrown up by Lacis and Benjamin's "Program for a Proletarian Children's Theatre," about what theatre might be able to do to the organization of the time of work. Perhaps this is why it insists on making an explicit parallel between itself and the "Dinner Theater," not just because, in a rather modest way, the audience at *No Dice* eats and drinks during the show, but because:

ANNE: We probably won't get back . . .
>for like . . . four or five hours

BOBBY: Mmm hm.

ANNE: It'll be, you know—
>the whole evening will be tied up.

BOBBY: Is your husband going?

ANNE: No, no. No. It's just a girl's thing.

BOBBY: Mm hm.

ANNE: He's . . . (breath. carefully)
>Let's see . . .
>He's—NOT—particularly—
>a lover of theater.

BOBBY: Mm hm.

ANNE: If he sees theater that
>he . . . (pause)
>stays awake for—
>it's usually a large—
>musical—Broadway type
>musical.

BOBBY: Mm hm.

ANNE: (pause) Um . . .

BOBBY: (long pause) That's good.

ANNE: Heh heh heh . . .

BOBBY: That's good. (big breath)[39]

That "the whole evening will be tied up" by the experience of theatre, and that the sleep required for the recreation of the worker in time for his morning's labor might be interrupted by "a large musical," starts to suggest a reorganization of the time of work inaugurated from within the time of play. Rather than occupying the time left over once work is done, play here threatens to relegate work to a secondary and subsidiary claim upon time. We'll start working once this is over, or, as one of the mostly young theatre professionals once said, back in 1988, in response to a manager's sarcastic question about whether he was going to do any work that day or just sit there reading the paper, "I think I'll just sit here and read the paper, if it's all the same to you."

The play—No Dice—proper starts rather as Uncle Vanya leaves off, with an explicit announcement about both the work of making the play and the work within the play. Everyone has their sandwiches and soda, and Pavol and Kelly have made their introductions:

ANNE: (*In a French accent*) Are you working?

ZACK: (*In an Irish accent*) Ohhh yeah! Heh heh![40]

Zack (Zachary Oberzan) affirms that he is now at work, making the play, while simultaneously reproducing an earlier conversation in which his "Ohhh yeah!" was uttered on the phone, in response to Pavol Liška's question "Are you working?" posed as part of the process of generating material for use in the play and answered in relation to some other, non- or pretheatrical work. In reproducing the response originally given to Liška's question, Zack announces that he is working too, or working again, working, presumably, at the sort of job—acting—that the person whose conversation he is imitating is doing their present job (for Walmart) in order to be able to do. That is to say that Zack is talking about and perhaps even doing two jobs at once: the clerical day job in the past and the (all) nighttime acting job in the present. It could even be the case—although there is nothing to suggest that it actually is—that Zack himself *was* the person Zack is imitating here: he is, after all, one of the nine people whose conversations are credited in the published text.[41] And in both work situations, the project is the organization of the time of work: in the theatrical present, by posing the question of our relationship to the time of play, and in the recorded past of the conversation with Liška, by "coding TARS right now."[42]

ANNE: Taurus? It's like—like the car?

ZACK: No. TAR.

   T—A—R

   Time Adjustment Request

   Form

ANNE: Oh, okay

   Time Adjustment Request Form

ZACK: Uh-huh,

ANNE: And that's—? Wha—

   When they're asking for time off?

   Or when they're coming in . . .

ZACK: Yeah when they're asking for—

   or they missed a punch?

   on the clock—?

ANNE: Mm hm.

ZACK: or um (*pause*)

   if they wanted to go on vacation . . .

ANNE: Mmmhm.
ZACK: . . . or, uh, if they're sick . . .
ANNE: Mmmhm.
ZACK: (*pause*) Um . . .
    Things like that.
    Yeah.[43]

This work in the past, then, is a function of the Taylorist micromanagement of employee time, presumably designed to ensure its maximum (rather than optimum[44]) use by the employer (Walmart) and the regulation by the clock of the distinction between the time of work and the nonwork times of illness or vacation. The work and nonwork time of the theatre, then, by calling into question the very distinctions upon which the work of "coding TARS" depends and to which it contributes, somehow appropriates the time regulation of the workplace for nonproductive and time-costly redeployment in the space and time of play, even as, despite its comic flirtation with excessive duration, *No Dice* itself remains lodged within the temporality governed by the logic of TARs, performed, as it is, after the end of the "normal" working day. Like the end of *Uncle Vanya*, then, the beginning of *No Dice* offers its audience an extended moment in which to consider their own place in the time of theatre and theatre's place in the time of their own work and leisure: it issues a time adjustment request.

It is a request with at least a hint of redemption to it, as long as our conception of redemption is limited to a sense somewhat closer to that used in relation to life insurance policies than it is to the messianic. What is to be redeemed, in and through the production and performance of *No Dice*, is precisely the (life)time spent on all those other jobs, some of which seem to have involved little more than the passing of time through the mere occupation of space:

ANNE: Like—I had to go to . . .
    work a little bit today . . . ?
ZACK: At the . . . um . . . real estate?
ANNE: Yeah . . . (*pause*) Yeah!
    Like you go sit in people's apartments, and . . .
    um . . . nobody's there, really . . .
    and like nobody hardly ever comes . . .
ZACK: Uh-huh.
ANNE: And then you just . . .
    then sometimes they walk in.

ZACK: Uh-huh. Like it's—the—
apartments are furnished?

ANNE: Yeah! Like uh—I could just go—if you wanted to sell your
apartment, like I'd go sit in your apartment . . . and you
weren't there, and—then people would come and look at it.
You know . . . ? And I'd just let them walk around and look at
it.

ZACK: Uh-huh. But I'd have to go out?

ANNE: Yeah. (*pause*)
But it's—(*breath*)
It's not a bad way to like make some money 'cause you just
sit there . . . you know,
you don't really do anything.[45]

The time redeemed by its translation to the stage is the time wasted on the way to doing whatever it is you really want to be doing; the time spent sitting in someone else's apartment, the time spent processing other people's time adjustment requests or calling them up to talk to them about nonexistent tire replacements or speculative supermarket constructions. Or, in other examples of wasted time redeemed during the course of *No Dice*, writing the "same story I've been writing for about 20–25 years," performing for web-cams in Times Square, working without pay for "a bunch of magicians," watching daytime television, doing a voiceover audition, playing a maniac in a Russian TV crime serial, all of which scenarios involve the subjection of one's own time to the demands of another's. Nowhere is this more emblematically the case than in the act of substituting for an absent apartment owner. It is this particularly meaningless occupation—more so, even, than playing the role of a maniac— that points most directly to the work of the actor, whose task is also to occupy the space that is someone else for a specified period of time (especially, perhaps, when the task of the actor is, literally, to speak that other person's words, word for word). When I was much younger I sometimes imagined that the time spent by an actor pretending to be someone else was time they were losing from their own life. I still think that there is some truth in this early theoretical intuition.

All these expenditures of time in their various wastes of shame are redeemed, either by the making of *No Dice* (and the payment eventually received for those who do so) or by the conversations (themselves part of the making of *No Dice*) that have lifted these expenditures themselves from the uninterrupted flow of "dead" commodified time.[46] The act of redemption is performed in order to cash in this time and its conversations at the next level: not, of course, in some "free" or uncommodified time, but rather in the commodification-squared temporality of the theatrical, where an additional portion of surplus value is squeezed from the process, as an almost unnoticed by-product of the industries of real estate, magic, advertising, and Russian television. Just as one might seek to cash in one's own "phone room" labor by repurposing it years later as academic research. The redemption doesn't return the time wasted, nor does it make anything all right. It merely reappropriates it by "taking the boring part of my life and making it into art."[47] For as Anne repeats, presumably reperforming Pavol Liška's side of the conversation with the TAR coder reperformed here by Zack, "Yeah, that's when you need me to—It's like my job is now to . . . (*pause*) perk people up [. . .] to make your work . . . productive."[48] Liška's affirmation of this goal—presented moments later in even more "redemptive" terminology as "to take the things that make us . . . (*pause*) suffer and turn them into something beautiful"—also sounds like the benign flipside (or ironic reappropriation) of contemporary digital capitalism's project of turning all our "free-time" social relations into productive work. For, as Tiziana Terranova has argued, this "free labour"—from voluntary participation in the development of "open source" software for corporations such as AOL to the minute-by-minute production of data for advertisers involved in participation in social media like Facebook—has become a structural feature of contemporary capitalism, tending, in the gloomiest analyses, to the complete abolition of any work/nonwork distinction.[49] At stake in this state of affairs, then, is the very survival of the amateur; of the subjects who are the focus, for example, of Jacques Rancière's studies of proletarian leisure, those whom Kristin Ross describes, in the introduction to her English translation of Rancière's *The Ignorant Schoolmaster*, as "workers who claimed the right to aesthetic contemplation, the right to dead time—and, above all, the right to think."[50] The assertion of such rights might be achieved by the act of closing the laptop and going for a walk or, alternatively, by the application of thought to the transformation of this "dead time" into an object for the aesthetic contemplation of others. Something like *No Dice*, for example.

While these might turn out to be the directions in which an audience might be encouraged to think in its contemplation of *No Dice* itself, something altogether different seems to be going on within the frame of its nonfictional action. Here words of encouragement tend instead towards the fulfillment of work. Twice during the first half of the show the same passage of conversation is reperformed, in which one speaker expresses his confidence in the other's capacity to work his or her way out of their slough of despond, offering such words of encouragement as

BOBBY: I—I'm sorry that, um . . . (*breath*)
　　things are not—(*pause*)
　　ROSY at—(*pause*)
　　at your workplace.
　　[. . .]
BOBBY: And I feel like there's a lot of—
　　lot of good WORK being
　　done . . . and a lot of
　　—GOOD ENERGY
　　[. . .]
BOBBY: Yeah. (*pause*)
　　Well—I think—
　　I think we're—we're workin'—
　　our way towards each other.
　　So . . .
　　Sounds good?
ANNE: Yes.
BOBBY: So let's get together and eat
　　some—
　　eat some hot dogs or
　　something.
ANNE: Okay.
BOBBY: Okay?
ANNE: Yeah. Yeah.
BOBBY: So hang in there . . . and . . .
　　um . . . I'll call you.[51]

In both iterations, the first performed by Bobby and Anne, the second by Bobby and Zack less than ten minutes later, the "words of encouragement" are reperformed in such a way as to ironize their apparent authenticity for comic effect. Or rather, the performance mode through which these words are made to appear (the accents, gestures, and costumes of risible inauthenticity) automatically consigns them to the category of the cliché and the secondhand, not least because they are so visibly and audibly and literally secondhand (like all verbatim theatre, even though so much of it still seems to insist upon the authenticity of its relation to the horse's mouth).[52] The effect is that the inauthenticity is ostended, even if it was never, in the first instance, actually intended. The repetition of the same passage so soon after its first appearance serves to heighten this effect. The idea that one might eventually succeed in moving on from all the dead-time nonwork occupation of space and, with "the beginning of the MILLENIUM," enter the promised land of fulfilling and productive achievement is presented here, then, as always already laughable. But not quite, or rather, only by virtue of its having been made "into art": whoever first spoke these words (as though words could ever be spoken first) presumably intended them sincerely and struggled with the language available for this interpenetration of the personal and the political to find a way of saying something, however dumb, to someone else, someone they cared about. It's only in the theatrical act of selecting and re-presenting them that these "words of encouragement," reentering the circulation of always-already-spoken speech from which they were "first" retrieved, or rather, "redeemed," gather back to themselves the scuffs and tears of the secondhand and inauthentic.

These "words of encouragement" will appear a third time, almost at the very end of the evening, to be redeemed (cashed in) yet again, but with a strikingly different value. Their value here relates, again, to the sequence of events in which they appear. Anne has just offered her rendition of her favorite scene from Jacques Rivette's film *Céline et Julie vont en bateau*, which she introduces as follows:

> ANNE: where Jule is pretending to be Celine . . .
> (*pause*) and Celine . . .
> (That's good!)
> Celine performs in a—Uh—
> And she's a magician . . .
> (*long pause*)
> But she's . . . currently
> OCCUPIED—uh—in a . . .
> (*pause*)
> . . . so she can't—go to the . . .
> But CELINE—
> is auditioning for a tour that's going to Beirut!
> (*pause*)
> But Julie . . . takes her place![53]

Anne then goes ahead and reperforms a scene from a film in which someone performs as and for someone else, an audition, an attempt to get a job. The scene of this reperformance redoubles the citational character of the performance in which it appears (*No Dice*) while presenting the mechanism of actorly substitution as the means by which theatrical employment itself might be obtained. The possibility of an infinite regress opens up, in which all performance becomes an audition, the whole of life an attempt to find work, and not even for oneself, but for someone else; as though the actors of the Nature Theatre of Oklahoma were at work in front of an audience now, in their performance of *No Dice*, hoping that one day someone, maybe one of those someones whose conversations they are reperforming here, might finally, in this new "MILLENIUM," get an actual and proper job, one that would not be some simulacrum of a job, nor a way of getting the job they really want, but would really and truly be the job itself. It is in the aftermath (in which "everyone seems lost and at an end") of this theatre of endless deferral, conjured up by the citation of Rivette's three-hour cinematic exploration of theatrical illusion, that the attempt to redeem the "words of encouragement" will be made.

First "KRISTIN, one of the musicians, who has been silent throughout the show, now steps forward and speaks."[54] She does so without the accoutrements of audio feed, dramatic gesture, or assumed accent, and she speaks directly to the audience, as herself as it were, about what it is that "we" might be looking for here in the theatre: "We don't want to enjoy ourselves ALONE . . . but we want to enjoy ourselves in SOCIETY, right?"[55] And our way of "enjoying ourselves" is through "our conversations, for instance, here," which constitute, she suggests, "a form of ENJOYMENT—actually."[56] As she speaks the other actors on stage— Anne Gridley, Robert Johanson, and Zachary Oberzan—remove their hats and wigs and earpieces and, thus unmasked, make their way to positions in the audience, from which, "in a normal, quiet, reassuring manner," they speak directly, each to an individual member of the audience, "the words of encouragement":

> WELL, GOOD TO TALK TO YOU! I—I'M SH-SORRY THAT , UM . . . (*BREATH*) THINGS ARE NOT—(*PAUSE*) ROSY AT— (*PAUSE*) AT YOUR WORKPLACE—BUT I KNOW THAT IF YOU, YOU KNOW, I MEAN . . . I—I THINK IT YOU—IF YOU—YOU SHOULD JUST GO FOR IT—YOU KNOW? YOU SHOULD JUST FOLLOW THAT.[57]

The familiar theatrical trope of removing the mask, accompanied by the meticulous construction of the tone and manner of the utmost sincerity, would seem to hold out the "authenticity" of the communicative act as an object for aesthetic contemplation: look at us doing the "reality effect." Yet at the same time, having brought into play the possibility that "we" might be here because we want to enjoy ourselves, in society, in conversation, and having done so after the dejected collapse of Anne's Rivettean hyper-theatricality, the performance somehow requalifies the seeming authenticity of these "words of encouragement," redeeming, perhaps, the affective force—the desire for things to be better—that forced them into speech in the "first" place. In this odd and undecideable moment it feels very hard not to accept at face value, whatever the words, this phatic communication of empathy and solidarity and to prefer such acceptance over the risk of feeling like condescending Marxists out to piss on everyone's chips:

MAYBE FROM THE—YOU—YOU SEE A CLEARER PICTURE, AND—BLEAKER THAN ME—? AND I'M JUST MORE NAÏVE AND—AND (BREATH)—AND STUPID—? PFFT!—AND— UNINFORMED—?[58]

The suggestion, then, is not that these words of encouragement will actually make things any better, nor that anyone will get the job itself—let alone that capitalism will be overthrown—but rather that getting together and eating some hot dogs sometime, having a little conversation, for the sake of it, might, for the time being, be a worthwhile way of spending one's time. Of being, in time, with others, "in SOCIETY."

The undecideability of this penultimate moment ebbs away in the concluding sequence of the piece, in favor of a more straightforward alignment of language and sentiment, as the audience hears, for the first time, one of the recordings made as part of the preparation for the show. It is a conversation between Pavol Liška and Teresa Gridley (Anne's mother), in which they discuss, among other things, how well the production of *No Dice* has gone and how Teresa had been deployed within the show as "our secret weapon." Gradually the recording fades out to leave only the projection of the transcript visible in the dark, as Pavol and Teresa talk about "choreography" and the pleasure Teresa takes from dancing in her wheelchair. The show ends with the lights back up and an "emphatic, energetic dance."[59] As an example of Virno's "being in the presence of others" this is of course, as always in the theatre, vitiated by the fact that some of the people in the room are clearly not involved in the "conversation" or the "dance." Indeed it is the clear recognition that the terms of participation are differentiated that distinguishes work like this from more utopian attempts to produce "community" in the theatre or to galvanize collective political action outside it.[60]

This work knows that it is just half of a conversation about conversation, and one in which it is as important that the conversation is possible as it is that something significant is said. One possible other half of this conversation—offered with some reciprocal signification in mind—might be to propose that *No Dice*, in both the manner of its making and the communication it seems to end up making, offers something not far from what Virno suggests regarding "idle talk." Virno's proposition is that "idle talk"—condemned along with "curiosity" by Heidegger, writes Virno, as "typical manifestations of the "unauthentic life," which is characterized by a conformist leveling of all feeling and all understanding,"[61] and as opposed to an authentic relation to the world to be found in work—is now to be understood as "the primary subject of the post-Fordist virtuosity discussed in the second day of our seminar,"[62] that is to say, as constituting precisely the talent for political action, derived in Autonomist thought from Marx's conception of the "general intellect," and from which work was once said (by Aristotle and Arendt, for example) to disqualify us. Lodged within work itself, then, is something that is both inimical and its precondition: the "idle talk" that is precisely the communicative capacity of the human that makes work today possible and equally precisely that capacity for solidarity and collective action that carries the potential to undo the terms upon which wage labor is established and that Virno calls "the communism of capital."[63] Taking a cue from the Nature Theatre of Oklahoma's use of the word "society"—"We want to enjoy ourselves in SOCIETY, right?"—might this communism be understood as a society rather than a community; a changeable association made of multiple conversations, across the intimate distances of the public space, rather than as a community that might close around its participants?

SIX

Solitude in Relation

The thing about Yetis is that no one knows what they want. They come from nowhere and return there. Not only do they live outside human society, but they are unconstrained by historical time. They are, of course, the productions of a utopian imaginary, mysterious inhabitants of a Shangri-La preserved among snowy peaks against the contaminations of capitalist modernity.[1] So when they intervene onstage in Socìetas Raffaello Sanzio's *B.#03*—setting up picket fences, kissing, performing an act of resurrection—part of their affective charge (their charm, perhaps) arises from a sense that they have no stake in human affairs. Their intervention appears amiably disinterested, as though they were purely and simply the hominid embodiment of the "unsentimental . . . pedagogic love" that Walter Benjamin recommends as the appropriate disposition for the leader of a proletarian children's theatre. Yetis are neither professionals nor amateurs—these are categories that only make sense in a human economy in which one works for one's living—they are the pure act of redemptive love itself. They are the possibility to which the amateur might aspire in the devotion of her energy to a labor that is its own reward and to which the revolutionary might aim in her visions of a humanity liberated from the alienation of wage labor. So while they may not be counted in the brief taxonomy that follows of the figure of the passionate amateur in the theatre, their fleeting and improbable appearance on the stage in Berlin in 2003 illuminates both the possibilities to which the work of passionate amateurs is directed and the impossibility of their realization, even within the imaginary worlds of theatrical production. What was so strange, and so utterly astonishing, in the appearance of the Yetis in Berlin was not that their intervention violated accepted norms of plausibility, but rather that it transgressed codes of theatrical or dramaturgical viability. Astonishment arose not from the failure to conform to a credible representation of "real-life" logics or likelihoods, but rather from a leap beyond what even the theatre might normally allow. For all those passionate amateurs who are not yet Yetis, the problems of what theatre allows (what one can do with it, within it) and what it does not (what it cannot do, what cannot happen there) are the stuff of everyday life, determined by needs, interests, and historical circumstances. Notwithstanding their passionate attachments to values that challenge those established by capitalist exchange—most of them are, after all, "romantic anti-capitalists"—none of them very fully lays claim to a Shangri-La beyond Marx's realm of necessity. All of them live and work on the inside.

Before proceeding to the substance of this final chapter, then, I offer a brief recapitulative summary of the various passionate amateurs whose historical circumstances and theatrical actions have figured so far. Theatre in Russia at the beginning of the twentieth century experienced a process of industrialization and specialization in which there emerged, as an increasingly dominant figure, the "professional": the worker who combined his or her livelihood with a commitment to wider social or cultural objectives. The "professional," as either doctor (Astrov) or manager (Stanislavski), is thus this book's first contradictory figure of the passionate amateur. She is the worker whose "love" is subsumed within capitalist production but who is also the bearer of "romantic anti-capitalist" values. There then followed a political response that involved an attempt to free recently professionalized and industrialized activities, including education and theatre, from their subsumption by capitalism and to repurpose them in the interests of a revolutionary politics. In the case of Walter Benjamin and Asja Lacis, the proletarian children's theatre was a practice that sought to actualize in the present a communism that Soviet-led orthodoxy was systematically consigning to a perpetual future. This orthodoxy, as Susan Buck-Morss has shown, brought Soviet communism and western capitalism into mutually reinforcing alignment for most of the rest of the twentieth century. Economic growth and technological progress were to be secured on the basis of a compact between capital and labor in which the exploitation of labor required for the constant production of surplus would be ameliorated by social welfare. As the terms of this compact began to unravel in the avowedly capitalist West, groups of workers and trainee workers (students) started to articulate demands that exceeded its terms by challenging not merely the conditions under which work was performed but the centrality of work itself. The student members of Godard's theatrical-revolutionary cell in *La chinoise* go to work in their summer holidays to make a theatre in which it might somehow be possible to live one's entire life, in a fictional project that could almost be a reenactment of Benjamin and Lacis's unrealized "program." In the post-Fordist moment of *No Dice*, the actors of the Nature Theatre of Oklahoma work constantly in the hope of getting work, redeeming the boredom and frustration of meaningless employment in an attempt to hold a conversation that the structure of the theatre simultaneously suggests and prohibits. They can talk to us about how important it is to talk, but we don't, or won't or can't, talk back. Unless, of course, we write. The spectator who writes rather than the spectator who participates is therefore the subject of this final chapter. The spectator who participates—the spect-actor of Boal's theatre or the convivial enthusiast of Bourriaud's relational art practices—might be said to join the conversation by becoming part of the event itself and may even be understood to experience some feelings of being part of a community constituted by the event. The spectator who writes—often understood as the critic—is normally understood to stand entirely outside the event and to perform a number of mediating functions, from scholarly interpretation to recommendations for a good night out. In practice most professional spectators—including those who choose to write about events in which they participate—move between the fictional polarities of community and detachment, principally because, in order to perform their professional function (as academics or journalists, for example), they generally need to enter into the relationships offered by the event on the same terms as all the other spectators with whom they share the experience (or at least try to do so, whatever the various complications offered by personal or professional relations with the producers). Thinking about the professional spectator as someone who does for a living what most people do mainly just for the love of it invites comparison with the figure of the passionate amateur, who may be doing out of love something from which others make a living, even if she may not always do so. In both cases clear distinctions between amateur and professional activity are hard to make, and it is vital to the formation of both categories—the professional spectator and the passionate amateur—that this should be the case.

Terry Eagleton identifies this confusion as constitutive of the historical formation of criticism as practice and institution:

> The contradiction on which criticism finally runs aground—one between an inchoate amateurism and a socially marginal professionalism—was inscribed within it from the outset. . . . The eighteenth-century gentleman was of no determinate occupation, and it was precisely this disinterested detachment from any particular worldly engagement which allowed him equally to survey the entire social landscape. The gentleman was custodian of the

comprehensive view, representative of a many-sided humanity which any specialist expertise could only impoverish.[2]

Criticism seeks to establish its objective and autonomous status as a disinterested practice free from either state or commercial control, and, in doing so, to help to legitimate literature, art, theatre, and music as autonomous activities too. The drive to autonomy is a self-contradictory one for both kinds of cultural producer, for artist and critic alike, as it encourages the very specialization that makes cultural production subject to the social division of labor, above which its claims to inhabit the realm of freedom might seek to elevate it. This involves a lived tension very similar to that articulated by Chekhov's Dr Astrov, between an impulse toward a commitment to universal human values on the one hand and the professional forms in which such values can be made useful in real social situations on the other. As Eagleton observes:

> Either criticism strives to justify itself at the bar of public opinion by maintaining a general humanistic responsibility for the culture as a whole, the amateurism of which will prove increasingly incapacitating as bourgeois society develops; or it converts itself into a species of technological expertise, thereby establishing its professional legitimacy at the cost of renouncing any wider social relevance.[3]

Eventually, according to Eagleton's historical narrative, the figure of the critic (who for Eagleton is primarily if not exclusively a literary critic) is able to secure this "professional legitimacy" in the university, as the "humanist" higher education generally associated with the "Humboldtian" university and its antecedents takes shape around the end of the nineteenth century. This incorporation has contradictory consequences, one of which is to provoke the mixture of conservatism and radicalism that characterized Walter Benjamin's critique of the university in his earliest writings. Eagleton sees the security achieved as a form of "professional suicide" in which criticism's "moment of academic institutionalization is also the moment of its effective demise as a socially active force."[4] But in order to resist or mitigate the effects and affects of this self-negation, criticism within the university seeks to develop and maintain a range of institutional conventions, variously substantial and fictional, to preserve the impression of autonomy. "Academic freedom" is one of the most powerful ideological tools in this process: it might be regarded as the central tenet of a "professional humanist" attempt to recreate the bourgeois public sphere to which modern criticism likes to trace its descent and to do so, as Eagleton notes, *"from within the very institutions which had severed criticism from it: the universities."*[5]

In her study of the disciplines of theatre studies and performance studies, Shannon Jackson traces a very similar pattern in the history of the American academy, drawing productively on Barbara Ehrenreich and John Ehrenreich's theorization of the "professional-managerial class": "salaried mental workers who do not own the means of production and whose major function in the social division of labor may be described broadly as the reproduction of capitalist culture and capitalist relations."[6] Jackson writes of the work of members of this professional-managerial class in the academy:

> Many academics, meanwhile, worked to maintain a separate professional position outside relations of capitalism and commerce, sometimes by adopting explicitly socialist language, other times by calling for the safe preservation of moral and cultural inquiry. Humanities professors in particular tried to create a separate sphere of cultural capital while simultaneously legitimating themselves curricularly and institutionally within professionalizing terms.[7]

We might consider that a significant factor in the complex set of circumstances leading to the university becoming the focus for anti-capitalist protest in the late 1960s was that a new crisis was taking shape, in which the "safe preservation of moral and cultural inquiry," or "the bourgeois public sphere" as recreated within the university, would face a powerful challenge from a drive to subsume education more fully to the requirements of capital. With the Fordist-Keynsian compromise under threat and a concomitant demand for a technical-managerial workforce, governments launching neoliberal projects would see the university as vocational training for immaterial labor. This would not, in the end, involve the expulsion of the critic from the university, of course, but would lead instead to the formation of a new set of contradictions in which the romantic anti-capitalist professional spectator in the academy would be seduced by the idea that the culture and creativity he or she supposedly espoused could be leveraged in a new economic compact between capitalism and its internal critics under the name of "creative industries." The make-believe revolutionaries of Godard's *La chinoise* now look, with hindsight, like the first generation to intuit the terms of this new deal.[8]

This book concludes therefore with three acts of criticism, each of which, whatever claims it may make to being a labor of love, constitutes an instance of professional activity. That is to say (that which normally goes without saying) that its communication with its "community" of readers and other writers is sustained and facilitated by institutions of higher education, professional associations, and processes of industrial production and distribution of what is sometimes called knowledge. As well as placing its producer in a condition of debt, acknowledged here as a matter of professional etiquette that can often overlap with expressions of what is sometimes called love, these conditions of production involve the expectation that some of the cultural capital accruing from publication will be traded in an economy of professional advancement. Each of these three acts of criticism seeks to account for specific feelings and experiences encountered in the contemporary theatre. A professional commitment to protocols of knowledge production in capitalism conspires here with affective affinities forged in these encounters, and others like them, in the form of an obligation to attend to the three theatre works discussed here as meaningful and intentional acts of communication in their own right. The very same commitment and affinities also require that this attention to their singularity should be articulated in relation to the broader argument or "contribution to knowledge" that might justify the publication of this book. Each of these accounts of moments in performance might therefore be understood as part of an examination of the place of theatre spectatorship in the romantic anti-capitalist subjectivity-formation of the professional-managerial class. In other words, they briefly sketch some of the contours of an affective affiliation with communism, not constructed as a utopian imaginary outside capitalist relations, but nurtured deep within the cultural form—theatre—that most often reproduces them. Each of these moments involves an experience of solitude in relation, the difficulty of which might also be captured in the idea of communism on your own.

LOVE AND ILLUSION

The first of these three moments is the briefest and serves as a prelude to two more substantial accounts of performance. It involves an apparently trivial error toward the end of a performance given at the 2005 Venice Theatre Biennale by the Slovenian collective Via Negativa. The error was both trivial and perhaps only apparent: its consequences were entirely in keeping with the logic of the production. The piece in question was *More,* and it was one of seven productions that formed part of a cycle of works by Via Negativa based on the seven deadly sins.[9] *More* was ostensibly a performance about gluttony, although this thematic sin, like the other six in the cycle, may best be understood as subsidiary to an exploration conducted across all seven pieces into the nature of theatrical communication. As Tomaž Krpić observes in an article on the company's work, this interest in theatre as a "sphere of communication" rather than as an aesthetic medium takes some inspiration—and hence the name of the collective project—from the practice of Jerzy Grotowski.[10] Unlike Grotowski, however, this project is interested in what happens to acts of communication between individuals when they are performed in a theatre, rather than in how theatre might help make community of any kind. *More* is composed of a series of twelve solo performances, each of which appears to involve some kind of personal narrative, confession, or ordeal. Something about the sociality of this particular theatrical set-up, however, works to turn this familiar and individualizing device into a reflection upon the extent to which it might be possible to establish anything collective on the basis of relations between individuals. In this respect it is interesting that Tomaž Krpić comments on the composition of the audience for Via Negativa performances as one way of distinguishing the work from projects that seek to realize a theatrical community:

> I am not saying that the aim of the theatre project *Via Negativa* is to raise a community or a collective consciousness in the traditional manner of speaking. Some of the spectators are friends or acquaintances of the performers; some are professionally interested in the work; many are cultured theatre-goers; some are just casual visitors.[11]

That work, leisure, and friendship rather than "community" are invoked here as motivations for individual attendance at Via Negativa's performances suggests that the work itself may do something to encourage spectators to pay particular attention to the ways in which they differ from and relate to one another and the performers, rather than just what brings them all together for this event.

More is presented by a group of seven performers and a "moderator," whose tasks include introducing the work, explaining the structure of the piece, and engaging the audience's participation. The piece works like this: the company sets out a wide range of food products across the front of the stage, and, the moderator explains, it is the task of the audience to nominate foodstuffs and, with the help of the moderator, determine which will be used in the performance. Each choice triggers a pre-prepared solo performance by one of the other performers, in which the selected foods are used: rice and sausage are eaten, fish gutted; a performer covers his face with cured meats; stories are told, memories recalled, confessions offered. The moderator brings the evening's encounter to a close by soliciting our applause for each of the other seven performers in turn. This gives the audience a chance to express for the first time the warmth with which they had earlier responded inwardly to the work of the red-haired woman who ate the processed chicken sausage, and who smiled with such charm, and also to engage again in boisterous enthusiasm for the work of Grega, almost recapitulating the earlier chants (Grega! Grega!) that had seen him through his rice-eating ordeal. But the moderator leaves one of the performers out, failing to introduce her so she can receive our applause, and the audience quickly starts shouting back to correct his mistake. The woman with the black hair, who had earlier stood on one leg in a bowl of spaghetti soup and then filled her eyes and her underpants with chocolates, stands up now and laughs as she acknowledges the audience's friendly applause. Her name is Barbara Kukovec.

This looks and feels like a straightforward encounter, a social transaction between people who have been in one another's company for a while. It feels like saying goodbye to two or three people with whom you have shared part of an evening at a bar, but whom you had never previously met and may never see again (something that happens often enough at theatre festivals). But this feeling is, to some extent, founded in illusion. The encounter, however fascinating in its mimesis of the social, is somehow missed. Earlier in the day the show's director, Bojan Jablanovec had said that the encounter between performers and spectators that their work sought to promote was not an encounter that looked to destroy the theatrical situation. Although the work would, he said, be "friendly" (no attempt to attack or expose the audience, for example), it would play with the conventions of the situation rather than attempt to do without them.[12] That is why our feelings toward the performers, as people, are a little more complicated than at first they may seem.

Our relationship, such as it is, with each performer is one that has been mutually constructed from those materials that the performance itself has allowed to appear. Although some of the feelings toward the performers— which might take the form, for example, of a desire to meet them for a drink for part of an evening in a bar—may arise from projections developed by solitary members of the audience, projections contingent, perhaps, upon appearance; they may also be understood as a result of the care with which the evening's performance has been constructed. They are to do with the presentation of faces and the calculation of distances, rather than with the psychology of identification or empathy upon which many accounts of the communication of feeling on stage depend. All seven performers sit perhaps two -thirds of the way back on a very deep stage. As they sit, they adopt casual positions on their chairs, from which they are able to exchange glances with one another and that they are at liberty to shift, into new casual poses. Their faces are a long way away, still, so we are initially invited instead, I think, to "read" character (moral rather than fictional) from posture. As each performer gets up from this starting position to present his or her individual performance, the position each adopts relative to the depth of the stage looks like it has been measured with great accuracy, as though each position has been assessed for its potential for social or affective heat or rather, in this case, warmth.

The case of the woman with black hair whom the moderator forgot (whom we now know to be Barbara Kukovec) is perhaps particularly revealing in this respect, and I will try briefly here to track the development of her "relationship" with the audience, through her stage position and the availability of her face. She performs two of the twelve "acts" that make up the evening. In the first (spaghetti soup) she comes right forward to collect the pan of soup itself from the lineup of foodstuffs across the very front of the stage. She retreats to about the same depth as that adopted by the previous (and first) performer (who skins and guts a fish while talking about herself: "I am a good fish"). However, the "good fish" has by now retreated to a position a little further back, so when the woman with the black hair stands on one leg in the soup, head forward a little, perhaps to help her balance, perhaps to help her slurp the spaghetti into her mouth, she is closer to the audience than any of the others. She also addresses us directly ("My mother has the illusion that I love her, only when I eat her soup") and in terms that already suggest that the generation of warm feeling between people may be constituted by action rather than, say, by something beneath the surface. We are invited, perhaps, to love her a little too, even though we know nothing of her, apart from the surface that she chooses to present to us in this performance. Next comes a development that reveals in a delightful impasse the logic of the show: the moderator returns to solicit the audience's choice of the next foodstuff to be used. Chocolates are called for by the audience, but no one responds. Eventually it transpires that this is because the performer responsible for the "chocolates" sequence is already engaged in a performance, and she can't move on to "chocolates" until she has finished her soup. When she has finished with the soup, Kukovec gathers up each of the four or five mainly heart-shaped boxes of chocolates from the front of the stage and parades in a gentle parody of a strip artist, chocolate box pressed against a hip, as though she were naked and trying to cover herself, teasingly. Once all the boxes have been gathered and carefully laid out, she takes two chocolates and presses them into her eyes. She then spends the next few minutes stuffing chocolates into her trousers (perhaps even into her own body) while standing in an awkward unseeing stance, legs apart, torso leaning forward. Eventually she ceases to be the focus of attention. A parody of self-revelation is thus followed by an act that is simultaneously a closing up of the self, a cutting off of the performer from the eye contact that had previously constituted a key element in her stage "persona" and also a difficult kind of self-exposure, in which nothing specifically personal is exposed, other than, perhaps, the exposure of the personal as such, as something other than what it had seemed, back then, to be. She has performed an act of self-exposure, but that which has been exposed remains secret.

A little while after this she returns to her seat at the back and gets the chocolate out of her eyes. Then she leaves the stage altogether by a door halfway back in the stage left wall, perhaps to remove more chocolate from herself. Once she returns she sits and watches the performance and the audience, legs crossed, and with what looks like, from this distance, the expression of someone enjoying a familiar amusement. With every minute that passes her face becomes more enigmatic. The site on which we had been encouraged to "read" her has turned, perhaps, into precisely the kind of secret that her self-exposure had revealed: the secret that points to a particular kind of opacity of the human. It is perhaps a paradox typical of the theatrical situation, that a work such as this that appears to offer complete transparency—the lights are on, there is no pretending, the audience determines the sequence of events—should in fact turn out, in the most "friendly" way imaginable, to be a reminder of just how little we know of one another and, at the same time, of the pleasures of the kind of social relation in which solitude does not preclude an entry into some apprehension of collectivity. It is in this apparent confusion between relation and unrelation that we might come to understand something theatrical in Jean-Luc Nancy's conception of "compearance," introduced briefly in chapter 1, in which it is the spatial distance across which one encounters someone else that permits or even produces relation. For Nancy this distance is both incontrovertible and necessary. In *Being Singular Plural*, for example, he writes:

> Even if being-social is not immediately "spectacular" in any of the accepted senses of the word, it is essentially a matter of being-exposed. It is a being-exposed; that is, it does not follow from the immanent consistency of a being-in-itself. The being-in-itself of "society" is the network and cross-referencing of co-existence, that is, of co-existences. That is why every society gives itself its spectacle and gives itself as spectacle, in one form or another. To this extent, every society knows itself to be constituted in the nonimmanence of co-appearance, although society does not expose this as a "knowledge." It exposes what it knows as its own stage and through its own stage praxis.[13]

This suggests that, in spite of any of the stories we tell ourselves about how community is founded in the theatrical-political-ritual togetherness that we imagine the Greek theatre to have been, and in spite of the fact that we recognize such stories as myth, we might yet make use of the theatre as a way of making known to ourselves the conditions of our being-social, understood not as a full community of individuals but as a network of relations of exposure, a "theatrical communism," perhaps.

CAT TIME

The second of these three acts of criticism involves cats. The study of animals in performance has taken on a life of its own in the last decade, and in some of my previous work I have attempted to contribute something to this strand of thought.[14] I suggested that there was no ontological distinction to be made between the functions of human and nonhuman animals in the theatre and felt fairly certain that the one thing they—animal animals, that is—could never be on stage was other, even if they seemed that way when imagined either to be or to stand for a natural existence outside the social relations shaped by capitalism. They could signify the conditions of labor in the theatre, they could nudge us into a consciousness of the history of their subjugation to human ends more generally (by making us think back to the substitutions of sacrifice), and they could stand in as figures for our own sense of what a life beyond our own might be or might be like. But they could never really be that life beyond our own because the moment they set their paws upon the stage they had become part of it, however much romantic anti-capitalist animal lovers might wish it were otherwise. But certain affective experiences persisted, and one of these furnishes my second example.

In the summer of 2004 Socìetas Raffaello Sanzio presented the London episode of *Tragedia Endogonidia* at Laban. During this performance there was a scene in which Saint Paul cut off his tongue and fed it to a group of cats and kittens. The tongue was not real, but the cats and kittens were. I found myself trying to account for how intriguing I found the way they padded quietly about the stage. It was as though the cats were my own prosthetic device, a set of furry feelers launched into a virtual space to explore and map it for me, their paws transmitting back to me an account of its dimensions, darknesses, folds, and intensities that I wouldn't have been able to pick up without them. I should make it clear at this point that I didn't actually receive any data in this way. That I felt that I might do was what mattered.

My interest in this experience was reawakened a few years later while reading Daniel Heller-Roazen's *The Inner Touch: Archaeology of a Sensation*. The first chapter concerns the *Life and Opinions of Tomcat Murr*, a novel, if we may call it that, by E. T. A Hoffmann. Murr is the author of a text that appears to interleave his own feline "life and opinions" with an account of the life of the musician Johannes Kreisler, a character around whom the composer Robert Schumann would later write a piano composition entitled *Kreisleriana*. Murr loves the feeling that he is feeling. He is skeptical of the reason supposedly located in the heads of humans: skeptical not so much of its existence as of its value. He speculates on the possibility of acquiring human consciousness but feels no need to do so. Heller-Roazen writes:

> At night, at least, Murr knows nothing; in the apparent absence of representation and cogitation, the dark night of the cat remains, by definition, utterly "conscious-less." The cat perceives "the princi-ple that holds sway over us" not by the organ of reason "that is supposed to sit in the heads" of men, but by an irreducibly animal faculty, namely sensation, or, as Murr puts it, "feeling."[15]

In this Murr is like the ancient philosophers, including Aristotle, who do not speak of consciousness at all, but speak rather of sensation or the sen-sitive faculty, as that by which animals may be said to be (as opposed, for instance, to plants, that have only nutrition but no sensation). Nonetheless, we recall, it was Aristotle himself who sought to make the distinction between human and nonhuman animals on the basis of reason and language, thereby distinguishing himself from many of the pre-Socratics, who, as Heller-Roazen notes, accepted "no such partition between man and other beasts."[16] What Heller-Roazen then advances, through a close reading of Aristotle's *De anima*, is the idea that all animals, human and nonhuman, share a "common sense," which is the sense of sensing. This is not really a sixth sense at all, but a kind of meta-sense that Heller-Roazen associates with Murr's delight in feeling himself feel. The key moment in Heller-Roazen's explication of Aristotle comes in relation to the philosopher's resolution of an apparent contradiction in his account of the senses. Because each sense has its proper organ, medium, and object, according to Aristotle, no single sense can sense its own sensing:

> If it is by the sense of sight that we perceive that we are seeing, he reasons, then the sense of sight must be said to have not one but two objects. The proper sensible quality of vision will be not only the visible, as he has until now maintained, but also the mere fact of vision, and it will be necessary to reject the doctrine developed in the preceding sections of the treatise, according to which there corresponds a particular quality, grasped by means of an organ in a medium at a point between two extremes. But if, instead, it is by a sense other than sight that we perceive that we are seeing, the problem still cannot be said to be solved. It seems, if anything, more pressing. For what will one say of this second sense: does it, too, perceive that it perceives the fact of vision?[17]

As Aristotle frames the problem: "Either the process will go to infinity, or there will be some sense that is [the sense] of itself."[18] This "common sense" is, for Heller-Roazen, not the candidate for the role of consciousness within Aristotle's thought, as subsequent commentators have sought to promote it, but rather, a form of sensation. It is in the sensation that is this "common sense" or "inner touch" that we know ourselves to be ourselves. And this is what we share with all the other animals, rather than, as in the model in which this "common sense" becomes "consciousness" and enables rationality and language, that which divides us from them. It is not surprising, then, that Heller-Roazen, who is, after all, a translator of Giorgio Agamben, should think about this possibility as a way of showing up and evading, conceptually at least, the operations of what Agamben has called the "anthropological machine" (the use of the exclusion of the animal in order to produce the category of the human).[19] The division of the human animal from the nonhuman animal requires also the division within each human between those qualities that are proper to the human and those that are not, that are understood as the nonhuman or animal within. The existence of this remainder—that which is left over inside the human once its human properties have been established—points, for Agamben and Heller-Roazen, to "a dimension of the living being in which the distinction between the human and the inhuman simply has no pertinence: a region common by definition to all animal life. In the idiom of classical philosophy the name of this shared region is 'sensation' (aisthesis)."[20]

What happens, then, is that in the dominant tradition of classical commentary the Aristotelian separation of humans from animals is shored up by claiming that the sense of "sensing that we are sensing" is the property not of all animals, as Aristotle himself has asserted, but the property of human animals alone, as Aristotle has subsequently come to mean. What matters for the present discussion is that it is precisely in the moment of the invention of consciousness as a faculty apart from sensation, and as something that will come to define the human, that upon which the human/nonhuman animal distinction is founded in classical thought, that we may also find the very concept that might help us unsettle that distinction again. And that therefore, it might be in moments of shared, mingled explorations of sensation that animal-human relations in the theatre might offer, again, some way of thinking about labor and our desire to be free of it. In the performance of the cats in the London episode of *Tragedia Endogonidia* it was perhaps my sense of their sense of their own and my senses of sensing that made me sense the cats and kittens as my own organs of sense. That what we had in common, in the theatre, was our sense of sensing, in my human animal case heightened perhaps by the fact that the theatre is an invention of my own kind expressly designed, one might say, to help us sense our own sensing.

What does this have to do with labor? Returning to the idea discussed in the previous chapter that the labor performed by performers in the theatre might be exemplary of what is variously called "affective" or "immaterial" labor, we might inquire as to the affects or emotional experiences that the cats produce in terms of our experience of work ordered by time. The theatre involves organized time. It measures the work time of its workers in relation to the work and leisure timetables of its consumers, and it makes this measurement audible and visible. Most theatre then

involves the organization of time within that time: the time of dramaturgy; sometimes the fictional time that runs alongside but at a different
speed from real time; sometimes simply real time made palpable in the
measure of the musical performance and count of the choreography; or,
in a most general sense, the organization of actions in and through space
and time that constitute more or less anything that happens on stage,
ever. Thus the theatre intensifies our experience of time as linear, progressive, and regular. The cats, and the feelings they provoke, undo this process. The cats do what the cats do, and they do it without reference to the
temporality of either the theatre as workplace or the theatre as time-
world. Or at least we feel this to be so. Imagine detaching your attention
for a few moments from the forward movement of the action on stage,
drifting away from the dramaturgy that is organizing the sequence of
events in time, and allowing your experience to be governed by the furry
antennae as the cats pad the stage, some with speedy paw-steps, some
tentatively, sniffing out and peering into its folds and corners and darknesses. Are you starting to hollow out an experience of an extended presence in space but without measurement or regulation—a kind of cat time
in which you can feel yourself slipping momentarily outside the time by
which our work and leisure (and the performance itself) are organized?
What is the quality or nature of this participation in the movement and
presence of the cats? I'd suggest that we might think of this attention not
in terms of our eyes following, tracking the cats, but, to follow through
with the idea that the cats themselves function like antennae, as a kind of
sensing more readily associated with listening.

This is where Jean-Luc Nancy makes his final appearance. For Nancy,
listening is a turning of the attention and the senses toward both the
world and the self. In fact he characterizes listening in terms that draw
upon precisely the same concept of *aisthesis,* or sense of oneself sensing,
that Heller-Roazen also takes from Aristotle. Nancy writes:

> Indeed, as we have known from Artistotle, sensing [sentir] (aisthe-
> sis) is always a perception [ressentir], that is, a feeling-onself-feel
> [se sentir sentir], or if you prefer, sensing is a subject or it does not
> sense. But it is perhaps in the sonorous register that this reflected
> structure is most obviously manifest.[21]

And, formulated slightly differently:

> To be listening is to be *at the same time* outside and inside, to be
> open *from* without and *from* within, hence from one to the other

and from one in the other. Listening thus forms the perceptible singularity that bears in the most ostensive way the perceptible or sensitive (*aisthetic*) condition as such: the sharing of an inside/outside, division and participation, de-connection and contagion.[22]

Listening, then, is the mode of attentiveness in which we simultaneously sense ourselves and ourselves sensing our relation with others. It is a mode of "compearance" and a becoming-audience. It might be practiced in the theatre auditorium as a kind of feeling-in-common that approaches but never closes into identification, participation, or community but that is also, nonetheless, a feeling-in-common of not being regulated by the temporality of capital. This experience might therefore be another specifically theatrical instance of Nancy's "literary communism": the production of a fragile being-in-common of singularities, produced, one might say, through the affective labor of the writer—and by extension the choreographer, the dramaturg, the actor, her soup, her chocolates, her face turned toward ours, our applause, her smile, her laughter, our love, and of course the cats. Such production might open onto the fleeting emergence of a feeling of feeling in which the temporality of work and leisure is undone, an emergence all the more poignant for its arising in precisely one of those places in which work and leisure articulate their relations with one another with peculiar force. To have such a feeling of liberation from the work-leisure dynamic in, say, a wilderness would be one thing. To have it in a theatre is quite another, especially as a professional spectator.

SOLITUDE IN RELATION

Chris Goode steps out onto the stage of the small upstairs theatre at the Oval House in London. He steps up from a seat on the front row stage right, to stand in the light in front of a full house of around sixty people. "So I step out onto the stage," he says, speaking of some other stage in a vast auditorium in front of a thousand people.[23] As he stands there, on this grand, heroic utopian stage, behind him there are children and foxes and squirrels, he says, and, as he opens his arm, snow falls. This, he will soon reveal, is the first of two dream sequences in this evening's performance. "I'm Chris," he announces now, in the kind of conversational but partly public tone of someone used to weighing and choosing every word. In tonight's show he is going to tell us about some things that have been going on in his life recently. It's not that these things are any more important than whatever might be going on in our lives right now, and, he even suggests to the audience, some other time we might all come round to "your place," and "you" can tell us all about "your" stuff. But tonight we're here, in this theatre, it is just us and this theatre, and although some of what is going to be said might be hard to say, and hard even to listen to, it is "just stuff." Theatre, Chris tells us, is where he comes, or what he uses, to think about things; it makes more sense to him, he tells us, to make that thinking social, than it does just to sit at home and write things down. And so that he is not entirely alone tonight—the life of a solo performer can be difficult—he has a guest who will join him on stage, a different guest each night, who will sit with him, listen, talk, and perform parts of the show with him. On March 12, 2012, his guest was Karen Christopher; on March 15 it was Theron Schmidt. Chris welcomes his guest to the stage, and the two of them sit down on straight-backed upholstered chairs on either side of a low table. Behind them a stretch of color-dappled flooring rises up to extend into a kind of backdrop, the kind that might look inoffensive on camera. There's a bookcase with a number of small objects on it. We are flirting with the format of the daytime talk show. At Chris's prompting his guest talks about how the two of them know each other. For a while it feels as though Chris is the host, and the show is really about the guest. Of course the idea that a talk show might ever really be about the guest is a fiction in which we all collude in order to make it happen.

He says that what he is going to tell us will be the truth. He has changed a few details to make things work better, but nothing significant enough to make what he will tell us anything other than the truth, the truth about himself, the only thing about which he thinks he is able to know the truth. He also wants this to be part of a social interaction. Although the show varies from night to night, not least because of the unpredictability of the interaction with the guest (which is in any case quite carefully orchestrated and prepared), it is, straightforwardly, that kind of theatre that is composed of a series of repeatable events, carefully organized in advance, and, very clearly, not the kind of theatre that is going to try to coerce its audience into extensive participation. So the extent to which the thinking in this theatre is going to be social is going to be shaped by qualities of mutual attention rather than any attempt at improvised conversation. In place of the false excitements of joining in, we are simply invited to give our attention, to assist, by means of our presence, at the making public of what might otherwise have been thought and imagined in solitude, in the hope, perhaps, that the simple but difficult act of making it public in this way, the act of offering it for the attention of others, might place that solitude in new relations. Or, in other words, that the person who speaks to us from this stage, who says "I'm Chris" to-night, and the next night, and the night after that, to different people each night, might be both Chris and "Chris," where the difference between them, and their truths, is so infinitesimal as not quite to matter, while, at the same time, so real and substantial and immediate and significant as to make this event just theatre enough. It is in the fine judgment of what it takes to make theatre just theatre enough that this performance finds its remarkable poise and communicates—however hard and painful its sub-ject matter—a kind of quiet public joy.

Chris Goode is a theatre-maker working as a writer, director, and per-former in a diverse range of projects. He has recently formed Chris Goode and Company with his producer, Ric Watts, having previously worked as artistic director of Camden People's Theatre in London (2001–4), as well as leading his own company, Signal to Noise, beginning in 1999, with which he presented a mixture of large-scale works for theatre spaces and more intimate pieces for performance in domestic spaces. He is also a poet and gives public readings and performances of his own poetry, as well as that of other experimental poets. Even when he works as a solo artist—in situations, like *God/Head,* that look like "one-man shows"—it is always clear that performance is understood and undertaken as a collab-orative project. Both *God/Head* and his 2012 touring production of an ear-lier "one-man show," *The Adventures of Wound Man and Shirley,* originally created in 2009, are directed by Wendy Hubbard, one of a constellation of artists who, so it seems, are going to be providing Chris Goode with his "and Company" in forthcoming work. From 2006 to 2011 he was the au-thor of a blog—Thompson's Bank of Communicable Desire—where he wrote about "theatre, art, poetry, music, London, the weather, airports, sudden fury, different music, still not cutting down on sugary snacks, film, horses, people doing sin, incidents, refractions, the entire dark dream outside." In an early entry on this blog he reports a conversation with "J" about the "blog voice," which he describes as "the strange hybrid of private journalling and the performance of intimacy to an unknown public."[24] The idea that theatre might be a way of giving form to acts of communication that might otherwise be impossible or at least uncomfort-ably difficult might even—with allowances for the convenience of narrative—account for Goode's continued interest in theatre and perfor-mance in preference to the more obviously solitary path of the writer. Asked about the "gregariousness and companionability" of the theatre-making process, in an interview with Chris Johnstone for the *Argument*

Room, Goode reveals, noting that "this is such a cliché," that even as a child he was interested in "using constructed events that I can control to engage with other people."[25]

In the process of closing Thompson's Bank of Communicable Desire he wrote about the way in which his various commitments to collaborative theatre-making had coalesced into the decision to create Chris Goode and Company as a way of sustaining a kind of discursive plurality of which theatre might be capable, but that a blog, he felt, can only rarely achieve:

> For now there are two things that feel profoundly important. One is to keep remaking and rethinking theatre as a polyvocal space, a social space, a space that's scrupulously hospitable to difference but also in itself a place we can hold in common. The other is to refuse—and to offer a welcoming alternative to—what we seem to see more and more, all over, which is the *simulation* of participation: whether that's about theatre that presents itself as interactive but actually has no room within itself for a consequential or causative interactivity, or about the free-reign multivoice playgrounds of below-the-line territories in blogs, on news sites and so on, in which contributors are reduced to one-person mobs, bullies enraged by their own impotence and by the apparent impossibility of being part of a virtual discourse that can ever, ever amount to anything, or would even wish to.[26]

Many of his recent works are much more self-evidently "poly-vocal" than *God/Head:* in 2011, for example, in a project called *Open House,* Goode and four other performers spent a week in a rehearsal room at the West Yorkshire Playhouse in Leeds, to which they invited anyone who cared to do so to join them and contribute to the making of a piece of theatre, from scratch, to be shown at the end of the week, which culminated in a one-off collaboration involving sixteen performers. But for all its similarity to the "one-man show," *God/Head* is quite clearly a social act, one that, as I hope to suggest in the discussion that follows, makes the question of social relation its most pressing preoccupation.

The sense of public joy that I have suggested the piece might be contributing is partly, perhaps substantially, a matter of attending to our attention to one another, and one of the key functions of the show's guest seems to be to draw attention to this attention; an ancient enough device, of course, with which an onstage surrogate allows the spectator to examine and calibrate her own responses to the action. If we are to imagine ourselves as having dropped in at Chris's place to hear about his stuff, it helps to have a plausible placeholder for ourselves, anchoring the social thinking in something that at least looks like a real conversation between two people, of the kind in which the truth might indeed be told. Sometimes it looks that way because that is precisely what it is, particularly in one exchange between Goode and Theron Schmidt, in which Schmidt, his speech fraught with hesitations and all the while acknowledging the particular difficulty of saying such things in public, says to Goode that he sometimes thinks it might be a better if he spent more time with other people and less time on his own. It also helps that the guest makes visible the relational nature of the whole enterprise, so that no member of the paying public can quite absorb themselves into the illusion that what Goode has to tell is for their ears only: if we have come round to Goode's place for the evening, it's more like a small party than a tête à tête.

So, after the dream with the squirrels and the stage and the snow, and after the explanations of what's going to happen, the introduction of the guest, and some conversation between host and guest, the main event of Goode's show is broached. It's a story from the everyday life of a writer. He's starting work a little late, on a day in April 2011, and after a little bit of faffing about, he decides he should do some grocery shopping before settling down to work. He is opening a show in a week's time, and he still hasn't finished writing it, and he has another show to write too—"the deadlines are piling up"—and so he doesn't have any time for either "monkey business" or "shenanigans." It is on his way back from the supermarket that it happens. He feels it "here" (he touches his chest, perhaps a little above the level of his heart) and "maybe here" (he touches his chest a little lower down), and here his speech slows as though it were absolutely necessary that precisely the right words should appear: "That there is nothing bigger and realer and more vivid in the world, in the world of my perceptions in this moment, there is nothing realer than the presence, the immediate and total presence of God." He pauses. "In whom I do not believe."

We will hear this story four or five times during the course of the rest of the evening. On each occasion Goode retains the rhythm and intonation of this first, very careful, clear telling, as well as the slightly apologetic gesture—two fists shaken from side to side at ear level—that accompanies his use of the phrase "mixing it up" to describe his occasional use of an alternate route between his home and the supermarket in Stoke Newington. But on each occasion there are variations, as aspects of the

story only touched upon in its first rendition are opened up and amplified. Perhaps the most significant amplification is his account of the show
he'll be writing once the show he's about to open is finished. This is a play
he has been asked to write, and he's decided that it's going to be about a
boy of thirteen, alone in his room, who's maybe queer and maybe not sure
whether he knows it yet and who might—that is, if Chris Goode chooses
to write it that way—be harming himself in some way. Another expansion
of the story of the encounter with God in Stoke Newington involves an
account of a visit to the doctor in Leytonstone ten years ago when it became clear to Chris that everyone else in the waiting room (which was itself merely a stage set) was a member of a religious cult, armed with
knives and ready to kill him. Chris recalls his rationalization of this experience some ten minutes after leaving the doctor's surgery: of course it
wasn't a stage set, of course no one was plotting to kill him, it was just his
brain doing something funny, something chemical. Except, and again of
course, he realizes that it could be the brain chemicals now, tricking him
into believing that no one really had any knives. We will hear, too, about
a second epiphanic moment, several months after the first, which took
place on the Royal Mile in Edinburgh as Chris was on his way, uncharac-
teristically a little late, to the theatre at which he was performing in the
Fringe Festival, and with the assistance of his guest, we will witness a reenactment of his conversation, in a dressing room at Bradford's Theatre in
the Mill, with an academic psychologist who gently suggests that the
epiphanic experience may have a neurochemical explanation and that it
may also have been precipitated by the encounter between Goode's own
"suggestibility" (he is an actor, after all) and the psycho-physical triggers
of the trance music and inspirational self-help material he had been listening to through headphones on the two occasions in question.

But the either/or scenario seemingly suggested by the dialogue with
the psychologist is not the scenario that Goode's performance is exploring. Whatever else it may be, *God/Head* is not really a piece about whether
or not God exists, and it is most certainly not the kind of science-versus-
religion discussion you might hear on BBC Radio 4, even if, as Goode
suggests at one point, this is what he first thought he might come up with
when he considered what he might make in response to the invitation
from Oval House. Goode's scenario has more to do with relations between people: it is, in a sense, about its own attempt to make relations
between people, but to do so from a position of solitude. Because it is
played out in a theatre, that scenario is always curiously subjunctive. For
the event to make sense its audience has to experience what Chris or

"Chris" presents as sincere and truthful and also to hold it at the very slightest distance; to take each act of communication as an experiment in communication, as an invitation to consider how it might be if someone were to say something like this:

> But turning love chemicals into love songs is a billion miles away from how basically fucking angry I feel about, um . . . the medicalizing of sadness: turning the fundamental sadness of being alive and being ultimately alone and wanting to fight that aloneness with love and art and fucking and being friends and hating capitalism and sometimes *sometimes* wishing you were dead, how angry I feel about a multi-billion dollar industry which depends on turning that reality into an illness that can be cured. That can just be suppressed.

The show offers numerous scenes of solitude (of "being ultimately alone"), each of which is experienced specifically in relation to theatre: there is the boy in his room in the play Chris is writing; there is Chris himself as a man at home with his theatre-writing deadlines; Chris on the way to his own performance, listening to music and speech through headphones while moving through public space; Chris in that peculiar airlock between the public and the private (the dressing room), conducting a conversation about the inside of his own head that he will later re-enact in the public space of another stage in another town. At the same time it is a show structured around the deeply disturbing experience of not being alone, of having one's solitude interrupted by the perception of a relation to the absolute. One aspect of the epiphanic encounters with the reality of God is that "God can see me. God can see inside me, see through me. Can see me. For myself. All that I am." God, then, is the overwhelming sensation of no longer and never being able to feel alone. An exposure so total that appearing in public to speak truthfully about oneself will, by contrast, feel like the most blessed solitude. Theatre emerges here as a paradoxical place of revelation; as a practice that makes it possible to say things in public but to do so in a sort of private capacity, to make disclosures without fully embracing them as one's own. Theatre figures as both refuge and liberation, as the place where one might go to satisfy a longing to be able to speak with the conviction that everyday life seems not to permit; to command a kind of certainty and the eloquence that goes with it; to possess the cadences of the preacher, the inspirational speaker, the self-help guru: in short, to emulate the example, in Goode's case, of Iyanla

Vanzant, whose appearances on the Oprah Winfrey show have awakened in him an enduring admiration and to whose words he was listening through his headphones on that morning in April when he encountered God in Stoke Newington. Which is precisely what happens here, as Goode announces that he "can feel the language that's been forming in my mouth," which, at the very start of the show, in the first dream, he was "not quite ready to speak yet."

It all comes together as ecstasy. Standing, as it were, to one side of his own show, producing from within his own show what the show itself seems to have been about the struggle to produce, Chris sets up a music stand in a kind of gear change that gently but firmly articulates the distance between him and his audience to perform, in the role of poet and preacher in one, a text whose materials are familiar to everyone who is listening, a recomposition of the words and phrases he has used so far, to talk about his epiphany, about his childhood dreams and his favorite book, about his hypno-therapy, and about his work in theatre:

Look up, my friends! Look up at the sky!

There is no shit-slinging dream monkey in the sky.

But the stars are interconnected and the snow is really coming down and the sky is falling in. And the truth is in action and we showed up to work.

Link this on! Link it on!

Here, and now, in this place, yield to the truth.

Our bodies are sad and we are separated from each other and our hearts are falling down. Link this on!

We are naked in plain sight. In our own sight of ourselves. Open your mouth. Open your fucking mouth! The stars are intimately connected. And this page is best.

The effect is stirring and beautiful and possessing. And "stirring" and "beautiful" and "possessing." Let the music stand between him and the audience, stand for and stand as the articulating of a distance between people who, however "intimately connected" and "in plain sight" of one another they may be, are also always "separated from each other" even in this moment at which Chris performs being so triumphantly beside himself for them. Let it stand also for the fault in the whole setup that, in the second and final dream of the show, makes a mystery of what the theatre does for communication. In this second dream Chris is in a huge theatre again, but this time he is in the auditorium rather than on the stage, close to the front of the stage, where eighteen actors, men and women, some dressed, some naked, stand in a line at the back of the stage looking out at the audience. One after another they run toward the front of the stage:

> And when they get to the front edge of the stage, they jump into the air.
>
> They leap into the air. Into the darkness of the auditorium.
>
> One after another. Running to the edge and leaping.
>
> And another, and another. Running to the edge of the stage and leaping.
>
> But the thing is . . .
>
> There's a fault. There's some kind of fault in the dream.
>
> Because I don't know what happens when . . .
>
> I'm watching them running and leaping but I don't know . . .
>
> I can't tell . . .
>
> I don't know whether they . . .

The "fault" in the dream is the gap between stage and auditorium imagined as though the theatre possessed a kind of inaccessible fold that prevented anyone from passing across it. It is a fold in which we can only imagine that something might be going on, through which something might be communicated, if only we could get to the place where it was being communicated, if only it weren't always disappearing, out of our grasp, into the fold. Chris leaves the stage. His guest opens an envelope and follows some final instructions to tidy up the space and leave. The audience applauds. They don't come back. They will never know whether they.

The things that Chris might say or want to say can only be said this way because of the possibility that it is only "Chris" saying them or that he might just be "saying" them. The theatre protects us from full communication, from the "immanence" that is the communion of community. This is maybe why it is one of those odd places outside the most intimate of personal relations where it is possible to attempt such communication. The theatre is where solitude in relation can begin to approach the experience of communism on your own. It is precisely because there can in fact be no community here in the place where it is always presupposed that the experience of listening among others acquires a peculiar condition, in which the intensities of both solitude and relation are amplified, so that inside a theatre auditorium one feels oneself both more alone and more related than one does on the outside in so-called real life. If the professional spectator has any special access to this experience, it may be due to a special kind of receptivity: not some special sensitivity, sensibility, or expertise, but rather a disposition arising from the extent to which the division of labor constitutes a more decisive element of the experience than it does for someone encountering such an experience in their leisure time. The feelings I have tried to account for in these three acts of theatre criticism are ordinarily thought either to exceed or to stand entirely outside the "realm of necessity," participating instead in the "realm of freedom" as love, friendship, and sensual perception. We are used to thinking and feeling that such feelings are authentic rather than commodified and, if we are romantic anti-capitalists, to value them accordingly. To experience something of such feelings within the realm of necessity—as part of one's professional activity, that is—is to enjoy (if that is the right word) a momentary disruption of the normal relations between freedom and necessity. It is to love one's work through the work of another, to find real pleasure in the manufacture of that love as a commodity.

Notes

PROLOGUE

1. For a fuller account of this production, of the entire *Tragedia Endogonidia* project, and of the work of the Socìetas Raffaello Sanzio, see Claudia Castellucci et al., *The Theatre of Socìetas Raffaello Sanzio* (London and New York: Routledge, 2007).

2. Benjamin Britten, "Cuckoo!," *Friday Afternoons*, op. 7. no. 3, 1935, choir of Downside School, Purley, with Viola Tunnard (piano), Decca Music Group Ltd., recorded 1967.

3. Joe Kelleher, in C. Castellucci et al., *Theatre of Socìetas Raffaello Sanzio*, 76–77.

4. Romeo Castellucci, "Tragedia Endogonidia" (unpublished production text, courtesy of Socìetas Raffaello Sanzio, 2004), my translation.

5. Nicholas Ridout, in C. Castellucci et al., *Theatre of Socìetas Raffaello Sanzio*, 88.

6. Chiara Guidi, in C. Castellucci et al., *Theatre of Socìetas Raffaello Sanzio*, 217.

7. Romeo Castellucci, in C. Castellucci et al., *Theatre of Socìetas Raffaello Sanzio*, 30.

8. Karl Marx, *Capital*, vol. 3, trans. David Fernbach (London: Penguin Books, 1981), 959.

CHAPTER 1

1. Jill Dolan, *Utopia in Performance: Finding Hope at the Theater* (Ann Arbor: University of Michigan Press, 2005).

2. My understanding of romantic anti-capitalism is substantially indebted to the work of Michael Löwy and Robert Sayre, as developed first in Robert Sayre and Michael Löwy, "Figures of Romantic Anti-Capitalism," *New German Critique* 32 (1984): 42–92, and subsequently in Michael Löwy and Robert Sayre, *Romanticisim against the Tide of Modernity*, trans. Catherine Porter (Durham: Duke University Press, 2001).

3. Paul Breines, "Marxism, Romanticism, and the Case of Georg Lukács: Notes on Some Recent Sources and Situations," *Studies in Romanticism* 16, no. 4 (1977): 482.

4. Löwy and Sayre, *Romanticism against the Tide of Modernity*, 108. Lukács' article, which they cite here, is "Über den Dostojevski Nachlass," *Moskauer Rundschau*, Marc. 22, 1931.

5. A sense that Benjamin is an exemplary figure of romantic anti-capitalism is explored more fully in chap. 3. In chap. 4 the idea that significant aspects of the romantic anti-capitalist tradition surfaced at street level in Paris in 1968 is implicit.

6. Sayre and Löwy, "Figures of Romantic Anti-Capitalism," 54–55.

7. Michael Löwy, *Fire Alarm: Reading Walter Benjamin's "On the Concept of History"* (London and New York: Verso, 2005), 5.

8. For a much more extensive consideration of questions about the politics of theatre's time and its repetitions, see Rebecca Schneider, *Performing Remains: Art and War in Times of Theatrical Reenactment* (Abingdon and New York: Routledge, 2011).

9. Miranda Joseph, *Against the Romance of Community* (Minneapolis: University of Minnesota Press, 2002).

10. See Jean-Luc Nancy, "La Comparution" [The Compearance: From the Existence of "Communism" to the Community of "Existence"], trans. Tracy B. Strong, *Political Theory* 20, no. 3 (1992): 371–98; and Jean-Luc Nancy, *Being Singular Plural*, trans. Robert D. Richardson and Anne E. O'Byrne (Stanford: Stanford University Press, 2000).

11. Jean-Luc Nancy, "Literary Communism," in *The Inoperative Community*, ed. Peter Connor, trans. Peter Connor, Lisa Garbus, Michael Holland and Simona Sawhney (Minneapolis and London: University of Minnesota Press, 1991), 80.

12. Jean-Luc Nancy, *La communeauté désoeuvrée* (Paris: Christian Bourgeois Editeur, 1986).

13. Jean-Luc Nancy, "Inoperative Community," in *Inoperative Community*, 2.

14. Philippe Lacoue-Labarthe and Jean-Luc Nancy, *The Literary Absolute: The Theory of Literature in German Romanticism*, trans. Philip Barnard and Cheryl Lester (Albany: State University of New York Press, 1988), 8.

15. Ibid., 5.

16. Ibid., 6.

17. Dorothea Schlegel (Mendelssohn-Veit) to her son, in Lacoue-Labarthe and Nancy, *Literary Absolute*, 6.

18. John Roberts, "Introduction: Art, 'Enclave Theory' and the Communist Imaginary," *Third Text* 23, no. 4 (2009): 353–67.

19. Ibid., 355. Since Roberts's "Introduction," the "enclave" has perhaps enlarged a little. In the context of the latest crisis of capitalism taking shape from 2008, one might point to such diverse but related events as a two-day conference in London, held in March 2009 under the title "The Idea of Communism," convened by Alain Badiou and Slavoj Žižek, contributions to which were later published in a book: Costas Douzinas and Slavoj Žižek, eds., *The Idea of Communism* (London and New York: Verso, 2010); the experiments in collective living as politics revived and developed by the "indignados" in Spain or the various "Occupy" movements; and the success of the neo- or

postcommunist radical left coalition Syriza at the Greek parliamentary elections of May and June 2012 (with the familiar caveat that the "old" communism as embodied in the KKE refused to have anything to do with it).

20. Roberts, "Introduction," 354.

21. See Nicolas Bourriaud, *Relational Aesthetics*, trans. Simon Pleasance and Fronza Wood (Dijon: Les Presses du Réel, 2002). Other work seeking to develop similar conceptions of artistic practice as social and communicative action includes Grant Kester, *Conversation Pieces: Community and Communication in Modern Art* (Berkeley and London: University of California Press, 2004). For its influence within theatre and performance studies, see Shannon Jackson, *Social Works: Performing Art, Supporting Publics* (Abingdon and New York: Routledge, 2011); for an overview of some of the potential for theatre studies, not just of Bourriaud's work, but also of the thought of Alain Badiou, Jacques Rancière, and Paolo Virno (the latter two will be of particular significance in this book), see Simon Bayly "Theatre and the Public: Badiou, Rancière, Virno," *Radical Philosophy* 157 (2009): 20–29.

22. A typical critique of Bourriaud may be found in Claire Bishop, "Antagonism and Relational Aesthetics," *October* 110 (2004): 51–79.

23. Roberts, "Introduction," 355.

24. Stewart Martin, "Critique of Relational Aesthetics," *Third Text* 21, no. 4 (2007): 379.

25. Stewart Martin, "Artistic Communism—A Sketch," *Third Text* 23, no. 4 (2009): 483.

26. Ibid., 485.

27. Ibid., 482, 481.

28. Ibid., 492. See Paolo Virno, *A Grammar of the Multitude: For an Analysis of Contemporary Forms of Life*, trans. Isabella Bertoletti, James Cascaito, and Andrea Casson (Los Angeles and New York: Semiotext(e), 2004).

29. Salvatore Settis, *The Future of the "Classical"* (Cambridge: Polity Press, 2006). The citation from Novalis is from his *Tagebücher und Briefe Friedrich von Hardenbergs* and is offered by Settis as an epigraph to his book. I have sought to indicate a few recent examples of such legitimization at work in both theatre and politics in Nicholas Ridout, "Performance and Democracy," in *The Cambridge Companion to Performance Studies*, ed. Tracy C. Davis (Cambridge: Cambridge University Press, 2008), 9–22, with particular reference to the supposed relation among theatre, democracy, and the political predispositions of performance studies itself:

> In its revived form, then, the myth may be stated as follows. Theatre and democracy were born together; both represent a sociality and a mode of appearing in public which is beneficial to the construction of community; performance itself, as an embodied practice, embeds the abstractions of democratic representation in a participatory constellation of activities (theatre-going, sports); and finally, performance studies reasserts these connections by giving voice to the under-represented, advocating for an anti-elitist culture, and restoring the body's performance to its place alongside the text in academic practice. (15)

30. Settis, *Future of the "Classical,"* 11–12.

31. The attempt to rethink Marx's "ontology of labour" and to replace it with a "political ontology" (see Christopher Holman, "Dialectics and Distinction: Reconsidering Hannah Arendt's Critique of Marx," *Contemporary Political Theory* 10, no. 3 [2011]: 332–53) in order properly to describe "the human condition" is regarded by many critics as abstract, idealizing and universalizing, and insufficiently attentive to the specific historical conditions of the economic and the social (from both of which Arendt sought to detach the political). See also Axel Honneth, "Work and Instrumental Action," *New German Critique* 26 (1982): 31–54.

32. Hannah Arendt, *The Human Condition* (Chicago and London: University of Chicago Press, 1998), 187.

33. Ibid., 198.

34. Ibid., 198.

35. Ibid., 198.

36. Sometimes this sort of distinction has been articulated in terms of "performance" and "theatre," with performance valorized for its capacity to escape valorization according to the logics of capitalist production and exchange. I prefer to keep the praxis-poesis distinction alive within the work of theatre, in view of theatre's tendency, which it is the project of this book to emphasize, to wobble a little between the productive and the nonproductive, the autotelic and the teleological.

37. Virno, *Grammar of the Multitude.*

38. For a consideration of Rancière's relationship to Arendt's thought, see Andrew Schaap, "Hannah Arendt and the Philosophical Repression of Politics," in *Jacques Rancière and the Contemporary Scene: The Philosophy of Radical Equality,* ed. Jean-Philippe Deranty and Alison Ross (London and New York: Continuum, 2012), 145–65.

39. See, variously, Jacques Rancière, *Aisthesis: Scènes du régime esthetique de l'art* (Paris: Editions Galilée, 2011); Jacques Rancière, *Staging the People: The Proletarian and His Double,* trans. David Fernbach (London and New York: Verso, 2011); and Jacques Rancière, *Disagreement: Politics and Philosophy,* trans. Julie Rose (Minneapolis: University of Minnesota Press, 2004).

40. Jacques Rancière, *The Emancipated Spectator,* trans. Gregory Elliott (London and New York: Verso, 2009). Rancière's theorization of politics as aesthetics, across a range of texts, but most recently in *Aisthesis,* traces a very similar set of historical connections to those suggested by Stewart Martin. Martin's perspective, however, differs substantially, from Rancière's. Reviewing the publication of the English volume of Rancière's writing, *The Politics of Aesthetics: The Distribution of the Sensible,* trans. Gabriel Rockhill (London and New York: Continuum, 2005), Martin writes:

> Far from reconstructing the conditions of possibility of debates around modernist art and politics, Rancière has merely reasserted its romantic heritage. But it was precisely the indifference of romanticism to the conditions of the political economy of capitalism that generated the aporias of these debates in the first place, and, in the process, rendered

romanticism culturally inadequate and politically harmless. Rancière's position should be judged in the same terms. The affection with which his oeuvre is held by many on the Left looks dangerously like nostalgia for yet another form of romantic anti-capitalism.

See Stewart Martin, "Culs de sac," *Radical Philosophy* 131 (2005): 42.

41. Rancière, *Emancipated Spectator*, 16.

42. Rancière, *Emancipated Spectator*, 17.

43. Settis, *Future of the "Classical,"* 102.

44. Jean-Pierre Vernant and Pierre Vidal Nacquet, *Myth and Tragedy in Ancient Greece*, trans. Janet Lloyd, (New York: Zone Books, 1988); Simon Goldhill, "The Great Dionysia and Civic Ideology," *Journal of Hellenic Studies* 107 (1987): 58–76; Simon Goldhill and Robin Osborne, *Performance Culture and Athenian Democracy* (Cambridge: Cambridge University Press, 1999); David Wiles, *Theatre and Citizenship* (Cambridge: Cambridge University Press, 2011). In his introduction Wiles notes that "my enquiry necessarily begins in Athens where theatre and the democratic citizen emerged at the same historical moment, apparently as part of a single process" (18).

45. Oddone Longo, "The Theatre of the Polis," in *Nothing to Do with Dionysos? Athenian Drama in Its Social Context*, ed. John J. Winkler and Froma I. Zeitlin (Princeton: Princeton University Press, 1990), 13.

46. See Jean-Luc Nancy, "Myth Interrupted," in *Inoperative Community*, 43–70; Romeo Castellucci, "The Animal Being on Stage," trans. Carolina Melis, Valentina Valentini, and Ric Allsopp, *Performance Research* 5, no. 2 (2000): 23–28.

47. Longo, "Theatre of the Polis," 16, 17, 18, 19.

48. See, e.g., George Thomson, *Aeschylus and Athens: A Study in the Social Origins of Drama*, 2nd ed. (London: Lawrence and Wishart, 1966), which draws heavily on Engels, Bachofen, etc.; for a substantial corrective to this view, also from a Marxist perspective, see G. E. M. de Ste. Croix, *The Class Struggle in the Ancient Greek World from the Archaic Age to the Arab Conquests* (London: Duckworth, 1981).

49. Longo, "Theatre of the Polis," 19.

50. For a survey of romantic anti-capitalism, which is one of the most significant "communist" tendencies for the purposes of this book, see Löwy and Sayre, *Romanticism against the Tide of Modernity*. For theatre's temporality, see Schneider, *Performing Remains*. The fullest engagement with this temporality is to be found in chap. 3's consideration of Walter Benjamin's conception of history, itself the work of a romantic anti-capitalist upon whom Schneider draws significantly.

51. Goldhill, "Great Dionysia and Civic Ideology," 114.

52. Wiles, *Theatre and Citizenship*, 47.

53. Edith Hall, Fiona Macintosh, and Amanda Wrigley, eds., *Dionysus since 69: Greek Tragedy at the Dawn of the Third Millennium* (Oxford: Oxford University Press, 2004). For Schechner's own account of *Dionysus in 69*, see Richard Schechner, *Environmental Theatre* (New York and London: Applause, 1994). Froma I. Zeitlin offers an analysis of Schechner's production in her contribu-

tion to *Dionysus since 69* ("Dionysus in 69," 49–75), in which she observes that Schechner's view of Greek culture is "romantic" in that it idealizes "their purported links with other quite different cultural manifestations" (58) and that "what strikes him most about the ancient theatre is the civic nature of performance in Athens," where, as Schechner himself writes, "Here in a single circular arena the whole community came to see its reality enacted" (Schechner, "Theater and Revolution," *Salmagundi* 2, no. 2 [Fall 1967–Winter 1968]: 11–27, cited in Zeitlin, "Dionysus in 69," 57).

54. Edith Hall, "Introduction: Why Greek Tragedy in the Late Twentieth Century?" in Hall, Macintosh, and Wrigley, *Dionysus since 69*, 29.

55. Ibid., 2.

56. Dipesh Chakrabarty, *Provincializing Europe: Postcolonial Thought and Historical Difference* (Princeton: Princeton University Press, 2000), cited in Page duBois, *Out of Athens: The New Ancient Greeks* (Cambridge and London: Harvard University Press, 2010), 5. Page duBois's project is to reveal alternative lines of historical and cultural transmission and exchange. In her critique of classical studies she suggests that even "the most enlightened of classicists" (she is referring here to Jean-Pierre Vernant) participates to some extent in this continuing fabrication: Vernant's characterization of "Greek civilisation," she writes, demonstrates "the great virtue of dethroning the Greeks from their pedestal as the point of origin of human civilisation *tout court*, but also the limitations of a Western perspective that sees the Greeks as autonomous and isolated from the Near East, Africa, and India, a perspective now eroded by our situation within globalization' (duBois, *Out of Athens*, 15).

57. Erika Fischer-Lichte, "Thinking about the Origins of Theatre in the 1970s," in Hall, Macintosh, and Wrigley, *Dionysus since 69*, 341. In proposing that they are "lost forever," Fischer-Lichte typically reckons without the capacity of performance to return things to us differently, discontinuously. It might be more accurate to say that we cannot return to origins, but that in performance, origins are somehow returned to us, but not as the origins they originally were.

58. Darko Suvin, "Modes of Political Drama," *Massachusetts Review* 13, no. 3 (Summer 1972): 311.

59. Arendt, *Human Condition*, 188.

60. Eugene van Erven, *Community Theatre: Global Perspectives* (London and New York: Routledge, 2001), 255.

61. Ibid., 1.

62. Augusto Boal, *Theatre of the Oppressed* (London: Pluto Press, 1979). For a persuasive critique of Boal's reading of Aristotle and the conclusions he draws about Greek theatre, see Paul Dwyer, "Theoria Negativa: Making Sense of Boal's Reading of Aristotle," *Modern Drama* 48, no. 4 (Winter 2005): 635–58.

63. Karl Marx, *Grundrisse: Foundations of the Critique of Political Economy (Rough Draft)*, trans. Martin Nicolaus (Harmondsworth: Penguin, 1973), 471–75.

64. Ellen Meiksins Wood, "Historical Materialism in 'Forms Which Precede Capitalist production,'" in *Karl Marx's Grundrisse: Foundations of the Critique of Political Economy 150 Years Later*, ed. Marcello Musto (Abingdon and New York: Routledge, 2008), 80.

65. Marx, *Grundrisse*, 471–72.

66. Marx, *Grundrisse*, 472.

67. Van Erven, *Community Theatre*, 257.

68. The story of capitalist regulation of the time of work is summarized in chap. 2, drawing substantially on the work of E. P. Thompson, himself a significant figure in British "romantic anti-capitalism."

69. Marx writes: "The true realm of freedom, the development of human powers as an end in itself, begins beyond it, though it can only flourish with this realm of necessity as its basis." Marx, *Capital*, vol. 3, 958–59.

70. Some of this work has recently been done for the substantial subfield of amateur productions of Shakespeare in Michael Dobson, *Shakespeare and Amateur Performance: A Cultural History* (Cambridge: Cambridge University Press, 2011).

71. Jon Oram, "The Social Actor," *Claque Theatre*, 2006, www.claquetheatre.com/wp-content/ . . . /Article_The-Social-Actor.pdf, 2.

72. Ann Jellicoe, *Community Plays: How to Put Them On* (London: Methuen, 1987), xvii.

73. Joseph, *Against the Romance of Community*, xxix–xxx.

CHAPTER 2

1. Anton Chekhov, *Uncle Vanya*, in *Plays*, trans. Peter Carson (London: Penguin Books, 2002), 200.

2. Karl Marx, *Capital: A Critique of Political Economy*, vol. 1, trans. Ben Fowkes (New York: Vintage Books, 1977).

3. E. P. Thompson, "Time, Work-Discipline, and Industrial Capitalism," *Past and Present* 38, no. 1 (1967): 56–97.

4. Ibid., 93–94.

5. Ibid., 60.

6. Ibid., 61.

7. Ibid., 81.

8. Ibid., 90.

9. Of course many such series make the working day and the working life their primary subject: the repackaging of daily work in the form of evening entertainment would be the basis for a study unto itself, ranging from *The Wire*, via innumerable police and hospital shows, to *The Office* and, most recently, *Parks and Recreation*. This is one rather literal way in which leisure is always a form of work.

10. Chris Rojek, *Capitalism and Leisure Theory* (London and New York: Tavistock Publications, 1985), 42.

11. Ibid., 46.

12. Ibid., 14.

13. David Harvey, *The Condition of Postmodernity* (Oxford: Basil Blackwell, 1989), 126.

14. Marx, *Capital*, vol. 1, 352.

15. Ibid., 409.

16. Ibid., 382.

17. Ibid., 409.

18. Ibid., 341.

19. Ibid., 364–65.

20. Ibid., 376.

21. Ibid., 416 n68.

22. Chekhov, *Uncle Vanya*, 152–53.

23. Ibid., 146.

24. Raymond Williams, *Modern Tragedy* (Stanford: Stanford University Press, 1966), 144.

25. Chekhov, *Uncle Vanya*, 178.

26. Neil B. Weissman, *Reform in Tsarist Russia* (New Brunswick, NJ: Rutgers University Press, 1981), 21.

27. Spencer Golub, *The Recurrence of Fate* (Iowa City: University of Iowa Press, 1994), 32.

28. Chekhov, *Uncle Vanya*, 147.

29. Ibid., 166.

30. Ibid., 178.

31. See John Tulloch, *Chekhov: A Structuralist Study* (London and Basingstoke: Macmillan, 1980).

32. See Weissman, *Reform in Tsarist Russia*.

33. Samuel C. Kramer, "The Zemstvo and Public Health," in *The Zemstvo in Russia: An Experiment in Local Self-Government*, ed. Terence Emmons and Wayne S. Vucinich (Cambridge: Cambridge University Press, 1982).

34. Tulloch, *Chekhov*, 53.

35. Arendt, *Human Condition*.

36. Marx, *Capital*, vol. 1, 133.

37. For a detailed exposition of the figure of the passionate amateur as a subcategory of the romantic anti-capitalist, see chap. 1.

38. Magali Sarfatti Larson, *The Rise of Professionalism: A Sociological Analysis* (Berkeley and Los Angeles: University of California Press, 1977), 220.

39. Ibid., 9.

40. Ibid., 221.

41. Harold Perkin, *The Rise of Professional Society: England since 1880* (London and New York: Routledge, 1989), xiv.

42. Sarfatti Larson, *Rise of Professionalism*, xviii.

43. Ibid., 237.

44. See also Joseph, *Against the Romance of Community*, on nonprofits, community, and "the spectre of communism."

45. Sarfatti Larson, *Rise of Professionalism*, 237–38.

46. Ibid., 234.

47. See, for example, Barbara Ehrenreich, *Bait and Switch: The (Futile) Pursuit of the American Dream* (New York: Metropolitan Books, 2001).

48. Laurence Senelick, *The Chekhov Theatre: Century of the Plays in Performance* (Cambridge: Cambridge University Press, 1997).

49. Nick Worrall, *The Moscow Art Theatre* (London and New York: Routledge, 1996), 7–8.

50. Marx, *Capital*, vol. 1, 133.

51. Theodor Adorno and Max Horkheimer, *The Dialectic of Enlightenment*, trans. John Cumming (London: Verso, 1997), 137.

52. Anton Chekhov, *Three Sisters*, in *Plays*, 216.

53. Anton Chekhov, *The Cherry Orchard*, in *Plays*, 312.

54. R. Williams, *Modern Tragedy*, 145.

55. There are, of course, some exceptions to this, including David Storey's *The Contractor* (London: Cape, 1970) and Arnold Wesker's *The Kitchen* (London: Oberon Modern Plays, 2012).

56. Joseph, *Against the Romance of Community*, 32.

57. Ibid., 33.

58. Ibid., 36.

59. Ibid., 34.

60. Peggy Phelan, *Unmarked: The Politics of Performance* (London and New York: Routledge, 1993), cited in Joseph, *Against the Romance of Community*, 66.

61. Joseph, *Against the Romance of Community*, 66.

62. Ibid., 66.

63. Ibid., 66.

64. Phelan, *Unmarked*, 146.

65. Anton Chekhov, *The Seagull*, in *Plays*, 83.

66. Chekhov, *Uncle Vanya*, 162–63.

CHAPTER 3

1. Narodnyi Komissariat Prosveschcheniya, which may be translated as People's Commissariat of either Education or Enlightenment. For an account of its earliest years, see Sheila Fitzpatrick, *The Commissariat of Enlightenment: Soviet Organization of Education and the Arts Under Lunacharsky, October 1917–1921* (Cambridge: Cambridge University Press, 1970). By 1928 Narkompros was becoming the target of a "class war on the cultural front" launched by radical proletarian elements in the Soviet Union who viewed it as part of a cultural establishment dominated by intellectuals and bureaucrats whose commitment to proletarian culture was suspect. See Sheila Fitzpatrick, "Cultural Revolution in Russia, 1928–32," *Journal of Contemporary History* 9, no. 1 (1974): 33–52. The role of Narkompros in the development of both theatre and education in the immediate post-revolutionary period will be considered further below.

2. "I will write the programme," he said, "and set out the theoretical basis for your practical work": Asja Lacis, *Revolutionär im Beruf: Berichte über proletarisches Theater, über Meyerhold, Brecht, Benjamin und Piscator*, edited by Hildegard Brenner (Munich: Rogner and Bernhard, 1971), 26. This autobiographical text is the principal source used here for the origins of the "Program for a Proletarian Children's Theater." See also Beata Paškevica, *In der Stadt der Parolen: Asja Lacis, Walter Benjamin und Bertolt Brecht* (Essen: Klartext Verlag, 2006).

3. Lacis, *Revolutionär im Beruf*, 26.

4. Walter Benjamin, "Program for a Proletarian Children's Theater," in

Selected Writings, Vol. 2, 1927—1934, trans. Rodney Livingstone and Others, ed. Michael W. Jennings, Howard Eiland, and Gary Smith (Cambridge and London: Belknap Press), 201–6 (hereafter cited in the text). The German text is in Benjamin, *Gesammelte Schriften*, vol. 2 (Frankfurt am Main: Suhrkamp Verlag, 1989), 763–69. The German text is also reproduced in Lacis, *Revolutionär im Beruf*, 26–31. It was unpublished in Benjamin's lifetime.

5. The KPD, for example, "idealized productive labour"; Eric D. Weitz, *Creating German Communism, 1890–1990: From Popular Protests to Socialist State* (Princeton: Princeton University Press, 1997), 7.

6. See, for example, Andrzej Wirth and Martha Ulvaeus, "The Lehrstück as Performance," *TDR/TheDrama Review* 43, no. 4 (1988): 113–21:

> The way the Lehrstück was performed during Brecht's lifetime stood in contradiction to the radicality of its theory, which emphasizes a sharp contrast between the Schaustück [a play for the benefit of the audience] and the Lehrstück [for the benefit of the players]. The radical core of Brecht's utopian theory is the idea of an autarkic (self-sufficient) metatheatre, a utopian objective accompanied by a utopian ideology. (116)

7. Lacis, *Revolutionär im Beruf*, 23 (my translation).

8. This is where Benjamin's text seems to have its most extraordinary contemporary resonance, with the Occupy movement, where the occupation of space seems to coincide with the refusal to articulate demands that might be met in the future: perpetual rehearsal for revolution as the only way to secure the space of revolution.

9. "Hier kommen Aufführungen nebenbei, man könnte sagen: aus Versehen, zustande, beinahe als ein Schabernack der Kinder, die auf diese Weise einmal das grundsätzlich niemals abgeschlossene Studium unterbrechen": Benjamin, *Gesammelte Schriften*, vol. 2, 765.

10. See also Marx, *Capital*, vol. 3, for the manager as orchestral conductor, or Regisseur.

11. His laborious attempts to get a waiter to serve him hot soup one evening resulted in a plate of sliced cheese. See also Jacques Derrida, *Moscou aller-retour* (Saint Etienne: Éditions de l'aube, 1995), 93.

12. Werner Hamacher, "'Now': Walter Benjamin on Historical Time," in *The Moment: Time and Rupture in Modern Thought*, ed. Heidrun Friese (Liverpool: Liverpool University Press, 2001), 172.

13. Walter Benjamin, "On the Concept of History," in *Selected Writings*, vol. 4, 1938–1940, trans. Edmund Jephcott and others, ed. Howard Eiland and Michael W. Jennings (Cambridge and London: Harvard University Press, 2003), 390.

14. Hamacher, "'Now,'" 165.

15. Ibid., 167.

16. Ibid., 171.

17. Walter Benjamin, "Paralipomena to 'On the Concept of History,'" in *Selected Writings*, vol. 4, 1938–1940, 400–401. This is the Thesis XVII that Agamben found.

18. Hamacher, "'Now,'" 164.

19. See Scott McCracken, "Idleness for All," *New Formations* 53 (2004): 65–76, for a more extended reflection on Benjamin's writing on "idleness" as a nonwork and antiwork practice, especially in *Convulute m* of the *Arcades Project*.

20. Benjamin, "On the Concept of History," 393.

21. Walter Benjamin, *The Arcades Project*, trans. Howard Eiland and Kevin McLaughlin (Cambridge: Belknap Press, 1999), 462.

22. Walter Benjamin, *One-Way Street and Other Writings*, trans. J. A. Underwood (London: Penguin, 2009), 110.

23. Alan Ball, "'The Roots of Bezprizornost' in Soviet Russia's First Decade," *Slavic Review* 51, no. 2 (1992): 247–70.

24. Ibid., 250.

25. Alan Ball, "State Children: Soviet Russia's Besprizornye and the New Socialist Generation," *Russian Review* 52, no. 2 (1993): 229.

26. Lacis, *Revolutionär im Beruf*, 21.

27. Ibid., 22.

28. See the introduction.

29. Fitzpatrick, *Commissariat of Enlightenment*, 20.

30. *Revolutionär in Beruf* (Revolutionary by profession) is the title of Lacis's (German) autobiography.

31. See Rei Terada, *Looking Away: Phenomenality and Dissatisfaction, Kant to Adorno* (Cambridge: Harvard University Press, 2009).

32. "That's robbers!": Lacis, *Revolutionär im Beruf*, 24.

33. Richard Wolin, *Walter Benjamin: An Aesthetic of Redemption* (Berkeley and Los Angeles: University of California Press, 1994), 37.

34. There were many different youth movements, whose participants were predominantly from the middle class. The *Wandervögel* was one of the earliest and largest of the groups, largely male and Protestant in composition and conservative and conformist in social orientation, with hiking or rambling as its core collective activity, reflecting a typically romantic affiliation with ideas about the value of nature as a corrective to the alienation of the urban industrial modernity upon which the prosperity of its members' parents largely depended. For a history of the various movements see Walter Laqueur, *Young Germany: A History of the German Youth Movement* (London: Routledge and Kegan Paul, 1962).

35. See Bernd Witte, *Walter Benjamin: An Intellectual Biography*, trans. James Rolleston (Detroit: Wayne State University Press, 1997), 19–23.

36. Philip Lee Utley, "Radical Youth: Generational Conflict in the Anfang Movement, 1912–January 1914," *History of Education Quarterly* 19, no. 2 (1979): 209.

37. Ibid., 211.

38. Ibid., 211–12.

39. Walter Benjamin, "Experience," in *Selected Writings*, vol. 1, 1913–1926, ed. Marcus Bullock and Michael W. Jennings (Cambridge and London: Belknap, 1996), 3.

40. Walter Benjamin, "The Life of Students," in *Selected Writings*, vol. 1, 1913–1926, 37.

41. U.N.E.F. Strasbourg, *On the Poverty of Student Life, Considered in Its Economic, Political, Psychological, Sexual, and Particularly Intellectual Aspects, and a Modest Proposal for Its Remedy*, http://library.nothingness.org/articles/SI/en/display/4 (1966).

42. Benjamin, "Life of Students," 38.

43. The idea of the "unity of knowledge" was central to romantic conceptions of education, as espoused by Fichte and Humboldt, which have come to be associated, widely but misleadingly, with the reform of the German university in the early nineteenth century and, in particular, with the foundation of the University of Berlin. See Charles E. McClelland, *State, Society, and University in Germany 1700–1914* (Cambridge: Cambridge University Press, 1980), for a detailed account of eighteenth- and nineteenth-century university reform; and Mitchell G. Ash, "Bachelor of What, Master of Whom? The Humboldt Myth and Historical Transformations of Higher Education in German-Speaking Europe and the US," *European Journal of Education* 41, no. 2 (2006): 245–67, for a summary and a debunking of the myth.

44. The damage caused by specialization to the work of the university, and to teaching in particular, was the target of a lecture given in Basel by Friedrich Nietzsche in 1872. For an account of this lecture, its reception. and its relation to post-1871 developments in Prussian education, see Christian J. Emden, *Friedrich Nietzsche and the Politics of History* (Cambridge: Cambridge University Press, 2008), 112–19.

45. See C. McClelland, *State, Society, and University in Germany*, 237.

46. Konrad H. Jarausch, *Students, Society, and Politics in Imperial Germany: The Rise of Academic Illiberalism* (Princeton: Princeton University Press, 1982), 156.

47. Geoff Eley, "Educating the Bourgeoisie: Students and the Culture of 'Illiberalism' in Imperial Germany," review of *Students, Society, and Politics in Imperial Germany: The Rise of Academic Illiberalism* by Konrad H. Jarausch, *History of Education Quarterly* 26, no. 2 (1986): 291.

48. Ibid., 291.

49. Jarausch, *Students, Society, and Politics*, 24.

50. Adolf von Harnack, "Von Großbetrieb der Wissenschaft," in *Wissenschaftpolitische Reden und Aufsätze* (Hildesheim, Zürich, and New York: Olms-Weidemann, 2001), 3–9.

51. Jarausch, *Students, Society, and Politics*, 24. Harnack's text refers directly to the development of academic exchanges between Berlin and Harvard universities.

52. Harnack, "Von Großbetrieb der Wissenschaft," 5 (my translation).

53. See Fitzpatrick, *Commissariat of Enlightenment*; Jon Lauglo, "Soviet Education Policy 1917–1935: From Ideology to Bureaucratic Control," *Oxford Review of Education* 14, no. 3 (1988): 285–99; and James C. McClelland, "Proletarianizing the Student Body: The Soviet Experience During the New Economic Policy," *Past and Present* 80 (1978): 122–46.

54. See Marjorie Lamberti, *The Politics of Education: Teachers and School Reform in Weimar Germany* (Oxford and New York: Berghahn Books, 2002); and Donald R. Tracey, "Reform in the Early Weimar Republic: The Thuringian Example," *Journal of Modern History* 44, no. 2 (1972): 195–212.

55. Walter Benjamin, "A Communist Pedagogy," in *Selected Writings*, vol. 2, 1927–1934, 273–75; Edwin Hoernle, *Grundfragen der Proletarischen Erziehung* (Berlin: Verlag der Jugendinterantionale, 1929).

56. Anson Rabinbach, *The Human Motor: Energy, Fatigue, and the Origins of Modernity* (Berkeley and Los Angeles: University of California Press, 1992), 2, 10, 191–94.

57. Ibid., 198.

58. Ibid., 282. For an account of the development of socialist and communist political organization in Germany, and the relationship of the German Social Democratic and Communist Parties (SPD and KPD) to questions of worker organization, management, and discipline, see Weitz, *Creating German Communism*.

59. Hoernle, *Grundfragen*, 139–41.

60. Benjamin, "Communist Pedagogy," 274.

61. Fitzpatrick, *Commissariat of Enlightenment*, xvi.

62. Ibid., 29.

63. Ibid., 30.

64. Cited in ibid., 33.

65. James C. McClelland characterizes both versions of the "polytechnic" approach to education as "utopian" in order to distinguish them from an alternative "heroic" attitude that he sees embodied by the Red Army under Trotsky and efforts to enforce military-style discipline and "monotechnical" vocational education. See James C. McClelland, "The Utopian and the Heroic: Divergent Paths to the Communist Educational Ideal," in *Bolshevik Culture*, ed. Abbott Gleason, Peter Kenez and Richard Stites (Bloomington: Indiana University Press, 1985), 114–30.

66. Hoernle, *Grundfragen*, 142.

67. See Lamberti, *Politics of Education*.

68. Hoernle, *Grundfragen*, 141.

69. Benjamin, "Communist Pedagogy," 274–75.

70. Edwin Hoernle, cited in Jack Zipes, ed. and trans., *Utopian Tales from Weimar* (Polygon: Edinburgh, 1990), 13.

71. Susan Buck-Morss, *Dreamworld and Catastrophe: The Passing of Mass Utopia in East and West* (Cambridge and London: MIT Press, 2002), 50.

72. Ibid., 60.

73. Ibid., 50.

74. Hamacher, "'Now,'" 164.

CHAPTER 4

1. "A film in the process of making itself" (my translation).

2. William Shakespeare, *Hamlet*, ed. Harold Jenkins (London: Methuen, 1982), 1.5. References are to act and scene.

3. "The French working class will not unify nor mount the barricades in order to win a twelve percent increase in wages": André Gorz, *Le socialisme difficile* (Paris: Du Seuil, 1967) (my translation: the published English translation does not quite convey the sense of the sentence as cited in the film).

4. In 1980 Gorz published *Adieux au proletariat* (Paris: Galilée, 1980). The English translation of this influential work is *Farewell to the Working Class:* André Gorz, *Farewell to the Working Class: An Essay on Post-Industrial Socialism,* trans. Michael Sonenscher (London: Pluto Press, 1997).

5. Gorz, *Socialisme difficile.*

6. Jean-Luc Godard, *La chinoise, ou plutôt à la chinoise,* dir. Jean-Luc Godard (1967; London: Optimum Releasing, 2005), DVD, 93 min.

7. "We are the speech of others": Godard, *La chinoise.*

8. Shakespeare, *Hamlet.*

9. In the period following 1968, some on the left explicitly sought to replace speech with action, in the turn toward armed struggle: "Shortly after forming, Weatherman declared the need 'to be a movement that fights, not just talks about fighting.' The RAF [Rote Armee Fraktion], in its first manifesto, announced, 'We will not talk about armed propaganda, we will do it'": Jeremy Varon, *Bringing the War Home: The Weather Underground, the Red Army Faction, and Revolutionary Violence in the Sixties and Seventies* (Berkeley and Los Angeles: University of California Press, 2004), 21.

10. Chekhov, *Uncle Vanya,* 186.

11. Ibid., 185.

12. Arendt, *Human Condition,* 178.

13. Ibid., 179.

14. Ibid., 198.

15. Ibid., 199.

16. See Ellen Meiksins Wood and Neal Wood, *Class Ideology and Ancient Political Theory: Socrates, Plato and Aristotle in Social Context* (Oxford: Basil Blackwell, 1978).

17. "They've got factories or something": Godard, *La chinoise* (my translation).

18. James S. Williams, "'C'est le petit livre rouge / Qui fait que tout enfin bouge': The Case for Revolutionary Agency in Jean-Luc Godard's *La Chinoise*," *Journal of European Studies* 40, no. 3 (2010): 206.

19. Cited in Jacques Bontemps, Jean-Louis Comolli, Michel Delahaye, Jean Narboni, and Jean-Luc Godard, "Struggle on Two Fronts: A Conversation with Jean-Luc Godard," *Film Quarterly* 22, no. 2 (Winter 1968–69): 20–35.

20. Pauline Kael, blurb of *La chinoise, ou plutôt à la chinoise,* dir. Jean-Luc Godard. Her review of the film upon its release in the United States, published in the *New Yorker,* is far more discriminating. See Pauline Kael, *Going Steady* (Boston: Little, Brown, 1970), 76–84.

21. J. Williams, "'C'est le petit livre rouge,'" 216.

22. "Shit, shit, stop"; Godard, *La chinoise.*

23. See Jean-Luc Godard, "Let's Talk about Pierrot: An Interview with Jean-Luc Godard," by Jean-Louis Comolli, Michel Delahaye, Jean-André Fieschi, and Gérard Guégan, *Cahiers du cinéma* 171 (Oct. 1965), reprinted in Tom Milne, ed. *Godard on Godard,* trans. Tom Milne (New York and London: Da Capo, 1972), 216.

24. The actual minister of culture of the USSR at this time was Yekaterina Furtseva, who was the only woman ever to become a full member of the Po-

litburo (until Galina Semyonova in 1990). She took a particular interest in the-atre and cinema in her fourteen years as minister of culture, a post to which she was appointed after her expulsion from the Politburo for criticizing Khrushchev, a suicide attempt, and political rehabilitation. Her obituary in the *Washington Post* reads: "Ekaterina A. Furtseva, Soviet minister of culture and the highest-ranking woman in the Soviet regime, died of a heart attack yesterday in Moscow at the age of 63. She was a handsome, blonde woman with a great zest for life and some very strong ideas." See Dorothy McCardle, "Soviet Official Ekaterina Furtseva Dies," *Washington Post*, Oct. 26, 1974. However, it is fairly clear that the "real" target of this unreal assassination was in fact the French minister of culture, André Malraux, to whom Godard had written an open letter in 1966, following the banning of Jacques Rivette's film *La religieuse* (which starred Godard's by-now-estranged wife, Anna Karina), in which he accused Malraux of being a "collaborator." The banning of *La religieuse* is cited by Véronique as a prime example of the oppression that, she argues, forces her into violence. *Le Nouvel Observateur*, April 6, 1966. Reprinted in *Cahiers du cinéma* (April 8–9, 1966), 177.

25. Jean-Luc Godard, interview with Andrew Sarris, *Village Voice*, Apr. 30, 1970. Winston Wheeler Dixon describes this claim as "disingenuous in the extreme": Wheeler Winston Dixon, *The Films of Jean-Luc Godard* (Albany: State University of New York Press, 1997), 85.

26. Other members of the Group listed in their manifesto were Gérard Martin, Nathalie Billard, and Armand Marco, but according to Steve Cannon, Jean-Henri Roger and Paul Burron "among others also participated": Steve Cannon, "'When You're Not a Worker Yourself . . .': Godard, the Dziga Vertov Group and the Audience," in *100 Years of European Cinema: Entertainment or Ideology?* ed. Diana Holmes and Alison Smith (Manchester: Manchester University Press, 2000), 102.

27. "As the summer ended, for me it was back to classes": Godard, *La chinoise* (my translation).

28. Might it even be worth wondering whether acting like a Marxist-Leninist cell while not really being one is either a kind of "fraud" or, alternatively, an attempt at a kind of alchemy? Or speculating that the choice of Jeanson as a "reality principle" who will seek to end the alchemy is a hidden reference to his Anglophone namesake, Jonson?

29. Jean-Luc Godard, *Pierrot le fou*, dir. Jean-Luc Godard (1965; London: Optimum Releasing, 2007), DVD, 106 min.

30. Jean-Luc Godard, *Weekend*, dir. Jean-Luc Godard (1967; London: Artificial Eye, 2005), DVD, 90 min.

31. "I am an actor . . . I am sincere": Godard, *La chinoise* (my translation).

32. "A true socialist theatre": Godard, *La chinoise* (my translation).

33. Louis Althusser, "The 'Piccolo Teatro': Bertolazzi and Brecht," part 4 of *For Marx*, trans. Ben Brewster (London: Verso, 1982).

34. Manny Farber, *Negative Space: Manny Farber on the Movies*, rev. ed. (New York: De Capo Press, 1998), 270.

35. Renata Adler, "Talking to the Young," *New York Times*, Apr, 4, 1967, 58.

36. Ibid., 58.

37. "Yes, sure it's fiction, but that gets me closer to the real": Godard, *La chinoise* (my translation).

38. See, for example, Paul De Man, "The Concept of Irony," in *Aesthetic Ideology*, ed. Andrzej Warminski (Minneapolis: University of Minnesota Press, 1996), 179.

39. "Completely unreal": Godard, *La chinoise* (my translation).

40. "They hadn't understood that it was theatre, real theatre": Godard, *La chinoise* (my translation).

41. James S. Williams, "C'est le petit livre rouge," 212. See also Jacques Rancière, *Film Fables*, trans. Emiliano Battista (Oxford and New York: Berg, 2006): "The political militant and the actor are alike: their work is to show us not visible horrors, but what cannot be seen" (150); "That is what we see in this cinema between two marxisms that concludes as a meditation on the theater" (152).

42. Benjamin, "Program for a Proletarian Children's Theater," 202.

43. Ibid., 203.

44. Henri Lefebvre, *The Explosion: Marxism and the French Revolution*, trans. Alfred Ehrenfeld (New York and London: Monthly Review Press, 1969), 104.

45. Jean Bertolino, *Les Trublions*, cited in Margaret Atack, *May 68 in French Fiction and Film: Rethinking Society, Rethinking Representation* (Oxford: Oxford University Press, 1999), 29 n15.

46. See Scott Lash and John Urry, *The End of Organized Capitalism* (Madison: University of Wisconsin Press, 1987); Henri Lefebvre, *The Production of Space*, trans. Donald Nicholson-Smith (Cambridge, MA: Blackwell, 1991); David Harvey, *A Brief History of Neoliberalism* (Oxford: Oxford University Press, 2005); Luc Boltanski and Ève Chiapello, *The New Spirit of Capitalism*, trans. Gregory Elliott (London: Verso, 2006).

47. Lefebvre, *Explosion*, 104.

48. U.N.E.F. Strasbourg, "On the Poverty of Student Life."

49. The term *edu-factory* has been used to describe the university in terms of the concept of "social factory" developed in Autonomist thought, in which the social, or in this case the educational institution, is understood as a site of production. It has been adopted as the name for a collective of activist scholars who jointly published *Toward a Global Autonomous University* (New York: Autonomedia, 2009).

50. According to Danielle Rancière and Jacques Rancière,

While the militants of the proletarian Left (GP, Gauche prolétarienne, was a post-68 Maoist party) proclaimed a revolt against bourgeois knowledge and academic authority, a new type of knowledge was establishing itself in the scholarship produced in the universities and in the specialization of its branches, a modern system for the development of the productive forces of theory that socialized the power of the professors. The system of credit units and continuous assessment marked the entry of the university apprenticeship into the age of Taylorist rationalization. A demand for continuous production replaced the artisanal work of the masters course and the annual examination, both for teachers and students, shaping a requirement for external support.

Danielle Rancière and Jacques Rancière, "La légende des philosophes (Les intellectuels et la traversée du gauchisme)," in *Les lauriers de mai, ou, Les chemins du pouvoir* (1968–1978), special issue, *Révoltes logiques* (Feb. 1978): 9 (my translation).

51. U.N.E.F. Strasbourg, "On the Poverty of Student Life."

52. Kristin Ross, *May '68 and Its Afterlives* (Chicago: University of Chicago Press, 2002), 32.

53. *Goguettes* were social groups that gathered in cafés and restaurants so that members could perform songs.

54. Jacques Rancière, "Good Times or Pleasure at the Barricades," in *Voices of the People: The Social Life of 'la sociale' at the End of the Second Empire*, ed. Adrian Rifkin and Roger Thomas, trans. John Moore (London: Routledge and Kegan Paul, 1988), 50.

55. Ibid., 50.

56. Ibid., 52.

57. Ibid., 51.

58. Jacques Rancière, *The Nights of Labor: The Workers' Dream in Nineteenth-Century France*, trans. John Drury (Philadelphia: Temple University Press, 1989), 54.

59. André Gorz, *Reclaiming Work: Beyond the Wage-Based Society*, trans. Chris Turner (Cambridge: Polity Press, 1999), 10.

60. Nancy, "Inoperative Community," 2.

61. Mao Tse-Tung, "Talks at the Yenan Forum on Literature and Art," May 1942, in *Quotations from Chairman Mao Tse-Tung* (Peking: Foreign Language Press, 1966), 302.

62. Rancière, "Good Times," 52.

63. Colin MacCabe, *Godard: A Portrait of the Artist at Seventy* (New York: Farrar, Strauss and Giroux, 2003), 180.

64. Jean-Luc Godard, "What Is to Be Done?" *Afterimage*, no. 1 (April 1970).

CHAPTER 5

1. Not what it meant, but what the rate set for that day was. The London Interbank Offered Rates (LIBOR), established in 1986, is derived from information supplied to the British Bankers Association and is used as an indicator of what financial institutions charge one another for loans. In the context of this discussion it is an interesting example of the way market behaviors are conditioned by what people say. It has been alleged that some banks under-reported their borrowing costs during the 2008 financial crisis, giving the impression that they were in better financial condition than was really the case, and that the LIBOR was therefore not reliable at times of financial crisis. See Carrick Mollencamp and Mark Whitehouse, "Study Casts Doubt on Key Rate," *Wall Street Journal*, May 29, 2008, 1.

2. Michael Hardt and Antonio Negri, *Empire* (Cambridge and London: Harvard University Press, 2000), 290. Hardt and Negri direct the reader in search of a fuller definition and analysis to Maurizio Lazzarato, "Immaterial Labor," trans. Paul Colilli and Ed Emory, in *Radical Thought in Italy*, ed. Michael Hardt and Paolo Virno (Minneapolis: University of Minnesota Press, 1996), 133–47.

3. Nature Theatre of Oklahoma, *No Dice*, transcription and arrangement by Kelly Copper (New York: 53rd State Press, 2007), 17.

4. Michel Foucault, *The Birth of Biopolitics: Lectures at the Collège de France, 1978–1979* (Basingstoke: Palgrave Macmillan, 2008), 226. Foucault's French original—"l'entrepreneur de soi-même"—does not specify gender.

5. Margaret Thatcher, interview for *Woman's Own*, by Douglas Keay, transcript, Sept. 23, 1987, http://www.margaretthatcher.org/document/106689.

6. K. Ross, *May '68*, 182.

7. See Alain Touraine, *The May Movement: Revolt and Reform* (New York: Random House, 1971).

8. K. Ross, *May '68*, 182.

9. K. Ross, *May '68*, 185.

10. In this respect—that capital was responding to the political action of labor—their analysis resembles that of autonomists such as Antonio Negri. See, for example, Michael Hardt and Antonio Negri, *Labors of Dionysus: A Critique of the State-Form* (Minneapolis: University of Minnesota Press, 1994):

> The history of the recent transformations should be centred, we believe, around the events of 1968. In that year the workers' attack against the organization of factory labor and against the social division of labor reached its summit. Through their struggles, the workers, up until then regimented in the factory and in society in the Taylorist, Fordist, and Keynesian mode of production, shattered the categories and the equilibria of the capitalist reproduction of society en masse through successive waves of extended struggles on an international level. To reformulate a Hegelian phrase, in 1968 the ferocious beast of living labor smashed every disciplinary limit. It was necessary, therefore, to tame it. In the years immediately after 1968, then, a new era of relationships began between capital (along with its State, be it bourgeois or socialist) and labor. (272)

11. Boltanski and Chiapello, *New Spirit of Capitalism*, 97.

12. They cite Vaneigem, for example, thus: "What people do officially is nothing compared to what they do in secret. People usually associate creativity with works of art, but what are works of art alongside the creative energy displayed by everyone a thousand times a day: seething unsatisfied desires, daydreams in search of a foothold in reality, feelings at once confused and luminously clear, ideas and gestures presaging nameless upheavals": Raoul Vaneigem, *The Revolution in Everyday Life*, trans. David Nicholson-Smith (London: Left Bank Books and Rebel Press, 1983), 147. This is cheeky because there is nothing to suggest that Vaneigem is suggesting that this

"creativity" is to be found in the workplace nor even that it should be. It is also cheeky because they claim that this and the other passages they cite were chosen "almost at random," a phrase in which the word "almost" reveals the deliberation involved. Boltanski and Chiapello, *New Spirit of Capitalism*, 101 n24.

13. Boltanski and Chiapello, *New Spirit of Capitalism*, 197–98.

14. Ibid., 98.

15. Ibid., 39.

16. Ibid., 39.

17. Ibid., xxxv.

18. Alberto Toscano, "Beginnings and Ends: For, Against and Beyond '68,'" *New Formations* 65, no. 1 (2008): 101.

19. Maurizio Lazzarato, "Mai 68, la 'critique artiste' et la révolution néolibérale," *La revue internationale des livres et des idées*, Sept. 21, 2009, http://www.revuedeslivres.net/articles.php?idArt=271:

> The misfortunes of the critique of the "artistic critique" conducted by Boltanski and Chiapello are numerous, but the greatest to have befallen it is precisely the resistance movement of theatre "artists" and "technicians" and the birth of the Coordination of Intermittent and Precarious Workers, which constitutes its foundational expression. The six words of one of the slogans of the intermittent movement, "no culture without social rights," are enough to unsettle the whole of Boltanski and Chiapello's theoretical construction and to make apparent the limits of their analysis of contemporary capitalism. Translated into their language, the slogan "no culture without social rights" becomes, in effect, "no liberty, autonomy and authenticity without solidarity, equality and security." That which Boltanski and Chiapello considered as potentially "aristo-liberal," as incompatible with social justice, becomes a field of struggle, perhaps the only one from which it might be possible to confront and undo the logic of neo-liberalism. (My translation)

20. Lazzarato, "Immaterial Labor," 131–32.

21. Virno, *Grammar of the Multitude*, 103.

22. Ibid., 109.

23. Rosalind Gill and Andy Pratt, "In the Social Factory? Immaterial Labour, Precariousness and Cultural Work," *Theory, Culture and Society* 25, nos. 7–8 (2008): 9. See also Angela Mitropoulos, whose work is cited in Rosalind Gill and Andy Pratt, "Precari-us," *Mute: Culture and Politics after the Net* 1, no. 29 (2005): 88–96.

24. Andrew Ross, "The New Geography of Work," *Theory, Culture and Society* 25, nos. 7–8 (2008): 31–49.

> On the face of it, an alliance of cleaners, web designers and adjunct teachers, to cite just three representative occupations from these sectors, is an unlikely prospect. It is easier to imagine on paper as a theo-

retically plausible construct than as a flesh-and-blood coalition in broad agreement on strategies and goals. For one thing, there is a sizeable imbalance in the social capital enjoyed by this range of constituents. Those in occupations with the most cachet would almost inevitably expect to be front and center, and, over time, would surely sideline the others. (41)

Nonetheless, Ross draws on his own empirical research into protests by janitors, job dissatisfaction among IT workers in "high-tech sweatshops" (43) and the political organization of adjunct labor in American universities, to suggest that we should be attentive to the "fellow-feeling" that is the precondition for such alliances (43).

25. Lazzarato, "Immaterial Labor," 134.

26. Virno, *Grammar of the Multitude*, 51.

27. This account of *No Dice* is based upon performances seen at the Theaterhaus Gessnerallee in Zurich in Oct. 2008 and at HAU3 in Berlin in Nov. 2009, as well as upon the published text.

28. Amber Reed, introduction to *No Dice*, by Nature Theatre of Oklahoma (New York: 53rd State Press, 2007).

29. Nature Theatre of Oklahoma, "We're in the Money," http://www.ok-theater.org/videomoney.htm.

30. See Mike Kelley, "In the Image of Man," in *Minor Histories: Statements, Conversations, Proposals*, by Mike Kelley, ed. John C. Welchman (Cambridge: MIT Press, 2004), 50–55.

31. Nature Theatre of Oklahoma, "We're in the Money."

32. Nature Theatre of Oklahoma, *No Dice*, 93.

33. Ibid., 94.

34. Ibid., 95.

35. That there is no way the gift can escape the logic of exchange is not lost on Nature Theatre of Oklahoma, any more than it is on Jacques Derrida, whose *Given Time 1: Counterfeit Money*, trans. Peggy Kamuf (Chicago: University of Chicago Press, 1992), is a rich exploration of this impossibility.

36. In material used on the website at the Theaterhaus Gessnerallee in Zürich, *No Dice* is described as "their entertaining three and a half hour version of the legendary and originally eleven hour melodrama-show": Theaterhaus Gessnerallee, *Gessnerallee Zürich*, http://www.gessnerallee.ch/en/programm/archive/vorstellung1/auffuehrung/91/index.html (accessed Nov. 2011).

37. There should be a study made into why it is that all kinds of uncommercial, broadly anti-capitalist people, some of them Marxists, both enjoy and seem strangely good at dreaming up crazy business ideas of this kind.

38. For critical accounts of Rimini Protokoll, see Miriam Dreysse and Florian Malzacher, eds., *Rimini Protokoll: Experts of the Everyday* (Berlin: Alexander Verlag, 2008).

39. Nature Theatre of Oklahoma, *No Dice*, 27.

40. Ibid., 16.

41. Listed as Marc Dale, Anne Gridley, Teresa Gridley, Robert M Johanson, Jo Liegerot, Zachary Oberzan, Adam Tsekman, Katarina Vizinova, and Kristin Worrall.

42. Nature Theatre of Oklahoma, *No Dice*, 16.

43. Ibid., 18.

44. See Richard Stites, *Revolutionary Dreams: Utopian Vision and Experimental Life in the Russian Revolution* (New York and Oxford: Oxford University Press, 1989), 147.

45. Nature Theatre of Oklahoma, *No Dice*, 34.

46. See Conrad Russell, "Against Dead Time," *Time and Society* 11, nos. 2–3 (2002): 193–208, for an extended discussion of a series of "romantic" critiques of capitalism's dead time, from Michael Löwy's account of romanticism as a critique of modernity, via the Situationists, to Paul Virilio.

47. Nature Theatre of Oklahoma, *No Dice*, 21.

48. Ibid., 21.

49. Tiziana Terranova, *Network Culture: Politics for the Information Age* (London and Ann Arbor: Pluto Press, 2004).

50. Kristin Ross, translator's introduction to *The Ignorant Schoolmaster*, by Jacques Rancière (Stanford: Stanford University Press, 1991), xviii.

51. Nature Theatre of Oklahoma, *No Dice*, 72–73.

52. The possibility that *No Dice* might be considered an instance of "verbatim theatre" might usefully be explored alongside the suggestion above that it is also an example of the kind of "documentary theatre" developed by groups like Rimini Protokoll. This might point to a broader category of "non-fiction" theatre.

53. Nature Theatre of Oklahoma, *No Dice*, 139.

54. Ibid., 145.

55. Ibid., 145.

56. Ibid., 145.

57. Ibid., 146.

58. Ibid., 147.

59. Ibid., 158.

60. See Rancière, *Emancipated Spectator*, for a critique of the myths of participation in theatre.

61. Virno, *Grammar of the Multitude*, 89.

62. Ibid., 90.

63. Ibid., 111.

CHAPTER 6

1. Stories of wild men who live in the snow appear to have entered the western imaginary from Nepalese and Tibetan culture during the nineteenth century and developed a distinctively modern life there from the 1930s, where, as Peter Bishop suggests, they comprised part of a utopian fantasy of the Himalayas as a sacred place. See Peter Bishop, *The Myth of Shangri-La: Ti-*

bet, Travel Writing and the Western Creation of Sacred Landscape (Berkeley and Los Angeles: University of California Press, 1989).

2. Terry Eagleton, *The Function of Criticism: From* The Spectator *to Post-Structuralism* (London: Verso, 2004), 69.

3. Ibid., 36–37.

4. Ibid., 65.

5. Ibid., 76–77.

6. Barbara Ehrenreich and John Ehrenreich, "The Professional-Managerial Class," in *Between Labor and Capital,* ed. Pat Walker (Boston: South End Press, 1979), 12; cited in Shannon Jackson, *Professing Performance: Theatre in the Academy from Philology to Performativity* (Cambridge: Cambridge University Press, 2004), 46. A full study of theatre criticism as a profession has yet to be written, although there is a brief book on the subject by a well-informed British newspaper critic: Irving Wardle, *Theatre Criticism* (London and New York: Routledge, 1992). Also Marcie Frank explores, very interestingly, the idea that, in England at least, literary criticism itself may have a particular historical relationship with the theatre: Marcie Frank, *Gender, Theatre, and the Origins of Criticism: From Dryden to Manley* (Cambridge: Cambridge University Press, 2003).

7. Jackson, *Professing Performance,* 46.

8. For a discussion of how a radical and socialist project might still be sustained by teachers and intellectuals who "sneak into the university and steal what they can," see Fred Moten and Stefano Harney, "The University and the Undercommons: Seven Theses," *Social Text* 22, no. 2 (2004): 101–15.

9. Via Negativa made these performances during the first seven years of their collective work, beginning in 2002 with *Starting Point: Anger* and continuing with *More* (2003), *Incasso* (2004), *Would Would Not* (2005), *Viva Verdi* (2006), *Four Deaths* (2007), and *Out* (2008). For more on the company's work see Marin Blažević, ed., *The No: Via Negativa 2002–2008* (Ljubljana: Maska, 2010); and the company's website: Via Negativa, http://www.vntheatre.com, accessed Nov. 5, 2012. The performance at Venice was presented as part of the Theatre Biennale, directed by Romeo Castellucci.

10. Tomaž Krpič, "The Spectator's Performing Body: The Case of the *Via Negativa* Theatre Project," *New Theatre Quarterly* 27, no. 2 (2011): 168. The interview with Via Negativa's director, Bojan Jablanovec, in which the idea of theatre as "a sphere of communication" is articulated, is available: Bojan Jablanovec, interview with Andrea Copać, trans. Polona Petek, *Maska* 20 (2005): 92–93, http://vntheatre.com/en/i-see-theatre-above-all-as-a-sphere-of-communication-not-as-a-medium-of-aestheticisation:

> Via Negativa is simply a return, a backward glance cast towards the reasons, the meaning, the goal and objectives, as well as the methods of theatre as such. It is not about developing a different theatre or inventing a new stylistic paradigm. It is simply a reconsideration of the meaning of theatre as a medium and an exploration of its mechanisms. Nowadays, I see theatre, above all, as a sphere of communication, not as a medium of aestheticisation. Institutional theatre, to some extent,

underestimates the audiences—in terms of how it communicates with them and what kind of language it uses. Negativa is all about opening up theatre as a space of communication.

11. Krpić, "Spectator's Performing Body," 172.

12. These comments were made in a public dialogue at the Venice Theatre Biennale, coordinated under the title *Fare e Rappresentare*, by Claudia Castellucci, and led by Joe Kelleher and myself.

13. Nancy, *Being Singular Plural*, 69.

14. A significant precursor to much recent work is Alan Read, ed., "On Animals," special issue, *Performance Research* 5, no. 2 (2000). My own contribution may be found in Nicholas Ridout, *Stage Fright, Animals and Other Theatrical Problems* (Cambridge: Cambridge University Press, 2006).

15. Daniel Heller-Roazen, *The Inner Touch: Archaeology of a Sensation* (New York: Zone Books, 2007), 17.

16. Ibid., 91.

17. Ibid., 34.

18. Ibid., 35.

19. Giorgio Agamben, *The Open: Man and Animal*, trans. Kevin Attell (Stanford: Stanford University Press, 2004).

20. Heller-Roazen, *Inner Touch*, 92.

21. Jean-Luc Nancy, *Listening*, trans. Charlotte Mandell (New York: Fordham University Press, 2007).

22. Ibid., 14.

23. Chris Goode, "God/Head," unpublished typescript, 2012, 2. All the subsequent direct quotations from this performance are from a version of the script that Chris Goode generously shared with me.

24. Chris Goode, "Corkafleeg," Thompson's Bank of Communicable Desire (blog), June 23, 2006, http://beescope.blogspot.co.uk/search?updated-min=2005-12-31T16:00:00-8:00&updated-max=2006-6-28T02:34:00%2B01:00&max-results=47&start=39&by-date=false.

25. Chris Goode, "A New Vision for Theatre," interview with Chris Johnstone, *Argument Room*, July 21, 2011, http://www.livestream.com/theargumentroom/video?clipId=pla_56a63c90-fd2b-4867-bc9d-af9b2376e8bb.

26. Chris Goode, "Season's Greeblings; And Another Year Over," Thompson's Bank of Communicable Desire (blog), Dec. 30, 2011, http://beescope.blogspot.co.uk/search?updated-min=2011-1-1T00:00:00Z&updated-max=2012-1-1T00:00:00Z&max-results=27.

Bibliography

Adorno, Theodor, and Max Horkheimer. *The Dialectic of Enlightenment.* Translated by John Cumming. London: Verso, 1997.

Agamben, Giorgio. *The Open: Man and Animal.* Translated by Kevin Attell. Stanford: Stanford University Press, 2004.

Althusser, Louis. *For Marx.* Translated by Ben Brewster. London: Verso, 1982.

Arendt, Hannah. *The Human Condition.* Chicago and London: University of Chicago Press, 1998.

Ash, Mitchell G. "Bachelor of What, Master of Whom? The Humboldt Myth and Historical Transformations of Higher Education in German-Speaking Europe and the US." *European Journal of Education* 41, no. 2 (2006): 245–67.

Atack, Margaret. *May 68 in French Fiction and Film: Rethinking Society, Rethinking Representation.* Oxford: Oxford University Press, 1999.

Ball, Alan. "'The Roots of Bezprizornost' in Soviet Russia's First Decade." *Slavic Review* 51, no. 2 (1992): 247–70.

Ball, Alan. "State Children: Soviet Russia's Besprizornye and the New Socialist Generation." *Russian Review* 52, no. 2 (1993): 228–47.

Bayly, Simon. "Theatre and the Public: Badiou, Rancière, Virno." *Radical Philosophy* 157 (2009): 20–29.

Benjamin, Walter. *The Arcades Project.* Translated by Howard Eiland and Kevin McLaughlin. Cambridge, MA: Belknap Press, 1999.

Benjamin, Walter. "A Communist Pedagogy." In *Selected Writings,* 2: 273–75.

Benjamin, Walter. "Experience." In *Selected Writings,* 1: 3–5.

Benjamin, Walter. *Gesammelte Schriften.* Vol. 2. Frankfurt am Main: Suhrkamp Verlag, 1989.

Benjamin, Walter. "The Life of Students." In *Selected Writings,* 1: 37–47.

Benjamin, Walter. "On the Concept of History." In *Selected Writings,* 4: 389–400.

Benjamin, Walter. *One-Way Street and Other Writings.* Translated by J. A. Underwood. London: Penguin, 2009.

Benjamin, Walter. "Paralipomena to 'On the Concept of History.'" In *Selected Writings,* 4: 401–11.

Benjamin, Walter. "Das Passagen-Werk." In *Gesammelte Schriften,* vol. 5, 577–78. Frankfurt am Main: Suhrkamp, 1982.

Benjamin, Walter. "Program for a Proletarian Children's Theater." In *Selected Writings,* 2: 201–6.

Benjamin, Walter. *Selected Writings.* Vol. 1, 1913–1926. Edited by Marcus Bullock and Michael W. Jennings. 3–5. Cambridge, MA, and London: Belknap, 1996.

Benjamin, Walter. *Selected Writings*. Vol. 2, 1927–1934. Translated by Rodney Livingstone and Others. Edited by Michael W. Jennings, Howard Eiland and Gary Smith. 273–75. Cambridge, MA, and London: Belknap Press, 1999.

Benjamin, Walter. *Selected Writings*. Vol. 4, 1938–1940. Translated by Edmund Jephcott and others. Edited by Howard Eiland and Michael W. Jennings. 389–400. Cambridge and London: Harvard University Press, 2003.

Benjamin, Walter. "The Concept of Art Criticism in German Romanticism." In *Selected Writings 1*: 116–200.

Bishop, Claire. "Antagonism and Relational Aesthetics." *October* 110 (2004): 51–79.

Bishop, Peter. *The Myth of Shangri-La: Tibet, Travel Writing and the Western Creation of Sacred Landscape*. Berkeley and Los Angeles: University of California Press, 1989.

Blažević, Marin, ed. *The No: Via Negativa 2002–2008*. Ljubljana: Maska, 2010.

Boal, Augusto. *Theatre of the Oppressed*. London: Pluto Press, 1979.

Boltanski, Luc, and Ève Chiapello. *The New Spirit of Capitalism*. Translated by Gregory Elliott. London: Verso, 2006.

Bontemps, Jacques, Jean-Louis Comolli, Michel Delahaye, Jean Narboni and Jean-Luc Godard. "Struggle on Two Fronts: A Conversation with Jean-Luc Godard." *Film Quarterly* 22, no. 2 (Winter 1968–69): 20–35.

Bourriaud, Nicolas. *Relational Aesthetics*. Translated by Simon Pleasance and Fronza Wood. Dijon: Les Presses du Réel, 2002.

Breines, Paul. "Marxism, Romanticism, and the Case of Georg Lukács: Notes on Some Recent Sources and Situations." *Studies in Romanticism* 16, no. 4 (1977): 473–89.

Britten, Benjamin. "Cuckoo!" *Friday Afternoons*, op. 7. no. 3. 1935. Choir of Downside School, Purley. With Viola Tunnard (piano). Decca Music Group Ltd. Recorded 1967.

Buck-Morss, Susan. *Dreamworld and Catastrophe: The Passing of Mass Utopia in East and West*. Cambridge and London: MIT Press, 2002.

Cannon, Steve. "'When You're Not a Worker Yourself . . . ': Godard, the Dziga Vertov Group and the Audience." In *100 Years Of European Cinema: Entertainment or Ideology?* edited by Diana Holmes and Alison Smith, 100–108. Manchester: Manchester University Press, 2000.

Castellucci, Claudia, Romeo Castellucci, Chiara Guidi, Joe Kelleher, and Nicholas Ridout. *The Theatre of Societas Raffaello Sanzio*. London and New York: Routledge, 2007.

Castellucci, Romeo. "The Animal Being on Stage." Translated by Carolina Melis, Valentina Valentini, and Ric Allsopp. *Performance Research* 5, no. 2 (2000): 23–28.

Castellucci, Romeo. "Tragedia Endogonidia." Unpublished production text, 2004. Microsoft Word file.

Chakrabarty, Dipesh. *Provincializing Europe: Postcolonial Thought and Historical Difference*. Princeton: Princeton University Press, 2000.

Chekhov, Anton. *The Cherry Orchard*. In *Plays*, 281–346.

Chekhov, Anton. *Plays*. Translated with notes by Peter Carson. London: Penguin Books, 2002.

Chekhov, Anton. *The Seagull*. In *Plays*, 81–141.

Chekhov, Anton. *Three Sisters*. In *Plays*, 201–80.

Chekhov, Anton. *Uncle Vanya*. In *Plays*, 143–200.

De Man, Paul. "The Concept of Irony." In *Aesthetic Ideology*, edited by Andrzej Warminski, 163–84. Minneapolis: University of Minnesota Press, 1996.

Derrida, Jacques. *Given Time 1: Counterfeit Money*. Translated by Peggy Kamuf. Chicago: University of Chicago Press, 1992.

Derrida, Jacques. *Moscou aller-retour*. Saint Etienne: Éditions de l'aube, 1995.

de Ste. Croix, G. E. M. *The Class Struggle in the Ancient Greek World from the Archaic Age to the Arab Conquests*. London: Duckworth, 1981.

Dixon, Wheeler Winston. *The Films of Jean-Luc Godard*. Albany: State University of New York Press, 1997.

Dobson, Michael. *Shakespeare and Amateur Performance: A Cultural History*. Cambridge: Cambridge University Press, 2011.

Dolan, Jill. *Utopia in Performance: Finding Hope at the Theater*. Ann Arbor: University of Michigan Press, 2005.

Douzinas, Costas, and Slavoj Žižek, eds. *The Idea of Communism*. London and New York: Verso, 2010.

Dreysse, Miriam, and Florian Malzacher, eds. *Rimini Protokoll: Experts of the Everyday*. Berlin: Alexander Verlag, 2008.

duBois, Page. *Out of Athens: The New Ancient Greeks*. Cambridge and London: Harvard University Press, 2010.

Dwyer, Paul. "Theoria Negativa: Making Sense of Boal's Reading of Aristotle." *Modern Drama* 48, no. 4 (Winter 2005): 635–58.

Eagleton, Terry. *The Function of Criticism: From* The Spectator *to Post-Structuralism*. London: Verso, 2004.

Edu-Factory Collective. *Towards a Global Autonomous University*. New York: Autonomedia, 2009.

Ehrenreich, Barbara. *Bait and Switch: The (Futile) Pursuit of the American Dream*. New York: Metropolitan Books, 2001.

Ehrenreich, Barbara, and John Ehrenreich. "The Professional-Managerial Class." In *Between Labor and Capital*, edited by Pat Walker, 5–49. Boston: South End Press, 1979.

Eley, Geoff. "Educating the Bourgeoisie: Students and the Culture of 'Illiberalism' in Imperial Germany." Review of *Students, Society, and Politics in Imperial Germany: The Rise of Academic Illiberalism*, by Konrad H. Jarausch. *History of Education Quarterly* 26, no. 2 (1986): 287–300.

Emden, Christian J. *Friedrich Nietzsche and the Politics of History*. Cambridge: Cambridge University Press, 2008.

Farber, Manny. *Negative Space: Manny Farber on the Movies*. Rev. ed. New York: De Capo Press, 1998.

Fischer-Lichte, Erika. "Thinking about the Origins of Theatre in the 1970s." In Hall, Macintosh, and Wrigley, *Dionysus since 69*, 329–60.

Fitzpatrick, Sheila. *The Commissariat of Enlightenment: Soviet Organization of*

Education and the Arts Under Lunacharsky, October 1917–1921. Cambridge: Cambridge University Press, 1970.

Fitzpatrick, Sheila. "Cultural Revolution in Russia, 1928–32." *Journal of Contemporary History* 9, no. 1 (1974): 33–52.

Foucault, Michel. *The Birth of Biopolitics: Lectures at the Collège de France, 1978–1979.* Basingstoke: Palgrave Macmillan, 2008.

Frank, Marcie. *Gender, Theatre, and the Origins of Criticism: From Dryden to Manley.* Cambridge: Cambridge University Press, 2003.

Gill, Rosalind, and Andy Pratt. "In the Social Factory? Immaterial Labour, Precariousness and Cultural Work." *Theory, Culture and Society* 25, nos. 7–8 (2008): 1–30.

Gill, Rosalind, and Andy Pratt. 'Precari-us.' *Mute: Culture and Politics after the Net* 1, no. 29 (2005): 88–96.

Godard, Jean-Luc. *La chinoise, ou plutôt à la chinoise.* Directed by Jean-Luc Godard. 1967. London: Optimum Releasing, 2005. DVD, 93 min.

Godard, Jean-Luc. Interview with Andrew Sarris. *Village Voice*, April 30, 1970.

Godard, Jean-Luc. "Let's Talk about Pierrot: An Interview with Jean-Luc Godard." By Jean-Louis Comolli, Michel Delahaye, Jean-André Fieschi, and Gérard Guégan, *Cahiers du cinéma* 171 (October 1965). Reprinted in *Godard on Godard,* translated by Tom Milne, edited by Tom Milne, 216. New York and London: Da Capo, 1972.

Godard, Jean-Luc. *Pierrot le fou.* Directed by Jean-Luc Godard. 1965. London: Optimum Releasing, 2007. DVD, 106 min.

Godard, Jean-Luc. *Weekend.* Directed by Jean-Luc Godard. 1967. London: Artificial Eye, 2005. DVD, 90 min.

Godard, Jean-Luc. "What Is to Be Done?" *Afterimage*, no. 1 (April 1970).

Goldhill, Simon. "The Great Dionysia and Civic Ideology." *Journal of Hellenic Studies* 107 (1987): 58–76.

Goldhill, Simon, and Robin Osborne. *Performance Culture and Athenian Democracy.* Cambridge: Cambridge University Press, 1999.

Golub, Spencer. *The Recurrence of Fate.* Iowa City: University of Iowa Press, 1994.

Goode, Chris. "Corkafleeg." Thompson's Bank of Communicable Desire (blog), June 23, 2006, http://beescope.blogspot.co.uk/search?updated-min=2005-12-31T16:00:00-08:00&updated-max=2006-06-28T02:34:00%2B01:00&max-results=47&start=39&by-date=false.

Goode, Chris. "God/Head." Unpublished typescript, 2012.

Goode, Chris. "A New Vision for Theatre." Interview with Chris Johnstone. *Argument Room*, July 21, 2011, http://www.livestream.com/theargument-room/video?clipId=pla_56a63c90-fd2b-4867-bc9d-af9b2376e8bb.

Goode, Chris. "Season's Greeblings; And Another Year Over." Thompson's Bank of Communicable Desire (blog), December 30, 2011, http://beescope.blogspot.co.uk/search?updated-min=2011-01-01T00:00:00Z&updated-max=2012-01-01T00:00:00Z&max-results=27.

Gorz, André. *Adieux au prolétariat.* Paris: Galilée, 1980.

Gorz, André. *Farewell to the Working Class: An Essay on Post-Industrial Socialism.* Translated by Michael Sonenscher. London: Pluto Press, 1997.

Gorz, André. *Reclaiming Work: Beyond the Wage-Based Society.* Translated by Chris Turner. Cambridge: Polity Press, 1999.

Gorz, André. *Le socialisme difficile.* Paris: Du Seuil, 1967.

Hall, Edith. "Introduction: Why Greek Tragedy in the Late Twentieth Century?" In Hall, Macintosh, and Wrigley, *Dionysus since 69,* 1–46.

Hall, Edith, Fiona Macintosh, and Amanda Wrigley, eds. *Dionysus since 69: Greek Tragedy at the Dawn of the Third Millennium.* Oxford: Oxford University Press, 2004.

Hamacher, Werner. "'Now': Walter Benjamin on Historical Time." In *The Moment: Time and Rupture in Modern Thought,* edited by Heidrun Friese, 161–96. Liverpool: Liverpool University Press, 2001.

Hardt, Michael, and Antonio Negri. *Empire.* Cambridge and London: Harvard University Press, 2000.

Hardt, Michael, and Antonio Negri. *Labors of Dionysus: A Critique of the State-Form.* Minneapolis: University of Minnesota Press, 1994.

Harvey, David. *A Brief History of Neoliberalism.* Oxford: Oxford University Press, 2005.

Harvey, David. *The Condition of Postmodernity.* Oxford: Basil Blackwell, 1989.

Heller-Roazen, Daniel. *The Inner Touch: Archaeology of a Sensation.* New York: Zone Books, 2007.

Hoernle, Edwin. *Grundfragen der Proletarischen Erziehung.* Berlin: Verlag der Jugendinterantionale, 1929.

Holman, Christopher. "Dialectics and Distinction: Reconsidering Hannah Arendt's Critique of Marx." *Contemporary Political Theory* 10, no. 3 (2011): 332–53.

Honneth, Axel. "Work and Instrumental Action." *New German Critique* 26 (1982): 31–54.

Jablanovec, Bojan. Interview with Andrea Copać. Translated by Polona Petek. *Maska* 20 (2005): 92–93. http://vntheatre.com/en/i-see-theatre-above-all-as-a-sphere-of-communication-not-as-a-medium-of-aestheticisation/.

Jackson, Shannon. *Professing Performance: Theatre in the Academy from Philology to Performativity.* Cambridge: Cambridge University Press, 2004.

Jackson, Shannon. *Social Works: Performing Art, Supporting Publics.* Abingdon and New York: Routledge, 2011.

Jarausch, Konrad H. *Students, Society, and Politics in Imperial Germany: The Rise of Academic Illiberalism.* Princeton: Princeton University Press, 1982.

Jellicoe, Ann. *Community Plays: How to Put Them On.* London: Methuen, 1987.

Joseph, Miranda. *Against the Romance of Community.* Minneapolis: University of Minnesota Press, 2002.

Kael, Pauline. Blurb of *La chinoise, ou plutôt à la chinoise.* Directed by Jean-Luc Godard. 1967. London: Optimum Releasing, 2005. DVD, 93 min.

Kael, Pauline. *Going Steady.* Boston: Little, Brown, 1970.

Kelley, Mike. "In the Image of Man." In *Minor Histories: Statements, Conversations, Proposals,* by Mike Kelley, edited by John C. Welchman, 50–55. Cambridge: MIT Press, 2004.

Kelly, Catriona. "Popular, Provincial and Amateur Theatres 1820–1900." In *A History of Russian Theatre,* edited by Robert Leach and Victor Borovsky, 124–45. Cambridge: Cambridge University Press, 2006.

Kester, Grant. *Conversation Pieces: Community and Communication in Modern Art.* Berkeley and London: University of California Press, 2004.

Kramer, Samuel C. "The Zemstvo and Public Health." In *The Zemstvo in Russia: An Experiment in Local Self-Government,* edited by Terence Emmons and Wayne S. Vucinich, 279–314. Cambridge: Cambridge University Press, 1982.

Krpić, Tomaž. "The Spectator's Performing Body: The Case of the *Via Negativa* Theatre Project." *New Theatre Quarterly* 27, no. 2 (2011): 167–75.

Lacis, Asja. *Revolutionär im Beruf: Berichte über proletarisches Theater, über Meyerhold, Brecht, Benjamin und Piscator.* Edited by Hildegard Brenner. Munich: Rogner & Bernhard, 1971.

Lacoue-Labarthe, Philippe, and Jean-Luc Nancy. *The Literary Absolute: The Theory of Literature in German Romanticism.* Translated by Philip Barnard and Cheryl Lester. Albany: State University of New York Press, 1988.

Lamberti, Marjorie. *The Politics of Education: Teachers and School Reform in Weimar Germany.* Oxford and New York: Berghahn Books, 2002.

Laqueur, Walter. *Young Germany: A History of the German Youth Movement.* London: Routledge and Kegan Paul, 1962.

Lash, Scott, and John Urry. *The End of Organized Capitalism.* Madison: University of Wisconsin Press, 1987.

Lauglo, Jon. "Soviet Education Policy 1917–1935: From Ideology to Bureaucratic Control." *Oxford Review of Education* 14, no. 3 (1988): 285–99.

Lazzarato, Maurizio. "Immaterial Labor." Translated by Paul Colilli and Ed Emory. In *Radical Thought in Italy,* edited by Michael Hardt and Paolo Virno, 133–47. Minneapolis: University of Minnesota Press, 1996.

Lazzarato, Maurizio. "Mai 68, la 'critique artiste' et la révolution néolibérale." *La revue internationale des livres et des idées,* September 21, 2009. http://www.revuedeslivres.net/articles.php?idArt=271.

Lefebvre, Henri. *The Explosion: Marxism and the French Revolution.* Translated by Alfred Ehrenfeld. New York and London: Monthly Review Press, 1969.

Lefebvre, Henri. *The Production of Space.* Translated by Donald Nicholson-Smith. Cambridge, MA: Blackwell, 1991.

Longo, Oddone. "The Theatre of the Polis." In *Nothing to Do with Dionysos? Athenian Drama in Its Social Context,* edited by John J. Winkler and Froma I. Zeitlin, 12–19. Princeton: Princeton University Press, 1990.

Löwy, Michael. *Fire Alarm: Reading Walter Benjamin's "On the Concept of History."* London and New York: Verso, 2005.

Löwy, Michael, and Robert Sayre. *Romanticisim against the Tide of Modernity.* Translated by Catherine Porter. Durham: Duke University Press, 2001.

MacCabe, Colin. *Godard: A Portrait of the Artist at Seventy.* New York: Farrar, Straus and Giroux, 2003.

Martin, Stewart. "Artistic Communism — A Sketch." *Third Text* 23, no. 4 (2009): 481–94.

Martin, Stewart. "Critique of Relational Aesthetics." *Third Text* 21, no. 4 (2007): 369–86.

Martin, Stewart. "Culs de sac." *Radical Philosophy* 131 (2005): 39–44.

Marx, Karl. *Capital: A Critique of Political Economy.* Vol. 1. Translated by Ben Fowkes. New York: Vintage Books, 1977.

Marx, Karl. *Capital.* Vol. 3. Translated by David Fernbach. London: Penguin Books, 1981.

Marx, Karl. *Grundrisse: Foundations of the Critique of Political Economy (Rough Draft).* Translated by Martin Nicolaus. Harmondsworth: Penguin, 1973.

McClelland, Charles E. *State, Society, and University in Germany 1700–1914.* Cambridge: Cambridge University Press, 1980.

McClelland, James C. "Proletarianizing the Student Body: The Soviet Experience during the New Economic Policy." *Past and Present* 80 (1978): 122–46.

McClelland, James C. "The Utopian and the Heroic: Divergent Paths to the Communist Educational Ideal." In *Bolshevik Culture,* edited by Abbott Gleason, Peter Kenez and Richard Stites, 114–30. Bloomington: Indiana University Press, 1985.

McCracken, Scott. "Idleness for All." *New Formations* 53 (2004): 65–76.

Meiksins Wood, Ellen. "Historical Materialism in 'Forms which Precede Capitalist Production.'" In *Karl Marx's Grundrisse: Foundations of the Critique of Political Economy 150 Years Later,* edited by Marcello Musto, 79–92. Abingdon and New York: Routledge, 2008.

Meiksins Wood, Ellen, and Neal Wood. *Class Ideology and Ancient Political Theory: Socrates, Plato and Aristotle in Social Context.* Oxford: Basil Blackwell, 1978.

Milne, Tom, ed. *Godard on Godard.* Translated by Tom Milne. New York and London: Da Capo, 1972.

Moten, Fred, and Stefano Harney. "The University and the Undercommons: Seven Theses." *Social Text* 22, no. 2 (2004): 101–15.

Nancy, Jean-Luc. *Being Singular Plural.* Translated by Robert D. Richardson and Anne E. O'Byrne. Stanford: Stanford University Press, 2000.

Nancy, Jean-Luc. *La communeauté désoeuvrée.* Paris: Christian Bourgeois Editeur, 1986.

Nancy, Jean-Luc. "La Comparution"/The Compearance: From the Existence of "Communism" to the Community of "Existence". Translated by Tracy B. Strong. *Political Theory* 20, no. 3 (1992): 371–98.

Nancy, Jean-Luc. "The Inoperative Community." In *The Inoperative Community,* edited by Peter Connor, translated by Peter Connor, Lisa Garbus, Michael Holland, and Simona Sawhney. Minneapolis and London: University of Minnesota Press, 1991.

Nancy, Jean-Luc. *Listening.* Translated by Charlotte Mandell. New York: Fordham University Press, 2007.

Nancy, Jean-Luc. "Literary Communism." In *The Inoperative Community,* edited by Peter Connor, translated by Peter Connor, Lisa Garbus, Michael Holland, and Simona Sawhney. Minneapolis and London: University of Minnesota Press, 1991.

Nancy, Jean-Luc. "Myth Interrupted." In *The Inoperative Community,* edited by Peter Connor, translated by Peter Connor, Lisa Garbus, Michael Holland, and Simona Sawhney. Minneapolis and London: University of Minnesota Press, 1991.

Nature Theatre of Oklahoma. *No Dice.* Transcription and arrangement by Kelly Copper. New York: 53rd State Press, 2007.

Nature Theatre of Oklahoma. "We're in the Money." http://www.oktheater.org/videomoney.htm. Accessed April 17, 2011.

Oram, Jon. "The Social Actor." *Claque Theatre*, 2006. www.claquetheatre.com/wp-content/ . . . /Article_The-Social-Actor.pdf.

Paškevica, Beata. *In der Stadt der Parolen: Asja Lacis, Walter Benjamin und Bertolt Brecht*. Essen: Klartext Verlag, 2006.

Perkin, Harold. *The Rise of Professional Society: England since 1880*. London and New York: Routledge, 1989.

Phelan, Peggy. *Unmarked: The Politics of Performance*. London and New York: Routledge, 1993.

Rabinbach, Anson. *The Human Motor: Energy, Fatigue, and the Origins of Modernity*. Berkeley and Los Angeles: University of California Press, 1992.

Rancière, Danielle, and Jacques Rancière. "La légende des philosophes (Les intellectuels et la traversée du gauchisme)." *Les lauriers de mai, ou, Les chemins du pouvoir* (1968–1978), special issue, *Révoltes logiques* (February 1978): 7–25.

Rancière, Jacques. *Aisthesis: Scènes du régime esthetique de l'art*. Paris: Editions Galilée, 2011.

Rancière, Jacques. *Disagreement: Politics and Philosophy*. Translated by Julie Rose. Minneapolis: University of Minnesota Press, 2004.

Rancière, Jacques. *The Emancipated Spectator*. Translated by Gregory Elliott. London and New York: Verso, 2009.

Rancière, Jacques. *Film Fables*. Translated by Emiliano Battista. Oxford and New York: Berg, 2006.

Rancière, Jacques. "Good Times or Pleasure at the Barricades." In *Voices of the People: The Social Life of 'la sociale' at the End of the Second Empire*, edited by Adrian Rifkin and Roger Thomas, translated by John Moore, 45–94. London: Routledge and Kegan Paul, 1988.

Rancière, Jacques. *The Nights of Labor: The Workers' Dream in Nineteenth-Century France*. Translated by John Drury. Philadelphia: Temple University Press, 1989.

Rancière, Jacques. *The Politics of Aesthetics: The Distribution of the Sensible*. Translated by Gabriel Rockhill. London and New York: Continuum, 2005.

Rancière, Jacques. *Staging the People: The Proletarian and His Double*. Translated by David Fernbach. London and New York: Verso, 2011.

Read, Alan, ed. *On Animals*. Special issue, *Performance Research* 5, no. 2 (2000).

Reed, Amber. Introduction to *No Dice*, by Nature Theatre of Oklahoma. New York: 53rd State Press, 2007.

Ridout, Nicholas. "Performance and Democracy." In *The Cambridge Companion to Performance Studies*, edited by Tracy C. Davis, 9–22. Cambridge: Cambridge University Press, 2008.

Ridout, Nicholas. *Stage Fright, Animals and Other Theatrical Problems*. Cambridge: Cambridge University Press, 2006.

Roberts, John. "Introduction: Art, 'Enclave Theory' and the Communist Imaginary." *Third Text* 23, no. 4 (2009): 353–67.

Rojek, Chris. *Capitalism and Leisure Theory*. London and New York: Tavistock Publications, 1985.

Ross, Andrew. "The New Geography of Work." *Theory, Culture and Society* 25, nos. 7–8 (2008): 31–49.

Ross, Kristin. *May '68 and Its Afterlives*. Chicago: University of Chicago Press, 2002.

Ross, Kristin. Translator's introduction to *The Ignorant Schoolmaster*, by Jacques Rancière, vii–xxiii. Stanford: Stanford University Press, 1991.

Russell, Conrad. "Against Dead Time." *Time and Society* 11, nos. 2–3 (2002): 193–208.

Sarfatti Larson, Magali. *The Rise of Professionalism: A Sociological Analysis.* Berkeley and Los Angeles: University of California Press, 1977.

Sayre, Robert, and Michael Löwy. "Figures of Romantic Anti-Capitalism." *New German Critique* 32 (1984): 42–92.

Schaap, Andrew. "Hannah Arendt and the Philosophical Repression of Politics." In *Jacques Rancière and the Contemporary Scene: The Philosophy of Radical Equality*, edited by Jean-Philippe Deranty and Alison Ross, 145–65. London and New York: Continuum, 2012.

Schechner, Richard. *Environmental Theatre*. New York and London: Applause, 1994.

Schechner, Richard. "Theater and Revolution." *Salmagundi* 2, no. 2 (Fall 1967–Winter 1968): 11–27.

Schneider, Rebecca. *Performing Remains: Art and War in Times of Theatrical Reenactment*. Abingdon and New York: Routledge, 2011.

Senelick, Laurence. *The Chekhov Theatre: Century of the Plays in Performance.* Cambridge: Cambridge University Press, 1997.

Settis, Salvatore. *The Future of the "Classical."* Cambridge: Polity Press, 2006.

Shakespeare, William. *Hamlet*. Edited by Harold Jenkins. London: Methuen, 1982.

Stites, Richard. *Revolutionary Dreams: Utopian Vision and Experimental Life in the Russian Revolution*. New York and Oxford: Oxford University Press, 1989.

Storey, David. *The Contractor*. London: Cape, 1970.

Suvin, Darko. "Modes of Political Drama." *Massachusetts Review* 13, no. 3 (Summer 1972): 309–24.

Terada, Rei. *Looking Away: Phenomenality and Dissatisfaction, Kant to Adorno.* Cambridge: Harvard University Press, 2009.

Terranova, Tiziana. *Network Culture: Politics for the Information Age.* London and Ann Arbor: Pluto Press, 2004.

Thatcher, Margaret. Interview for *Woman's Own*. By Douglas Keay. Transcript. September 23, 1987. http://www.margaretthatcher.org/document/106689.

Theaterhaus Gessnerallee. *Gessnerallee Zurich*. http://www.gessnerallee.ch/en/programm/archive/vorstellung1/auffuehrung/91/index.html. Accessed November 2011.

Thompson, E. P. "Time, Work-Discipline, and Industrial Capitalism." *Past and Present* 38, no. 1 (1967): 56–97.

Thomson, George. *Aeschylus and Athens: A Study in the Social Origins of Drama.* 2nd ed. London: Lawrence and Wishart, 1966.

Toscano, Alberto. "Beginnings and Ends: For, Against and Beyond '68.'" *New Formations* 65, no. 1 (2008): 94–104.

Touraine, Alain. *The May Movement: Revolt and Reform*. New York: Random House, 1971.

Tracey, Donald R. "Reform in the Early Weimar Republic: The Thuringian Example." *Journal of Modern History* 44, no. 2 (1972): 195–212.

Tse-Tung, Mao. "Talks at the Yenan Forum on Literature and Art." May 1942. In *Quotations from Chairman Mao Tse-Tung*, 1–43. Peking: Foreign Language Press, 1966.

Tulloch, John. *Chekhov: A Structuralist Study*. London and Basingstoke: Macmillan, 1980.

U.N.E.F. Strasbourg. *On the Poverty of Student Life, Considered in Its Economic, Political, Psychological, Sexual, and Particularly Intellectual Aspects, and a Modest Proposal for Its Remedy*. http://library.nothingness.org/articles/SI/en/display/4 (1966).

Utley, Philip Lee. "Radical Youth: Generational Conflict in the Anfang Movement, 1912–January 1914." *History of Education Quarterly* 19, no. 2 (1979): 207–28.

Vaneigem, Raoul. *The Revolution in Everyday Life*. Translated by David Nicholson-Smith. London: Left Bank Books and Rebel Press, 1983.

van Erven, Eugene. *Community Theatre: Global Perspectives*. London and New York: Routledge, 2001.

Varon, Jeremy. *Bringing the War Home: The Weather Underground, the Red Army Faction, and Revolutionary Violence in the Sixties and Seventies*. Berkeley and Los Angeles: University of California Press, 2004.

Vernant, Jean-Pierre, and Pierre Vidal Nacquet. *Myth and Tragedy in Ancient Greece*. Translated by Janet Lloyd. New York: Zone Books, 1988.

Virno, Paolo. *A Grammar of the Multitude: For an Analysis of Contemporary Forms of Life*. Translated by Isabella Bertoletti, James Cascaito, and Andrea Casson. Los Angeles and New York: Semiotext(e), 2004.

von Harnack, Adolf. "Von Großbetrieb der Wissenschaft." In *Wissenschaftpolitische Reden und Aufsätze*, 3–9. Hildesheim, Zürich, and New York: Olms-Weidemann, 2001.

Wardle, Irving. *Theatre Criticism*. London and New York: Routledge, 1992.

Weissman, Neil B. *Reform in Tsarist Russia*. New Brunswick, NJ: Rutgers University Press, 1981.

Weitz, Eric. D. *Creating German Communism, 1890–1990: From Popular Protests to Socialist State*. Princeton: Princeton University Press, 1997.

Wesker, Arnold. *The Kitchen*. London: Oberon Modern Plays, 2012.

Wiles, David. *Theatre and Citizenship*. Cambridge: Cambridge University Press, 2011.

Williams, James S. "'C'est le petit livre rouge / Qui fait que tout enfin bouge': The Case for Revolutionary Agency in Jean-Luc Godard's *La Chinoise*." *Journal of European Studies* 40, no. 3 (2010): 206–18.

Williams, Raymond. *Modern Tragedy*. Stanford: Stanford University Press, 1966.

Wirth, Andrzej, and Martha Ulvaeus. "The Lehrstück as Performance." *Drama Review* 43, no. 4 (1988): 113–21.

Witte, Bernd. *Walter Benjamin: An Intellectual Biography*. Translated by James Rolleston. Detroit: Wayne State University Press, 1997.

Wolin, Richard. *Walter Benjamin: An Aesthetic of Redemption*. Berkeley and Los Angeles: University of California Press, 1994.

Worrall, Nick. *The Moscow Art Theatre*. London and New York: Routledge, 1996.

Zeitlin, Froma I. "Dionysus in 69." In Hall, Macintosh, and Wrigley, *Dionysus since 69*, 49–75.

Zipes, Jack, ed. and trans. *Utopian Tales from Weimar*. Polygon: Edinburgh, 1990.

Index